SCHIRMER

PRONOUNCING

POCKET MANUAL

of

MUSICAL TERMS

SCHIRMER
PRONOUNCING
POCKET MANUAL
of
MUSICAL TERMS

FOURTH EDITION

Edited by
THEODORE BAKER

Revised by
NICOLAS SLONIMSKY

SCHIRMER BOOKS
A Division of Macmillan Publishing Co., Inc.
New York

COLLIER MACMILLAN PUBLISHERS
London

SCHIRMER BOOKS
A Division of Macmillan Publishing Co., Inc.
866 Third Avenue, New York, N.Y. 10022

Collier Macmillan Canada, Ltd.

Library of Congress Catalog Card Number: 77-5236

Printed in the United States of America

printing number

  3 4 5 6 7 8 9 10

Library of Congress Cataloging in Publication Data

Baker, Theodore, 1851–1934, ed.
  Schirmer pronouncing pocket manual of
musical terms.
  1905 and 1947 editions published under title:
A pronouncing pocket-manual of musical terms.
  1. Music—Terminology.   Slonimsky,
Nicolas   II. Title.
ML109.B16 1978   780'.3   77-5236
ISBN 0-02-870250-6

CONTENTS

PREFACE

Some years back I received a letter in schoolboy handwriting, all in capital letters, the nub of which was this: "Somebody told me there were about 6,800 types of music. Could you tell me the correct number? How many musical instruments are there in the world since prehistoric times?" The letter included a list of musical forms, which seemed to be taken from titles of recordings, for it contained such items as "Vexations" (obviously from a recording of a Satie piece) and "Jealousy." My first impulse was to lay the letter aside, but on second thought I decided to answer it; after all, the letter was inspired by a sincere, if naive, desire to learn the facts of music. In my reply, I explained that it is impossible to name the exact number of "types of music," because not every title of a composition represents a generic category; I explained that the same holds true of the exact number of instruments in the world "since prehistoric times." My reply must have come as a disappointment to my correspondent, for another letter soon arrived, saying, "I am extremely sorry to bother you again, sir, but I asked you what is the exact overall correct number of types of music and instruments." Would that there were such a magic number! But I could proffer none, and so let the matter rest.

In revising the present miniature dictionary of musical terms I have been guided by the simple criterion: what is the likelihood of an earnest student looking up a specific term relating to a musical form, a technique of composition, or an expression mark in the chief European languages? The first edition of the dictionary was compiled before the advent of modern musical phenomena, such as rock 'n' roll, and avant-garde techniques such as dodecaphony. Consequently, many terms of recent origin had to be added. Pronunciation is indicated, as in the original edition, according to standard phonetic symbols.

The appendix, "Biographical Dates of Noteworthy Musicians," has been greatly extended to include a number of
musicians, composers, performers, and musicologists who
have become "noteworthy" in recent times, as well as some
important music makers of the past centuries. The briefest of
all possible characterizations have been added in this section
for each musician listed; biographical dates have been appended to each name, indicating the years of birth and death,
as well as the national origin. These dates have been verified
according to the latest findings, so that an alert student should
not be surprised to find that they do not necessarily agree with
those in standard music dictionaries. Thus it transpires that
MacDowell was born in 1860 and not in 1861, that Leoncavallo was born in 1857 and not in 1858, that Cole Porter was
born in 1891, not 1893, and that Lily Pons was born in 1898,
not 1904. In some other entries, as for instance that of Vivaldi,
indefinite dates given in the original edition have been
changed to precise dates in the light of recent research.

Nicolas Slonimsky
1978

INTRODUCTORY

Elements of Notation

Notation is a system of signs used in writing music. The written signs for the time value (length, duration) of musical tones are called *Notes;* the written signs for pauses (intervals of silence) between the tones are called *Rests*.

Notes and Rests

Whole note ○   Half note ♩   Quarter note ♩

Whole rest ▬   Half rest ▬   Quarter rest ♪

Eighth note ♪   16th note ♪   32d note ♪

64th note ♪

Eighth rest ♪   16th rest ♪   32d rest ♪

64th rest ♪

1 Whole note ○ equals 2 ♩, or 4 ♩, or 8 ♪,

or 16 ♪, or 32 ♪, or 64 ♪

1 Half note ♩, = 2 ♩, or 4 ♪, or 8 ♪,

or 16 ♪, or 32 ♪

1 Quarter note ♩, = 2 ♪, or 4 ♪, or 8 ♪, or 16 ♪

1 Eighth note ♪ = 2 ♪, or 4 ♪, or 8 ♪

1 16th note ♪ = 2 ♪, or 4 ♪; and

1 32d note ♪ = 2 ♪

The Staff

The *Staff* consists of five parallel horizontal lines. Notes are written on the lines, or in the spaces between. For higher or lower tones, additional short lines are provided, called *Leger lines*.

— — Leger lines

5th line ———————————
                                      4th space
4th line ———————————
                                      3d space
3d line ———————————
                                      2d space
2d line ———————————
                                      1st space
1st line ———————————

— — Leger lines —

The Clefs

A *Clef* is a sign written at the head (beginning) of the staff to fix the position of one note. The most common clefs are

the *G* Clef , fixing the place of the
(Treble Clef)   note *g*[1]

the *F* Clef , fixing the place of
(Bass Clef)   the note *f;* and

the *C* Clef, which designates a line on the staff as *c*[1] (middle *C*); it acquires a different name according to the line used:

Tenor Clef   Alto Clef   Soprano Clef

See next entry, SCALES.

The Scales

The Staff and Clefs together fix the Pitch of the notes,
showing whether they are high or low. A series of 8 successive
notes on the staff forms what is called a *Scale*. To name the
notes of the scale, we use the first seven letters of the alphabet,
A B C D E F G. Scales are named after the note on which they
begin, which is called the *Keynote*. The scale of *C*, written in
whole notes, in the bass and treble clefs is as follows:

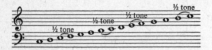

The *C* written on the leger line just below the treble staff
and just above the bass staff, is called Middle *C*.

The notes in the same vertical line are of the same pitch
and have the same name. For ordinary purposes, any note
marked *C* (*c*) is called simply "*C*." But, in order to fix the
place which any given note occupies among all the others
(that is, to fix its "Absolute Pitch"), the whole range of musical tones is divided into sections of seven notes each, called
"Octaves," and lettered and named as shown in the Table.
N.B.—The next octave below the Great Octave is the "Contra-octave": below that again is the "Double Contra-octave."

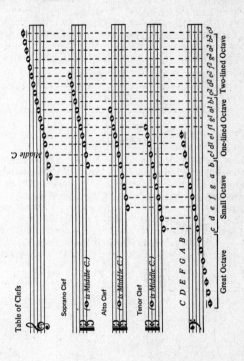

Chromatic Signs

The *Chromatic Signs* are set before notes to raise and lower their pitch.

The Sharp ♯ raises its note a semitone;

The Flat ♭ lowers its note a semitone;

The Natural ♮ restores its note to the natural pitch on the staff (without chromatic signs);

The Double sharp ✕ raises its note 2 semitones;

The Double flat ♭♭ lowers its note 2 semitones;

The sign ♮♯ restores a double sharped note to a sharped note;

The sign ♮♭ restores a double flatted note to a flatted note.

The Intervals

An *Interval* is the difference in pitch between two notes. In measuring an interval, it is customary to take the lower note as the basis, and to measure up to the higher note. When the measurement is made downward, the interval is called "inverted."

Diatonic Intervals of the Major Scale

All Standard Intervals and Their Inversions

The Keys

A *Key* is a scale employed harmonically, that is, employed to form chords and successions of chords. On the keynote *C*, or on any other note, two different species of scale or key may be built up:

Such a key or scale is called *Major* when its third and sixth are major intervals; it is *Minor* when its third and sixth are minor intervals. The succession of intervals in every major key is the same as that in *C* major; in every minor key, as in *C* minor. To adjust the intervals properly, chromatic signs are employed, as shown below·

Table of Major Keys

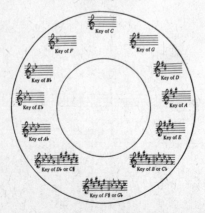

It will be seen, on passing round the circle in either direction, that the keynotes of the successive keys always follow each other at the interval of a perfect fifth; hence, this circle of keys, ending where it began, is called the *Circle of Fifths.*

Chords

A *Chord* is formed by a succession of from 3 to 5 different tones, built up in intervals of diatonic thirds from a given tone, or Root. A 3-tone chord is a Triad; a 4-tone chord is a Seventh chord (chord of the Seventh); a 5-tone chord is a Ninth chord (chord of the Ninth).

Ninth chords

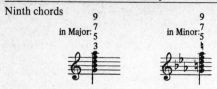

in Major:
$\begin{matrix}9\\7\\5\\3\end{matrix}$

in Minor:
$\begin{matrix}9\\7\\5\\\flat\end{matrix}$

When the root of the chord is the lowest tone, the chord is in the fundamental position; when some other tone is the lowest, the chord is inverted. Each triad has 2 inversions; each Seventh chord has 3.

Inversions of Triad   Inversions of 7th Chord

1st inv.   2nd inv.   1st inv.   2nd inv.   3rd inv.

The 1st inv. of a triad is called a $\begin{smallmatrix}6\end{smallmatrix}$ chord.
The 2nd inv. of a triad is called a $\begin{smallmatrix}6\\4\end{smallmatrix}$ chord.
The 1st inv. of a seventh chord is called a $\begin{smallmatrix}6\\5\end{smallmatrix}$ chord.
The 2nd inv. of a seventh chord is called a $\begin{smallmatrix}4\\3\end{smallmatrix}$ chord.
The 3rd inv. of a seventh chord is called a $\begin{smallmatrix}2\end{smallmatrix}$ chord.

Time Signatures

The *Time Signature* appears after the clef, at the beginning of a movement; the lower figure shows the *kind* of notes taken as the unit measure, while the upper figure shows the number of these notes that can fit a measure, and the grouping of beats.

For instance $\frac{3}{4}$ (3/4 time) means "3 quarter notes to the measure": | ♩ ♩ ♩ |

$\frac{12}{16}$ (12/16 time) means "12 sixteenth notes to the measure":

Rules for Pronouncing
German, French, and Italian

(Read these Rules carefully, and always refer to them in case of
doubt.)

The vowels are often not pronounced as in English. The
system of pronunciation employed in this Manual is
explained below.

ah is the broad *a* in *father*.

ăh is the same sound, only not dwelt upon; like *ah* in the
college cheer "'*rah! 'rah! 'rah!*" Never pronounce ăh
like the short English ă in *bat*.

ă is the short English *a*, as in *bat*.

â is like *a* in *bare*.

ä is nearly like â, but closer. Short ä (ä̆) is nearly like *e* in
bet, but more open.

ā is nearly like *a* in *bate*; only the long English *a* ends with a
soft sound like short ĭ, called a "vanish," caused by
slightly raising the root of the tongue (ā¹); whereas the
long "Continental" *a* has no vanish.

ĕh is the short sound of long *a* (closer than *e* in *bet*).

ĕ is short *e*, as in *bet*.

ē is long *e*, like *ee* in *beet*.

ī is long *i*, as in *bite*.

ĭ is short *i*, as in *bit*, though sometimes shaded towards *ee*.

oh is like *o* in *bode*; only the long English *o* ends with a
soft sound like *u* in *bull*, called a "vanish," caused by
drawing the lips together (ō̆ᵘ); whereas the long "Continental" *o* has no vanish.

ŏh is short *o*, like the first *o* in *opinion*. Never pronounce it
like the short English *o* in *blot*.

ô is the so-called broad Italian *o*, pronounced like *aw* in
law.

ö is a sound not found in English. To pronounce long ö, set
the lips as if to say "oh," and then say "ā" (as in *bate*),
keeping the lips fixed in the first position; for short ö (ö̆)
set the lips as before, but then say "ĕ" (as in *bet*), *keeping
the lips fixed* in the first position.

oo is like long *oo* in *boot*.

ŏŏ is like short *oo* in *book*.

ŭ is short *u,* as in *but*.

ŭh is like the *u* in *fur*.

ü is a sound not found in English. To pronounce long ü, set
the lips as if to say "oo" (as in *boot*), and then say "ee"
(as in *beet*), *keeping the lips fixed* in the first position; for
short ü (ü̆), set the lips as before, but then say "ĭ" (as in
bit), *keeping the lips fixed* in the first position. (N.B.—
This ü, long or short, is the so-called *French* u.)

DIPHTHONGS:

ahü represents the German *äu* or *eu*; pronounce as one
syllable quickly drawn together, accent on the "ah"
(ah´ü). It is somewhat like the English *oy* in *boy* (aw´ĭ).

wäh represents the French *oi*; pronounce as if written o͟͟äh,
in one syllable quickly drawn together, accent on the
"ah" (o͟͟äh´).

ow is like *ow* in *brow*.

THE CONSONANTS are usually pronounced as in English.
The following signs need explanation:

yh represents a sound not found in English, namely, the
soft German *ch*. Set the tongue as if to pronounce "ye,"
and then breathe (whisper) "he" through between
tongue and hard palate (see ALLMÄHLICH).

h represents a sound not found in English, namely, the *hard*
German *ch*. It is merely a rough breathing, as if one were
trying gently to clear one's throat. **Never** pronounce it
like *k,* unless explicitly so marked.

ng^k represents the sound *ng* at the end of German words,
which finish, after the usual *ng*-sound (*ng* as in *ring*),
with a light *k*-sound (see AUFSCHWUNG).

n represents a sound not found in English, namely, the
French nasal *n*. To get the correct nasal sound, the *n*
must be pronounced, not *after* the vowel, but *together
with* the vowel; that is, **the vowel must be spoken through**

the nose, thus becoming a nasal vowel. **Never** pronounce like "ang," "ong," etc., as the pronunciation is often printed; there is no *ng*-sound about the French nasal *n*. For example, to get the sound of *ain,* as in the French word *main* (măn), first sound "n," setting the tongue firmly against the hard palate so that the vocal air (air vibrating with tone) passes through the nose instead of between the lips; then, **letting the "n" still vibrate through the nose, drop the tongue and instantly blend the vowel "ă" (as in** *bat*) **with the "n."** This **blending** of "ă" and "n" gives the exact sound desired, if cut off short like a staccato trumpet tone. To say "main," simply put an "m" before the nasal vowel "ăn." The nasal vowels "ăhn" and "ŏhn" are obtained similarly.

r is to be pronounced with a roll, tip of tongue against hard palate.

s must be pronounced *sharp,* wherever it occurs in the marked pronunciation; *soft* s is represented by z.

zh represents the *z* in *azure*.

The consonants *d* and *t* are usually formed, in the Continental languages, by touching the root of the upper front teeth with the tip of the tongue. To make this point clear, first pronounce the English word "dry" in the ordinary way, tip of tongue against the hard palate; then pronounce the German "drei," but taking the *dr* with tip of tongue against root of upper front teeth.—Form *l* in the same manner.

The German *w* is a compound of the English *w* and *v*; i.e., to get it right, the lips must almost close and, *at the same time,* the lower lip must lightly touch the upper front teeth.

N.B.—All accents (vowel marks) found on the key words, such as à, ä, â, é, è, ê, ö, ü, etc., belong to the words as correctly written in their respective languages.

Comparative Table of Tempo Marks

CLASS I

INDICATING A STEADY RATE OF SPEED

Larghissimo, molto largo ⎫	
Largo (broad, stately)	
Largamente	
Larghetto	Group I.
Grave (heavy, dragging)	General
Lento (slow)	signification
Adagissimo	of terms is
Adagio (slow, tranquil)	SLOW.
Adagietto	
Andantino ⎭	

Andante (moving, going along) ⎫	
Moderato	
Allegretto	Group II.
Allegramente	General
Allegro (brisk, lively) [con moto,	signification
vivace] [agitato, appassionato]	of terms is
Presto (rapid) [con fuoco, veloce]	FAST.
Prestissimo ⎭	

CLASS II

INDICATING ACCELERATION

Accelerando (with increasing rapidity)

Stringendo ⎫
Affrettando ⎬ (swiftly accelerating, usually with a *crescendo*)
Incalzando ⎭

Doppio movimento (twice as fast)

Più mosso ⎫
Più moto ⎬ (a steady rate of speed, *faster* than preceding movement)
Veloce ⎭

CLASS III

INDICATING A SLACKENING IN SPEED

Rallentando
Ritardando
Allargando
Tardando } (gradually growing slower)
Slentando
Strascinando

Molto meno mosso ($\musQuarter = \musHalf$ del movimento precedente) } (half as fast)

Ritenuto
Meno mosso } (a steady rate of speed, *slower* than preceding movement)
Meno moto

Calando
Deficiendo
Mancando
Morendo } (growing slower and softer)
Sminuendo
Smorzando

A

A. 1. (Ger. *A*; Fr. and It., *La*). The sixth tone and degree in the typical diatonic scale of *C*-major.—2. In musical theory, capital *A* stands for the *A*-major triad, small *a* for the *a*-minor triad.—3. In Italian, *a* [ăh] (in French, *à* [ăh]) signifies to, at, for, by, in, etc.—4. In this Manual, an **-a** following an Italian word means that in the feminine form of the word **a** takes the place of the masculine ending **o**.

Ab (Ger., ăhp). Off (in organ music).

A B A. A symbolic representation for ternary form, in which the first statement (*A*) is repeated after (*B*). Most classical songs follow this formula. *A B A* is, therefore, also known as Song form. See Song form.

A ballata (It., ăh băhl-lah′tăh). In ballad style.

Abandon, avec (Fr., ăh-vek′ ăh-băhn-dŏhn′). See Abbandono, con.

A battuta (It., ăh băht-too′tăh). "With the beat"; in strict time.

Abbandonandosi (It., ăhb-băhn-dŏh-năhn′dŏh-sē).
Abbandonatamente (It.,—năh-tăh-men′tĕh).
Abbandono, con (It., kŏhn ăhb-băn-doh′nŏh).
    Yielding wholly to emotion; with a burst of passion; carried away by feeling.

Abbandonare (It., ăhb-băhn-dŏh-nah′rĕh). To abandon, to quit; *senza abbandonare la corda,* without quitting the string.

Abbellimenti (It., ăhb-bĕl-lē-men′tē). Embellishments.

Abendmusik (Ger., ăh′bend-moo-zīk). Evening music.

A bene placito (It., ăh bâ′nĕh plah′chē-tŏh). At pleasure; meaning that the tempo may be altered, graces or cadenzas added, or that certain specified instruments may be used, or not, at the performer's pleasure.

Aber (Ger., ah′behr). But.

Abgemessen (Ger., ăhp′gĕ-mes′sen). Measured; in strict time.

Abgestossen (Ger., ăhp′gĕ-shtoh′sen). "Struck off"; detached; *staccato.*

Ablösen (Ger., ahb′lö-zen). To loosen; to separate one note from another.

Abnehmend (Ger., ăhp′nā′ment). *Diminuendo.*

Abschnitt (Ger., ahb′shnitt). Section.

Abschwellen (Ger., ăhp′shvel′len). *Decrescendo.*

Absetzen (Ger., ahb′zet-zen). To separate; to detach.

Absolute music. Music without extra-musical connotation. See PROGRAM MUSIC.

Absolute pitch. Ability to name instantly and without fail any note struck on the piano keyboard or played on an instrument. This is an innate faculty, which appears in a musical child at a very early age, distinct from relative pitch, common among all musicians, in which an interval is named in relation to a previously played note. Absolute pitch is rare, even among professional musicians and is not a sure indication of great musical talent. Wagner and Tchaikovsky lacked it, but many obscure musicians possess it to an astonishing degree, being able to name the most complicated dissonant chords. Absolute pitch is also known as PERFECT PITCH.

Abstract music. A term often used for ABSOLUTE MUSIC.

Abwechseln (Ger., ăhp′vek′seln). To alternate ... *Mit abwechselnden Manualen* [măh-noo-ah′len], with alternating manuals.

A cappella (It., ăh căhp-pel′läh). "As in chapel," that is, as in the church style; choral singing without instrumental accompaniment.

A capriccio (It., ăh căhp-prit′chŏh). "As a caprice," according to one's own fancy.

Accarezzevole (It., ăhk-̇käh-ret-tsä′vŏh-lĕh). }
Accarezzevolmente (It.,—tsä-vŏhl-men′tĕh). }
Caressfully, caressingly, coaxingly.

Accelerando (It., ăht-chĕh-lĕh-rähn′dŏh). "Accelerating," growing faster.

Accelerato (It., ăht-chĕh-lĕh-rah′tŏh). "Accelerated," livelier, faster.

Accent. A stress.

Accentato (It., ăht-chen-tah′tŏh). }
Accento, con (It., kŏhn ăht-chen′tŏh). }
Accented, marked ... *Accentate* (—tah′tĕh) [plural form of *accentata,* or imperative], accent the notes.

Accentuando (It., ăht-chen-tŏŏ-ăhn′dŏh). Accenting.

Accentuare (It.,—ah′rĕh). To accent; *senza accentuare,* without accenting.

Accentuato (It.,—ah′tŏh). Accented.

Accentué (Fr., ăhk-sahnt-tyoo-a′). Accented.

Acciaccato, -a (It., ăht-chäh-kah′tŏh, -täh). Vehemently.

Acciaccatura (It., ăht-chäh-käh-too′räh). 1. A short accented appoggiatura.—2. A note a second above, and struck with, the principal note, and instantly released.

Acciaio (It., ăh-chäh′yo). "Steel." *Instrumento d'acciaio,* "instrument of steel," is Mozart's designation for the Glockenspiel part in *The Magic Flute.*

Accidental. Any chromatic sign not found in the key signature, occurring in the course of a piece.

Accompagnamento (It., ăhk-kŏhm-păhn-yăh-men′tŏh). Accompaniment.

Accompagnato (It., ahk-kohm-pahn-yah′-toh). 1. Accompanied.—2. A recitative with ensemble accompaniment.

Accompagnement (Fr., ăh-kŏhm-păhn-yŭ-măhn′). Accompaniment.

Accompanied fugue. A fugal form sometimes occurring in oratorios, in which the choral fugue is accompanied by instruments.

Accompaniment. Any part or parts which attend the voices or instruments bearing the principal part or parts in a musical composition. It is *ad libitum* when the piece can be performed without it, and *obbligato* when it is necessary to the piece. . . . *Additional accompaniments* are parts added to a composition by some other person than its original author . . . *Accompaniment of the scale,* the series of chords used to harmonize the ascending or descending diatonic scale.

Accopiato (It., ăhk-kŏp-pē-ăh′tŏh). Tied, bound.

Accord (Fr., ah-kor′). Chord.

Accordando (It., ăhk-kor-dăhn′dŏh). "Accordant," in tune. (In comic stage scenes it means that the tuning of an instrument is imitated by the orchestra.)

Accordatura (It., ăhk-kor-dăh-too′răh). The "tuning," or series of tones according to which a stringed instrument is tuned; g-d^1-a^1-e^2 is the *accordatura* of the violin.

Accorder (Fr., ah-kor-day′). To tune.

Accordion. A free-reed instrument invented by Damian, of Vienna, in 1829. The elongated body serves as a bellows, to be drawn out and pushed together; the bellows is closed at either end by a keyboard, that for the right hand having a diatonic (or incomplete chromatic) scale, while that for the left hand has 2 or more keys for harmonic bass tones. See Concertina.

Accordo (It., ahk-kor′doh). Chord.

Accoupler (Fr., ahk-koo-play′). "To couple," as in organ playing.

Achtelnote (Ger., ah′-tel-no′-tay). Eighth note.

Acoustic (ăh-koo′stĭk) **color.** The *timbre* (character or quality) of a musical tone.

Acoustics. Musical acoustics is the science of musical tones distinguished from mere noises. A *tone* of sustained and equal pitch is caused by regular and constant vibrations of the air, set in motion by similar vibrations in the body producing the tone (for instance, a piano string, a violin string, an organ pipe, or the vocal cords); while a *noise* is caused by irregular and unequal vibrations.

Action. In keyboard instruments, the mechanism set in motion by the player's fingers, or by the feet (organ pedals). —In the harp, the "action" (a set of pedals) does not directly produce the sound, but changes the key by shortening the strings by a semitone or whole tone.

Action song. A children's song in which bodily movements depict the action of the words, such as folding the hands and closing the eyes to represent sleep, fluttering of the fingers downward to represent rain, crossing the arms in a circular movement to represent the sun, and flapping the hands to imitate a bird in flight.

Act-tune. Music played between the acts of a drama; an *entr'acte.*

Acuta (L., ăh-koo′tah, "sharp," "shrill"). In the organ, a mixture stop having from 3 to 5 ranks.

Acute. High in pitch, sharp, shrill; opposed to Grave.

Adagietto (It., ăh-dăh-jet′tŏh). 1. A movement slightly faster than Adagio.—2. A short Adagio.

Adagio (It., ăh-dah′jŏh). Slow, leisurely; a slow movement . . . *Adagio adagio, adagio assai, adagio molto,* very slow . . . *Adagio non molto,* or *non tanto,* not too slow.

Adagissimo (It., ăh-dăh-jis′sē-mŏh). Extremely slow.

Adaptation. An ARRANGEMENT.

Added seventh. A minor or major seventh added to the concluding major triad. In jazz, the minor seventh (e.g., *C*, *E*,
G, *B* flat) is one of the blue notes (along with the flatted
third) and is characteristic of the blues. Much more acrid is
the major seventh in a tonic major triad at the end of a
piece, often played in tremolo by jazz pianists.

Added sixth. A sixth added to the major tonic triad, usually at
the end of a phrase, and treated as a consonance. First used
by Debussy and composers early in the 20th century, the
added sixth chord (*C*, *E*, *G*, *A* in *C* major) became extremely popular in jazz piano playing.

Additional accompaniments. See ACCOMPANIMENT.

Additional keys. Those above f^3.

Addolorato (It., ăhd-dōh-lōh-rah′tōh). Plaintive; in a style
expressing grief.

Adel, mit (Ger., mit ah′del). "With nobility"; in a lofty style.

À demi-jeu (Fr., ăh dŭ-mē-zhö′). With half the power of the
instrument.

À demi-voix (Fr., ăh dŭ-mē-vwăh′). MEZZA VOCE.

À deux (Fr., ăh dö′). A DUE: *à deux mains,* for two hands.

Adjunct. Closely related, as one key or scale to another . . .
Adjunct note, an unaccented auxiliary note not essential to
the harmony.

Ad libitum (L., ăhd lĭ′bi-tŭm, "at will"). A direction signifying (1) that the performer may employ the tempo or expression that suits him; (2) that any vocal or instrumental
part so marked may be left out, if desired. *Cadenza ad
libitum* means that a given cadenza may be performed or
not, or another substituted for it, at the performer's pleasure.

A due (It., ăh doo′ĕh). See DUE.

A dur (Ger., ah door′). *A* major.

Aengstlich (Ger.). See Ängstlich.

Aeolian harp or **lyre.** A stringed instrument sounded by the wind. It is a narrow, oblong wooden box, with low bridges at either end, across which are stretched a number of gut strings. The harp is placed in an open window, or some other aperture where a draft of air will sweep the strings.

Aeolian mode. A mode beginning on the sixth degree of the major scale, as in *A, B, C, D, E, F, G, A.*

Aequal (Ger., ä-kvahl'). A prefix to a stop-name, indicating that it is an 8-foot register.

Affabile (It., ähf-fah'bē-lĕh).

Affabilità, con (It., kŏhn ähf-fäh-bē-lē-tah').

Affabilmente (It., ähf-fäh-bēl-men'tĕh).
Sweetly and gracefully; suavely.

Affannato (It., ähf-fäh-nah'tŏh). Uneasily, distressfully.

Affannosamente (It., ähf-fäh-nŏh-säh-men'-tĕh). Anxiously, restlessly.

Affannoso (It., ähf-fäh-nŏh'sŏh). Anxious, restless.

Affetto, con (It., kŏhn ähf-fet'tŏh).

Affettuosamente (It., ähf-fet-tŏŏ-ŏh-säh-men'-tĕh).

Affettuoso (It., ähf-fet-tŏŏ-oh'sŏh).
With passion, emotion, feeling; very expressively; tenderly.

Affezione, con (It., kŏhn ähf-fĕh-tsē-oh'nĕh). In a style expressive of tender emotion.

Afflitto (It., ähf-flēt'tŏh). Melancholy, sad.

Afflizione, con (It., kŏhn ähf-flē-tsē-oh' nĕh). Sorrowfully, mournfully.

Affrettando (It., ähf-fret-tähn'dŏh). Hurrying.

Affrettare (It., ähf-fret-tah'rĕh). To hasten . . . *Senza affrettare,* without hastening.

Affrettato (It., ăhf-fret-tah′tŏh). Hurried; *tempo più affrettato,* at a swifter pace.

Affrettoso (It., ăhf-fret-toh′sŏh.) Hurriedly.

A fior di labbra (It., ăh fē-or′ dē lăhb′bräh). Very lightly and softly sung or spoken.

After beat. An ending to a trill, comprising two notes, the lower auxiliary and the principal note.

After note. 1. Unaccented appoggiatura.—2. The unaccented note of a pair.

After-striking. The reverse of Anticipation by the bass.

Agevole (It., ăh-jā′vŏh-lĕh). Easy, light.

Agevolezza, con (It., kŏhn ăh-jā-vŏh-let′-săh). ⎫
Agevolmente (It., ăh-jā-vŏhl-men′tĕh).   ⎬
  Easily, lightly. ⎭

Aggiustatamente (It., ăh-jŏŏs-tăh-tăh-men′-tĕh). Strictly in time.

Agiatamente (It., ăh-jă-tăh-men′tĕh). Easily, indolently.

Agilità (It., ăh-jē-lē-tah′). ⎫
Agilité (Fr., ah-zhē-lē-tā′). ⎬
  Agility, sprightliness, vivacity . . . *Con agilità,* in a light and lively style.

Agilmente (It., ăh-jēl-men′tĕh). Lightly, vivaciously.

Agitamento (It., ăh-jē-tăh-men′tŏh). Agitation.

Agitatamente (It., ăh-jē-tăh-tăh-men′tĕh). Excitedly, agitatedly.

Agitato (It., ăh-jē-tah′tŏh). Agitated . . . *Agitato con passione,* passionately agitated.

Agitazione, con (It., kŏhn ăh-jē-tăh-tsē-oh′-nēh). Agitatedly.

Agogic. A relatively modern term, from the Greek verb, "to lead," applied to slight deviations from the main rhythm.

Agraffe (ăh-grähf′). In the piano, a small metallic support of a string, between bridge and pin, serving to check vibration in that part.

Agréments (Fr., ah-grā-mahn′). Plural noun for ornaments and grace notes as used in Baroque music.

Ai (It., ah′ē). See **ALL′**.

Air. A tune or melody.

Air (Fr., är). Air, melody, tune; also, a song . . . *Airs detachés,* single numbers taken from operas, etc.

Aïs (Ger., ah′iss). *A* sharp.

Aisis (Ger., ah′iss-iss). *A* double sharp.

À l'aise (Fr., ah lehz′). "At ease"; in a relaxed manner.

À la mesure (Fr., äh läh mŭ-zür′). In strict time.

Alberti bass. A bass in broken chords, like

Alborada (Sp., ăhl-bŏ-räh′-däh). Type of Spanish music; originally a morning serenade. See **AUBADE**.

Albumblatt (Ger., ăhl′-bŭm-blăht). }
Album-leaf.
Title of a short and (usually) simple vocal or instrumental piece.

Alcuno, -a (It., ăhl-koo′nŏh, -năh). Some; certain. . . . *Con alcuna licenza,* "with a certain freedom" (as regards tempo).

Aleatory. A modern word as applied to music, from the Latin *alea,* "a game of dice." In Aleatory music, rhythmic values and even notes themselves are subject to multiple choices by the performer. Sometimes only duration is specified by the composer; in extreme cases even the length of the piece itself is aleatory. Aleatory music is sometimes called *chance music.*

Aliquot strings. Strings placed above the regular strings of the piano and tuned according to sympathetic vibrations so as to reinforce the tone of the instrument.

Al fine (It., ăhl fē′-něh). "To the finish"; used in phrases like *Dal segno al fine,* "from the sign to the end marked *Fine.*"

All', Alla (It., ăhl, ăhl′-lăh). To the, in the, at the, etc.; in the style of, like.

Alla breve (It., brâ′vĕh). 𝄵 In modern music, a meter of 2/2; i.e., two beats per measure with the half note carrying the beat; also called "cut time." The implication is of a faster tempo than 4/4.

Alla caccia (It., căht′chăh). In the hunting style.

Alla camera (It., kah′mĕh-răh). In the style of chamber music.

Alla cappella (It., kăh-pel′lăh). A CAPPELLA.

Alla marcia (It., mahr′chăh). In march style.

Alla militare (It., mē-lē-tah′rĕh). In military style.

Alla moderna (It., mŏh-dâr′năh). In modern style.

Allargando (It., ăhl-lar-găhn′dŏh). Growing slower.

Allagare, senza (It., sen′tsăh ăhl-lar-gah′rĕh). Without slackening speed.

Allargate (It.,—gah′tĕh). Go slower.

Alla russa (It., rŏŏs′săh). In the Russian style.

Alla scozzese (It., skŏht-tsa′zĕh). In Scotch style.

Alla siciliana (It., sē-chēl-yăh′năh). Like a Siciliana.

Alla stretta (It., strĕ′tăh). 1. Growing faster and faster.—2. In the style of a Stretta (or Stretto).

Alla tromba (It., trôm′băh). Like a trumpet.

Alla turca (It., toor′kăh). In Turkish style.

Alla veneziana (It., vĕh-nĕh-tsē-ah′năh). In the Venetian style (like a Gondoliera).

Alla zingara (It., tsin′găh-răh). In the style of Gypsy music.

Alla zoppa (It., tsôp′păh). Lamely, haltingly; in syncopated style.

Allegramente (It., ăhl-lĕh-grăh-men′tĕh). Nimbly, lightly, gaily, vivaciously.

Allegrettino (It., ăhl-lĕh-gret-tē′nŏh). 1. A short Allegretto movement.—2. A tempo slower than allegretto.

Allegretto (It., ăhl-lĕh-gret′tŏh). Quite lively; moderately fast (faster than andante, slower than allegro).

Allegrezza, con (It., kŏhn ăhl-lĕh-gret′săh). }
Allegria, con (It., kŏhn ăhl-lĕh-grē′ăh). }
With liveliness, vivacity.

Allegrissimo (It., ăhl-lĕh-gris′sē-mŏh). Very rapidly.

Allegro (It., ăhl-lā′grŏh). Lively, brisk, rapid. An Allegro (movement) is not quite as fast as a Presto . . . *Allegro assai, Allegro di molto,* very fast (usually faster than the foregoing movement) . . . *Allegro di bravura,* a technically difficult piece or passage to be executed swiftly and boldly . . . *Allegro giusto,* a movement the rapidity of which is suited to its subject . . . *Allegro risoluto,* rapidly and energetically. Etc., etc.

Allegro ma non troppo (It., ăhl-lā′grŏh măh nŏhn trŏp′pŏh). "Fast, but not too much."

Allein (Ger., ăhl-līn′). Alone; only.

Alleluia. The Latin form of Hallelujah (Praise the Lord!) as used in the Roman Catholic church service.

Allemanda (It., ăhl-lĕh-măhn′dăh). }
Allemande (Fr., ăhl-l′-mahn′d). }
1. A German dance in 3/4 time, like the Ländler.—2. A lively German dance in 2/4 time.—3. A movement in the Suite (either the first, or next to the Prelude) in 4/4 time and moderate tempo (*andantino*).

Allentamento (It., ăhl-len-tăh-men′tŏh). Slowness.

Allentato (It., ăhl-len-tah′tŏh). Slower.

All' espagnuola (It., ăhl ĕh-spăhn-yŏ′lăh). In the Spanish style.

All' inglese (It., ăhl in-glā′zĕh). In the English style.

All' italiana (It., ăhl ē-tăh-lē-ah′năh). In the Italian style.

Allmählich (Ger., ăhl-mä′lïyh). Gradually, by degrees. Also spelled *allmählig, allmälig.*

Al loco (It., ăhl lô′kŏh). "To the place"; a direction following *"8va,"* and meaning "perform the music as written."— Also directs a violinist to return to a former position after a shift.

Allongé (Fr., ăhl′lŏhn-zhā′). Prolonged stroke (of the bow).

Allontanando(si) (It., ăhl-lŏhn-tăh-năhn′dŏh [-sē]). Withdrawing; dying away.

Allora (It., ăhl-loh′răh). Then.

All' ottava (It., ăhl ŏht-tah′văh). "At the octave"; meaning, "play the notes an octave higher than written." The sign *8va*------------ or *8*----------- is usually employed.

All'unisono (It., ăhl oo-nē′sŏh-nŏh). In unison (or octaves).

Alma, con (It., kŏhn ăhl′măh). With soul, spirit; loftily; ardently.

Alphorn. A very long Swiss horn which is used by shepherds in the Alps to call the sheep back home at sunset.

Al segno (It., ăhl sen′yoh). "To the sign," directing the performer to go on playing until the sign in the form of the large letter *S* superimposed on a large *X*.

Alt (from the It., *alto*). Notes "in alt" are those of the next octave above *f*². Notes in the octave higher than this are said to be "in altissimo."

Alt (Ger., ăhlt). Alto (voice or part).

Alt-clarinet. An alto clarinet. See ALTO.

Altered chords. Chords containing chromatic alterations of chords properly belonging to the tonality of the music; also called *chromatic chords.*

Alterezza (It., ăhl-tĕh-ret′săh). Pride, loftiness.

Alternamente (It., ăhl-târ-năh-men′tĕh).

Alternando (It., ăhl-târ-nahn′dŏh). Alternating, alternatively.

Alternativo (It., ăhl-târ-näh-tē′voh). Alternative, or rather a contrasting section in dance forms, such as a trio in a minuet.

Alt-horn. The alto Saxhorn.

Altieramente (It., ăhl-tē-ĕh-räh-men′tĕh). In a lofty, majestic style.

Altíssimo (It., ăhl-tis′sē-mŏh). Highest. See ALT.

Alto (from the It., *alto*). 1. The deeper of the two main divisions of women's or boys' voices, the Soprano being the higher. (Also called *Contralto*.) Ordinary compass from *g* to *c*^{2}; in voices of great range, down to *d* and up to *f*^{2}, or even higher.—2. An instrument of similar compass; as the alto Saxhorn.—3. The counter-tenor voice.—4. The viola, or tenor violin.

Alto, -a (It., ăhl′tŏh, -tăh). High . . . *Alta viola,* tenor violin . . . *Ottava alta,* an octave higher.

Alto clef. A *C*-clef on the 3d line.

Altro, -a (It., ăhl′trŏh, -träh). Other . . . *Altri, Altre,* others.

Alzamento (It., ăhl-tsăh-men′tŏh). A raising or lifting.

Alzando (It., ăhl-tsähn′dŏh). Raising . . . *Alzando un po' la voce,* raising the voice a little.

Am (Ger., ăhm). By the.

Amabile (It., ăh-mah′bē-lĕh). Sweet, tender, gentle.

Amabilità, con (It., kŏhn ăh-măh-bē-lē-tah′). With sweetness; tenderly.

Amaramente (It., ăh-măh-räh-men′tĕh). ⎫
Amarevole (It., ăh-măh-rä′vŏh-lĕh). ⎬
Amarezza, con (It., kŏhn ăh-măh-ret′säh). ⎭
   Bitterly; mournfully, grievingly.

Amarissimamente (It., ăh-măh-ris-sē-măh-men′-tĕh). ⎫
Amarissimo (It., ăh-măh-ris′sĕ-mŏh). ⎬
   Very bitterly, with great anguish.

Amaro (It., ăh-măh′-rŏh). Grief, bitterness.

Amateur (Fr., ăh-măh-tör′). A "lover" of art, who, while possessing an understanding for and a certain practical knowledge of it, does not pursue it as a profession.

Ambrosian chant. This is the system of liturgical singing connected with the practice established by St. Ambrose in the 4th century. Its structure is much freer than that of the Gregorian chant, which followed two centuries later, and there are some "modern" applications (such as very long cadenzas, wandering from one mode to another) that are attractive to contemporary musicians.

Amen. The concluding word in a Jewish, or Christian, prayer, which means "so be it." Sometimes an Amen section in an oratorio is extended so as to become a concluding chorus of considerable length.

American organ. See REED ORGAN.

A mezza aria (It., ăh med′zăh ah′rē-ăh). Half-way between an aria and a recitative.

A mezza voce (It., voh′chĕh). With half the power of the voice (or an instrument).

A moll (Ger., ah mŏhl′). *A* minor.

Amore, con (It., kŏhn ăh-moh′rĕh).

Amorevole (It., ăh-mŏh-rā-vŏh-lĕh).

Amorevolmente (It., —rā-vŏhl-men′tĕh).

Amorosamente (It., —rŏh-săh-men′tĕh).

Amorously; lovingly, fondly, devotedly, tenderly.

Amoroso (It., ăh-mŏh-roh′sŏh). Amorous; loving, fond.

An (Ger., ăhn). On, by; "add" (in organ music).

Anacrusis (Gk., ăn-ŭ-kroo′sĭs). One or two unaccented syllables beginning a verse of poetry. In music, the weak beat, or weak part of a measure, with which a piece or phrase may begin. See AUFTAKT.

Anapest. A metrical foot of 3 syllables, 2 short and 1 long:
‿‿—.

Anche (Fr., ăhnsh). Reed . . . *Jeu d'anches* [zhö dähnsh], reed stop.

Anche (It., ăhn′kĕh). Also, too, likewise; even.

Ancor (It., ăhn-kohr′). ⎫
Ancora (It., ăhn-koh′răh). ⎬
Again, also, yet, still, even . . . *Ancora più mosso,* still faster . . . *Ancora piano,* continue singing (*or* playing) softly . . . *Ancora più piano,* still more softly.

Andacht, mit (Ger., mit ăhn′dăht). ⎫
Andächtig (Ger., ăhn′dĕyh′tĭyh). ⎬
With devotion; devotionally, devoutly.

Andamento (It., ăhn-dăh-men′-tŏh). Literally, "going"; an energetic tempo.

Andando (It., ăhn-dăhn′dŏh). "Going on"; easy and flowing.

Andante (It., ăhn-dăhn′tĕh). "Going," "moving"; a tempo mark indicating a moderately slow, easily flowing movement between *adagio* and *allegretto.—Andante affettuoso,* rather slowly and pathetic . . . *A. cantabile,* flowingly, in a singing style . . . *A. con moto, A. mosso, A. un poco allegretto,* a flowing and rather more animated movement . . . *A. non troppo,* easily flowing, but not too fast . . . *A. maestoso,* a flowing and stately movement . . . *A. pastorale,* flowing with tranquil simplicity . . . *A. sostenuto,* rather slow, flowing smoothly . . . *Meno andante,* slower.

Andantemente (It., ăhn-dăhn-tĕh-men′teh). Smoothly and flowingly.

Andantino (It., ăhn-dăhn-tē′nŏh). This word is a diminutive of *Andante,* and means, properly, a little slower than *andante*; but it is often used as if meaning a little faster.

Andare (It., ăhn-dah′rĕh). To move on . . . *Andare diritto,* go straight on . . . *Andare in tempo,* keep strict time.

Anfang (Ger., ăhn′făhng[k]). Beginning . . . *Vom Anfang,* same as DA CAPO.

Angemessen (Ger., ăhn′gĕ-mĕssen). Suitable, comfortable.

Angenehm (Ger., ăhn′gĕ-nāhm). Pleasing, agreeable.

Angklung. A Japanese rattle made of bamboo, and included in a gamelan, producing a pleasing sound in irregular rhythm.

Anglaise (Fr., ăhn-gläz′). The English country dance.

Anglican chant. Liturgical singing generally adopted in English speaking Protestant liturgy; it is usually harmonized with simple chords.

Angoscia, con (It., kŏhn ăhn-gŏh′shăh).
Angosciosamente (It., ăhn-gŏh-shŏh-săh-men′tĕh).
Angoscioso (It., ăhn-gŏh-shŏh′sŏh).
    With anguish, with agony of mind.

Ängstlich (Ger., engst′lĭyh). Anxiously, fearfully.

Anhang (Ger., ăhn′hăhngᵏ). Coda, codetta.

Anima, con (It., kŏhn ah′nē-măh). ANIMATO.

Animando (It., ăh-nē-măhn′dŏh). With increasing animation; growing livelier ... *Animando e crescendo,* growing livelier and louder ... *Animando sempre (più),* growing more and more animated ... *Animando un poco,* with somewhat more animation ... *Lo stesso tempo e animando sempre più,* the same rate of speed, with ever increasing animation (of expression).

Animato (It., ăh-nē-mah′tŏh). With spirit, spiritedly, vivaciously ... *Animato di più,* with greater animation.

Animosissimamente (It., —sis-sē-măh-men′tĕh).
Animosissimo (It., ăh-nē-mŏh-sis′sē-mŏh).
    With utmost animation, spirit, boldness.

Animoso (It., ăh-nē-moh′sŏh). Animated, spirited.

Anlaufen (Ger., ăhn′low-fen). To increase in volume.

Anmut(h), mit (Ger., ăhn′moot).
Anmut(h)ig (Ger., ăhn′moo′tĭyh).
    With grace, charm; gracefully, suavely.

Anomaly. The slight deviation from true pitch caused by tempering intervals on fixed-tone instruments; hence, an *anomalous chord* is a chord containing an interval rendered, by unequal tempering, extremely sharp or flat.

Anschlag (Ger., ăhn′shlăh). 1. The touch in pianoforte playing.—2. An appoggiatura or ornament.—3. A stroke, or the striking of a chord.

Anschwellen (Ger., ăhn′shvel′len). To swell, increase in loudness.

Anschwellend (Ger.,—lent). *Crescendo.*

Ansietà, con (It., kŏhn ăhn-sē-ĕh-tah′).

Ansiosamente (It., ăhn-sē-ŏh-săh-men′tĕh).

Ansioso (It., ăhn-sē-oh′sŏh).

In a style expressive of anxiety or hesitation.

Anstimmen (Ger., ăhn′shtĭm-men). To tune, to begin to sing.

Anstimmung (Ger., ăhn′shtĭm-moong^k). Tuning, intonation.

Answer. In a fugue, the taking-up by the *second* part (at a different pitch) of the subject proposed by the *first* part.

Antecedent. The theme or subject of a canon or fugue, as proposed by the first part; the Leader. Also, any theme or motive proposed for imitation, or imitated further on.

Anthem. A piece of sacred vocal music usually founded on biblical words, with or without instrumental accompaniment, and of moderate length.

Anticipation. The advancing of one or more of the parts constituting a harmony before the rest; which part or parts would, if all the parts progressed together, enter later.

Antico (It., ăhn-tē′kŏh). Antique, ancient . . . *All'antico,* in the ancient style.

Antiphon, or Antiphone. Originally, a responsive system of singing by two choirs (or divided choir), an early feature in the Catholic service of song; later applied to responsive or alternate singing, chanting, or intonation in general, as practiced in the Greek, Roman, Anglican, and Lutheran churches.—Also, a short sentence, generally from Holy Scripture, sung before and after the Psalms for the day.

Antiphonal. 1. A book or collection of antiphons or anthems.—2. In the style of an antiphon; responsive, alternating.

Antiphony. Responsive singing by two choirs (or divided choir) of alternate verses of a psalm or anthem.

Antique cymbal. A very small pair of brass cymbals, such as were used in accompanying dances in ancient Greece. They are sometimes used in modern scores for special effects.

Anvil. A metal bar used as a percussion instrument for special effects, as in the famous Anvil Chorus in Verdi's opera *Il Trovatore.*

Anwachsend (Ger., ähn′vähk′sent). *Crescendo.*

Aperto (It., äh-pâr′tōh). Open, without a mute . . . *Allegro aperto,* an allegro with broad, clear phrasing.

Aphony. Loss of voice.

A piacere (It., ah pee-ah-cher′-eh). "As you please"; that is, free in tempo and dynamics.

Aplomb (Fr., äh-plōhn′). Coolness, self-possession, steadiness.

Appassionamento (It., ähp-pähs-sē-ōh-näh-men′tōh). Passion, ardor.

Appassionatamente (It.—näh-täh-men′tĕh). Passionately, ardently.

Appassionato, -a (It.,—näh′tōh, -täh). Impassioned, with passion.

Appena (It., ähp-pā′näh). Hardly, very little . . . *Appena animando,* a trifle more animated . . . *Appena meno,* a very little slower . . . *Appena sensibile,* hardly audible.

Appenato (It., ähp-pĕh-nah′tōh). Distressed; in a style expressive of distress or suffering.

Appoggiando (It., ăhp-pŏhd-jähn′dŏh). "Leaning on," "supported." Said of a tone (note) gliding over to the next without a break, like an appoggiatura or the portamento.

Appoggiato (It., ăhp-pŏhd-jah′tŏh). "Leaned against," "supported." Calls for same style of execution as *Appoggiando*. In the following example, it is equivalent to *mezzo legato*.

appoggiato e piano

Appoggiatura (It., ăhp-pŏhd-jäh-too′räh). An *accented appoggiatura* is a grace note which takes the accent and part of the time value of the *following* principal note. The *long appoggiatura*

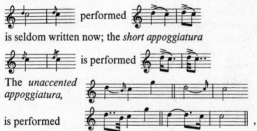

performed

is seldom written now; the *short appoggiatura*

is performed

The *unaccented appoggiatura*,

is performed

,

taking its time value from the *preceding* principal note, to which it is smoothly bound.

A punta d'arco (It., ăh pŏŏn′täh dar′kŏh). With the point of the bow.

À quatre mains (Fr., ăh kăh′tr măn). }
A quattro mani (It., ăh kwăht′trŏh mah′nē). }
For 4 hands; duets on piano or organ.

À quatre voix (Fr., ăh kăh′tr vwăh). }
A quattro voci (It., ăh kwăht′trŏh voh′chē). }
For 4 voices or parts.

Arabesque. A type of fanciful pianoforte piece; ornamental passages accompanying or varying a theme.

Arbitrio (It., ar-bē′trē-ŏh). Will, pleasure . . . *A suo arbitrio,* at your pleasure.

Arcato (It., ar-kah′tŏh). With the bow.

Arch-(Engl.), **Archi-**(L., ar′kē), **Arci-**(It., ar′chē). A prefix signifying "chief, pre-ëminent," formerly applied to instruments in the sense of "largest," and to official titles in the sense of "head."—*Archchanter,* precentor . . . *Archlute* (Fr., *Archiluth* [ar-shē-lüt′]; It., *Arciliuto* [archē-lē-oo′tŏh]), a large kind of bass lute.

Arco (It., ar′kŏh). Bow . . . *Arco in giù* (joo′), down-bow; *arco in su* (soo′), up-bow.

Ardente (It., ar-den′tĕh). Ardent, fiery, passionate.

Ardentemente (It., ar-den-tĕh-men′tĕh). Ardently.

Arditezza, con (It., kŏhn ar-dē-tet′săh). With boldness, boldly, spiritedly.

Ardito (It., ar-dē′tŏh). Bold, spirited.

Ardore, con (It., kŏhn ar-doh′rĕh). With ardor, warmth.

Arctinian syllables. The syllables *ut, re, mi, fa, sol, la,* first used to name the tones of the hexachord by Guido d'Arezzo (Guido Aretinus).

Aria (It., ah′rē-ăh, plural **Arie** [ah′rē-ĕh]). An air, song, tune, melody. The *grand* or *da-capo aria* (*Aria grande* [grähn′dĕh]) is in 3 divisions: (I) The theme, fully developed; (II) a more tranquil and richly harmonized section; (III) a repetition *da capo* of the first, with more florid ornamentation.

Aria buffa (It., bŏŏf′făh). A comic or burlesque aria.

Aria concertante (It., kŏhn-châr-tähn′tĕh). An aria for concert singing, with obbligato instrumental accompaniment.

Aria da chiesa (It., dăh k′yâ′zăh). Church aria.

Aria da concerto (It., dăh kŏhn-châr′tŏh). An aria for concert singing.

Aria d'entrata (It., den-trah′tăh). An aria sung by any character in an opera, on his or her first entrance.

Aria di bravura (It., dē brăh-voo′răh). An aria replete with ornaments and difficulties for showing off the singer's skill.

Aria di sortita (It., dē sohr-tē′tăh). See Sortita.

Arie (Ger., ah′rē-ĕ). Aria.

Arietta (It., ahrē-et′tăh).

Ariette (Fr., ăh-rē-et′).

Ariettina (It., ăh-rē-et-tē′năh).

A short air or song; a short aria.

Arioso (It., ăh-rē-oh′sŏh). In vocal music, a style between aria and recitative; or, a short melodious strain interrupting or ending a recitative.—Also, an impressive, dramatic style suitable for the *aria grande;* hence, a vocal piece in that style.—In instrumental music, the same as *cantabile*.

Armoniosamente (It., ăr-mŏh-nē-ŏh-săh-men′tĕh). Harmoniously.

Armonioso (It., ar-mŏh-nē-oh′sŏh). Harmonious.

Arpa (It., ar′-pah). Harp.

Arpeggiando (It., ar-ped-jăhn′dŏh). Playing in harp-style; sounding broken chords.

Arpeggiato (It., ar-ped-jah′tŏh). Arpeggiated, arpeggio'd.

Arpeggio (It., ar-ped′jŏh; plural **Arpeggi** [ar-pĕd′jē]). Playing the tones of a chord in rapid, even succession; playing broken chords. Hence, a chord so played; a broken or spread chord, or chord-passage.

Arrangement. The adaptation of a composition for performance on an instrument, or by any vocal or instrumental combination, for which it was not originally written. Hence, any composition so adapted or arranged.

Ars antiqua (L., ahrz ăn-tē′kwŭ). A contrapuntal, sometimes dissonant style of 12th–13th century France.

Arsin et thesin, per. Imitation of a weak beat (arsis) by a strong beat (thesis) in a canon. Also, imitation by inversion.

Arsis and thesis (Gk., ahr′sēs, thēs′ēs). Upbeat and downbeat.

Ars nova (L., ahrz nō′vŭ, "new art."). The period of 14th century music which contrasted with the Ars antiqua by its more complex counterpoint.

Articolato (It., ar-tē-kŏh-lah′tŏh). "Articulated"; *ben articolato,* clearly and neatly pronounced and phrased.

Artificial harmonics. Harmonics produced on a *stopped* string rather than on an open string (as on the violin).

Artiglich (Ger., ar′tiyh-lĭyh). Prettily, neatly, gracefully.

As (Ger., ăhss). *A♭* (*A* flat).

Asas, or **Ases** (Ger., ăhss′ăhss, ăhss′ess). *A* double flat.

As dur (Ger., dōōr). *A♭* major.

Asprezza, con (It., kŏhn ăh-spret′săh). With harshness; harshly, roughly.

Aspro (It., ăh′sprŏh). Harsh, rough.

Assai (It., ăhs-sah′ē). Very ... *Allegro assai,* very fast ... *Adagio assai,* very slow ... *Assai moderato,* very moderate.

Assez (Fr., ăhs-sā′). Enough; rather.

Assottigliando (It., ăh-sŏh-tē-l'yăhn′dŏh). Diminishing, softening.

A string. The 2d string of a violin; the 1st of a viola. or 'cello; the 3d of a double bass; the 5th of a guitar.

A suo arbitrio (It., ăh soo′ŏh ar-bē′trē-ŏh). ⎫
A suo bene placito (It., bâ′nĕh plah′chē-tŏh). ⎬
A suo comodo (It., kŏh′mŏh-dŏh). ⎭
At the pleasure or discretion of the singer or player.

Atempause (Ger., ah′tŭm-powze). Literally, "breath-pause"; a slight break to catch the breath before a strong beat.

A tempo (It., ăh tem′pŏh). In time; at the preceding rate of speed.

At(h)emlos (Ger., ah'tem-lohs). Breathlessly.

Atonality. The absence of tonality. A type of modern music in which the traditional tonal structures are abandoned, and the key signature is absent.

Attacca (It., ăht-tăhk'kăh). "Attack" or begin what follows without pausing, or with a very short pause . . . *Attacca* (or *attaccate* [ăht-tăhk-kah'těh]) *subito,* attack instantly.

Attacco (It., ăht-tăhk'kŏh). Attack; stroke of the glottis.

Attack. The act (or style) of beginning a phrase, passage or piece.

Attendant keys. Of a given key are its relative major or minor, together with the keys of the dominant and subdominant and their relative major or minor keys. For instance, the attendant keys of *C* major are *a* minor, *G* major, *F* major, *e* minor, and *d* minor.

Attenzione, con (It., kŏhn ăht-ten-tsē-oh'něh). "With attention"; in a marked style; significantly.

Aubade (Fr., ōh-băhd). Morning music.

Audacia, con (It., kŏhn ăh-oo-dah'chah). With boldness.

Aufführung (Ger., owf'füh-rŏŏng^k). Performance.

Aufgeregt (Ger., owf'gĕ-rayht'). Agitated, excited.

Aufgeweckt (Ger., owf'gĕ-věkt). Animated, brisk.

Aufhalten (Ger., owf'hăl-ten). To stop or retard.

Aufschwingend (Ger., owf'shving'ent). Soaring, impetuous.

Aufschwung (Ger., owf'shvŏŏng^k). Lofty flight, soaring impetuosity; *mit Aufschwung,* in a lofty, impetuous, impassioned style.

Aufstrich (Ger., owf'strīyh). An up bow.

Auftakt (Ger., owf'tähkt). Upbeat, anacrusis; a fractional measure beginning a movement, piece or theme.

Auftritt (Ger., owf'trĭtt). A scene of an opera.

Aufzug (Ger., owf'zŭg). An act of an opera.

Augmentation. Doubling (or increasing) the time-value of the notes of a theme or motive in imitative counterpoint.

Augmented fourth. The interval a semitone bigger than the perfect fourth, as from *C* to *F* sharp.

Augmented second. An interval a semitone larger than a major second. It is used between the sixth and the seventh degrees of the minor harmonic scale, as between *F* and *G* sharp in the *a* minor scale. It is characteristic of oriental melodies.

Augmented sixth. An interval a semitone larger than a major sixth, as from *C* to *A* sharp. It is the basic interval of the so-called French Sixth, German Sixth and Italian Sixth.

Augmented triad. A triad consisting of 2 major thirds, as in *C, E, G* sharp.

Aulos. An ancient Greek wind instrument resembling an oboe. It usually had two connected pipes, blown simultaneously.

Aumentando (It., ăh-ŏŏ-men-tăhn′dŏh). CRESCENDO.

Ausdruck (Ger., ows′drŏŏk). Expression. *Mit innigem Ausdruck,* with heart-felt expression.

Ausdrucksvoll (Ger., ows′drŏŏks-fŏhl′). Expressively.

Ausgabe (Ger., ows′găbe). Edition.

Ausgelassen (Ger., ows′gĕ-lässen). Boisterous, exuberant.

Auszug (Ger., ows′tsŭh). Arrangement or reduction, as in *Klavierauszug,* piano reduction from a full score.

Authentic cadence. See CADENCE.

Authentic melody. One whose range covers all, or nearly all, the octave-scale above its tonic or final; opposed to PLAGAL.

Authentic mode. In an *authentic* church mode, the keynote is the lowest tone; in a *plagal* mode, the keynote is a fourth above the lowest tone.

Authentic part of the scale. That part lying between the keynote and its *higher* dominant; the part between keynote and *lower* dominant being called *plagal*.

Autoharp. A zither-like educational instrument having devices for playing preset chords; used to demonstrate harmonic progressions and to accompany simple songs.

Auxiliary note. A note not essential to the harmony or melody; particularly, a grace note a second above or below a given melody note.

Auxiliary scales. Those of attendant keys.

Auxiliary stop. See STOP.

Avec (Fr., ăh-věk′). With . . . *Avec âme* [ahm], the same as *con anima* . . . *Avec le chant* [shähn], the same as *col canto*.

Avoided cadence. See CADENCE.

À volonté (Fr., ăh vŏh-lŏhn-tā′). At pleasure.

Ayre. An English court song of the 16th and 17th century, usually accompanied on the lute. The word is an old English spelling of "air."

B

B. 1. (Ger. *H*; Fr. and It. *si*). The seventh tone and degree in the diatonic scale of *C* major.—2. In musical theory, capital *B* designates the *B*-major triad, small *b* the *b*-minor triad.—3. In German, *B* stands for B♭.—4. *B.* is also an abbreviation for *Bass* or *Basso* (*c. B.* = col Basso; *B. C.* = basso continuo).

Baby grand. The smallest size of the grand piano.

B-A-C-H. These letters of Bach's name represent in German nomenclature the notes *B* flat, *A, C,* and *B* natural. Bach used this chromatically sounding theme in the unfinished last fugue of his work, *The Art of the Fugue,* and many composers since then have paid tribute to Bach by writing pieces based on the same 4 notes.

Bachelor of (or **in**) **Music.** In U.S., the lower of the academic musical degrees, Master of Music being the higher, and Doctor of Music the highest. In Great Britain, the two academic degrees are Bachelor and Doctor of Music.

Backfall. An obsolete grace, played like an accented appoggiatura.

Backturn. A melodic ornament which begins on a lower note; so if *C* is followed by an inverted turn, the ornament will be *C, B, C, D, C.*

Badinage (Fr., bäh-di-nă′zh). Playful banter.

Badinerie (Fr., bah-dee-neh-ree′). "Teasing"; occasionally used in Baroque music as the title of a quick movement in 2/4 time.

Bagatelle. A trifle; usually a short, fairly easy piece.

Bagpipe. A very ancient wind instrument of Eastern origin, still popular in Great Britain. The commonest form has 4 pipes; 3 drones (single-reed pipes tuned to a given tone, its fifth and its octave, respectively, and sounding on continuously), and 1 chanter or melody-pipe (a double-reed pipe with 6 or 8 holes), on which the tune is played. The "bag" is a leathern sack, filled with wind either from the mouth or from small bellows worked by the player's arm; the pipes are inserted in and receive wind from the bag.

Baguette (Fr., bah-get′). Conductor's baton; also a drumstick.

Baile (Sp., bi′-leh). A dance.

Balalaika (Russian, băl-a-lī′kăh). Popular Russian instrument of the guitar type.

Balance swell-pedal. See PEDAL.

Ballabile (It., băhl-lah′bē-lĕh). 1. A piece of dance music.—2. Ballet-music.—3. In the style of, or suitable for, dance music.

Ballad. Originally, a song intended for a dance-accompaniment; hence, the air of such a song.—In modern usage, a ballad is a simple narrative poem, generally meant to be sung.—As a purely musical term, it was originally applied to a short, simple vocal melody, set to one or more stanzas, with a slight instrumental accompaniment. It now includes instrumental melodies of a similar character; also compositions for single instruments, or for orchestra, supposed to embody the idea of a narrative.

Ballade (Ger., băhl-lah′dĕ). ⎫
Ballade (Fr., băhl-lăhd′). ⎬
A ballad-like art song, or an instrumental solo piece.

Balladenmässig (Ger., băhl-lah′d′n-mä′sīyh). In ballad style.

Ballad opera. An opera chiefly made up of ballads and folk-songs.

Ballata (It., băhl-lah′täh). A ballad.—*A ballata,* in ballad style.

Ballet (băl-lay′, *or* băl-let′). 1. A spectacular dance introduced in an opera or other stage-piece.—2. A pantomime, with music and dances setting forth the thread of the story.

Ballet (Fr., băh-lā′). ⎫
Ballett (Ger., băhl-let′). ⎬
A ballet.

Balletto (It., băhl-let′tŏh). 1. A ballet.—2. The title of an Allegretto by Bach, in common time.

Ballo (It., băhl′lŏh). A dance; a ballet . . . *Balli inglesi,* English dances . . . *Balli ungaresi,* Hungarian dances . . . *Da ballo,* in dance-style, light and spirited.

Band. 1. A company of musicians playing martial music (brass-band, military band).—2. An orchestra.—3. A section of the orchestra playing instruments of the same class (brass-band, string-band, wind-band, wood-band).

Banda (It., băhn′däh). 1. A military band.—2. The brass wind-instruments and the instruments of percussion in the Italian opera orchestra.—3. An orchestra playing on the stage.

Bandmaster. Conductor of a military band.

Bandola (Sp., băhn-doh′läh). [Also the *Bandolon, Bandora, Bandura.*] Instruments of the lute family, with a greater or smaller number of steel or gut strings, and played with a plectrum ("pick"); all very similar to the Mandolin.

Banjo. American folk instrument with 5 strings, which are plucked by the fingers or a pick; it was made popular in Negro minstrelsy, country mountain music, and early jazz.

Bar. A vertical line dividing measures on the staff, and indicating that the strong beat falls on the note just after it.—2. The popular name for "measure" (the notes and rests contained between two bars). (N.B.—It is better to call a bar a *bar,* and a measure a *measure.*)

Barbaro (It., bar′băh-rŏh). Same as FEROCE.

Barbershop harmony. The type of close harmony, often with chromatic passing notes, which singing barbers made popular in America at the turn of the century.

Barcarola (It., bar-kăh-rô′läh).
Barcarole (Ger., bar-kăh-roh′lĕ).
Barcarolle (Fr., bar-kăh-rŏhl′).
Barcaruola (It., bar-kăh-rŏŏ-ô′läh).
1. A gondoliera; song of the Venetian gondoliers.—2. A vocal or instrumental solo, or concerted piece, imitating the Venetian boat-songs, and usually in 6/8 time (Chopin's, for piano, is in 12/8 time).

Bare fifth, octave. See NAKED FIFTH.

Bariolage (Fr., băh-rē-ŏh-läh′zh). 1. A medley.—2. A group of several notes played in the same position on 2, 3, or 4 strings (violin).

Baritone. 1. The male voice between bass and tenor, and

more or less similar in quality to both. Compass from G to f^1. Also, a singer having such a voice.—2. A bow instrument like the *viola da gamba*.—3. The Euphonium (bass Saxhorn).

Baritone clef. The obsolete F clef on the *third* line:

Baroque music. The type of contrapuntal music developed within the historical period of about 1600–1750. Bach and Handel belonged to this era. Although the word "Baroque" originally implied a bizarre and even crude quality, it has acquired the opposite meaning of dignity and precise craftsmanship.

Baroque organ. A highly developed Gothic organ with several manuals and a variety of stops, such as was used by Bach.

Baroque suite. CLASSICAL SUITE.

Barocco (It., băh-rôhk′kŏh). Eccentric, strange, odd, whimsical.

Barré (Fr., bar-rā′). In lute or guitar playing, the stopping of several or all the strings with the left-hand forefinger.— *Grand* [grähn] *barré,* a stop or more than 3 strings.

Barrel organ. A species of mechanical organ. The Orchestrion is a large kind of barrel organ.

Barytone. Another spelling of BARITONE.

Bass. 1. The lowest tone in a chord, or the lowest part in a composition.—2. The lowest male voice; ordinary compass from F to c^1 (or d^1); extreme compass from C to e^1:—3. A singer having such a voice.

Bass (Ger., băhs). Besides the 3 English meanings given above, it denotes (*a*) an old bowed instrument between 'cello and double bass, with 5 or 6 strings; (*b*) the same as *Kontrabass* (double bass); (*c*) at the end of the name of an organ-stop, it means that the stop is on the pedal (for example, *Gemshornbass*).

Bass-bar. In violins, etc., a long narrow strip of wood glued to the inner surface of the belly parallel with and just beneath the *G*-string, put in to strengthen the belly and equalize vibration.

Bass clef. *F* clef on the 4th line:

Bass drum. The biggest and lowest pitched drum. It does not produce a definite note, however.

Bass fiddle. A colloquial name for the DOUBLE BASS.

Basse (Fr., băhs). Bass.

Basse danse. (Fr., băhs dăhns). A medieval French dance, characterized by feet shuffling across the floor.

Basset horn. A tenor clarinet of mellow, though somber, timbre, with a compass from *F* to *c*³.

Basso (It., băhs′sŏh). Bass; also, the double bass.

Basso buffo (It., bŏŏf′fŏh). A comic bass.

Basso cantante (It., kăhn-tăhn′tĕh). A bass-baritone.

Basso continuo (It., kŏhn-tē′nŏŏ-ŏh). In Baroque ensemble music, the part played by a keyboard instrument (organ or harpsichord) and a low stringed instrument (equivalent to the modern cello); sometimes a bassoon is also included. See FIGURED BASS.

Basso giusto (It., jŏŏ′stŏh). A basso cantante.

Basso obbligato (It., ŏhb-blē-gah′tŏh). An indispensable bass part or accompaniment.

Bassoon. A woodwind instrument of the oboe family; the double tube bears the long, curving, metallic mouthpiece with its double reed. Compass from *B*₁♭ to *c*², or even to *f*². Tone soft and mellow.

Basso ostinato (It., ŏh-stē-nah′tŏh). See GROUND BASS.

Basso profondo (It., prŏ-fŏhn′dŏh). Literally, "profound bass"; the lowest bass voice.

Basstuba (Ger., băhs′tŏŏ′băh). See TUBA 2.

Baton. A conductor's stick.

Battery (also Fr., **batterie**). 1. The group of percussion instruments.—2. A drum roll.—3. 18th-century term for broken chord figures.

Battuta (It., băht-tŏŏ'tăh). Beat; downbeat; measure ... *A battuta,* in strict time.

B dur (Ger., bā door). *B* flat major.

Be (Ger., bā). The flat sign (♭).

Beat. 1. A movement of the hand in marking ("beating") time.—2. A division of a measure marked by a beat.—3. In a trill, the pulsation of 2 consecutive tones.—4. An appoggiatura.—5. A throbbing caused by the interfering tone waves of 2 tones of different pitch.

Beating reed. See REED.

Bebop. A type of JAZZ that emerged in America in the 1940's; associated with Charlie Parker and Dizzy Gillespie.

Bebung (Ger., beh'boong). Literally, "trembling"; a vibrato effect on string instruments or on a clavichord.

Bécarre (Fr., beh-car'). Natural sign.

Becken (Ger., bek'en). Cymbal (singular); cymbals (plural).

Bedeutungsvoll (Ger., bĕ-dahü'tŏŏngs-fōhl'). Full of meaning; significantly.

Bedrohlich (Ger., bĕ-drŏh'lĭyh). Menacing.

Begeisterung, mit (Ger., mit bĕ-gī'stĕ-rŏŏngᵏ). With enthusiasm, spirit.

Begleitung (Ger., bĕ-glī'tŏŏngᵏ). Accompaniment.

Beguine. A Latin American dance in a lively syncopated rhythm.

Behaglich (Ger., bĕ-hahg'lĭyh). Easily, comfortably; *comodo.*

Bel canto (It., bel kăhn'tŏh). The art of beautiful song, as exemplified by the finest Italian singers of the 18th and 19th centuries, and their pupils or imitators. Opposed to Recitative, and to the "declamatory" style of singing brought into such prominence by Wagner.

Belebt (Ger., bĕ-lāpt'). Animated, brisk.

Bell. A hollow metallic instrument of percussion, sounded by a clapper hanging inside, or a hammer outside.—Also, the flaring end of various wind-instruments.

Bell diapason. An organ stop, usually of 8′ pitch, with open, bell-mouthed pipes.

Bellezza con (It., kŏhn bel-let′säh). With beauty; gracefully, suavely.

Bell gamba. An organ stop having conical pipes surmounted by bells.

Bell harp. A kind of dulcimer used in the 18th century in England.

Bellicosamente (It., bel-lē-kŏh-säh-men′tĕh).⎫
Bellicoso (It., bel-lē-kŏh′sŏh).   ⎬
    In a martial, warlike style. ⎭

Bell metronome. A metronome with a bell attachment which may be set to strike with every second, third, fourth, or sixth beat of the pendulum.

Bell piano. See GLOCKENSPIEL.

Belly. The face (upper side) of the resonance-box of the violin, etc.—Also, the soundboard of the piano.

Bémol (Fr., bā-mŏl). The flat sign (♭).

Bene (It., bâ′nĕh). [Abbreviation, *ben.*]. Well. . . . *Ben marcato,* well marked; *a bene placito,* at pleasure; *ben ritmato,* with careful and precise observance of the rhythm; *ben sostenuto, ben tenuto,* well sustained.

Benedictus. In Latin, "blessed"; the concluding portion of the Sanctus in the Roman Catholic Mass.

Bequem (Ger., bĕ-kväm′). Easily, comfortably.

Berceuse (Fr., bâr-söz′). A cradle song, lullaby.

Bergamask. A clownish dance like that of the peasants of Bergamasca, Italy.

Bergerette (Fr., bâr-zhâr-et′). A pastoral or rustic song; also a type of 18th-century French lyrical poetry.

Beruhigend (Ger., bĕ-roo′-ĭyhent). Becoming calm.

Beschleunigen (Ger., bĕ-shlăhü′nĭ-gen). To hasten.

Beschwingt (Ger., bĕ-shvingt′). Winged ... *Leicht beschwingt,* lightly and swiftly; *volante.*

Beseelt (Ger., bĕ-zālt′). "Soulfully," animated.

Bestimmt (Ger., bĕ-shtimt′). With decision, energy.

Betont (Ger., bĕ-tohnt′). Accented, marked.

Betonung, mit (Ger., mit bĕ-toh′nŏŏngᵏ). With emphasis.

Betrübt (Ger., bĕ-trü′bt). Grieved, afflicted.

Bewegt (Ger., bĕ-vāyht′). Moved, agitated.

Bewegter (Ger., bĕ-vāyh′ter). Faster; *più mosso.*

Bewegung (Ger., bĕ-vā′gŏŏngᵏ). Movement; agitation.

Bichord. Having two strings. A bichord instrument is one (like the mandolin, lute, and certain pianos) having a pair of strings, tuned in unison, for each tone.

Bicinium. A song for 2 voices.

Bien (Fr., b'yĕn). Well ... *Bien chanté,* same as MOLTO CANTABILE; *bien rythmé,* same as BEN RITMATO.

Bifara. An organ stop, the pipes of which are either double mouthed, or in pairs; the two members of each pair are tuned at slightly different pitches, so that the interference ("beating") of the sound waves produces a gentle tremolo.

Binary. Dual; two-part ... *Binary form,* a form of movement founded on two principal themes (see SONATA), or divided into 2 distinct or contrasted sections ... *Binary measure,* that of common time, the first of every 2 members taking the accent (regular and equal alternation between downbeat and upbeat).

Bind. 1. A tie.—2. A brace.

Bio-music. A term denoting the physiological and psychological response to musical stimuli.

Bis. Twice; commonly used in Europe to request an encore.

Also used in printed music to indicate that a passage is to be repeated.

Biscroma. In Italian, a thirty-second note.

Bisogna (It., bē-zŏhn′yăh). "Is necessary," "must"; as, *si bisogna da capo al segno,* must be repeated from the beginning to the sign.

Bitonality. Harmony in 2 different tonalities, as *C* major and *F* sharp major played simultaneously. Bitonality is often used in modern compositions.

Bizzarramente (It., bid-zar-răh-men′tĕh). ⎫
Bizzarria, con (It., kŏhn bid-zar-rē′ăh). ⎬
    In a bizarre, whimsical, fantastic, extravagant style.

Bizzarro,-a (It., bid-zar′rŏh, -răh). Bizarre, whimsical, odd, fanciful.

Black bottom. A rapid ballroom dance of the roaring twenties characterized by sinuous hip movements.

Blasinstrumente (Ger., blaz′in-stru-men-teh). Wind instruments.

Blech (Ger., bleh). Brass; *Blechmusik,* brass music.

Blochflöte (Ger., blŏh′flö′tĕ). ⎫
Blockflöte (Ger., blŏhk′flö′tĕ). ⎬
    1. An old kind of *flute à bec.*—2. An organ stop having pyramid-shaped flue pipes of 2′, 4′, 8′, or 16′ pitch, and sometimes stopped.

Block. In violins, etc., the blocks are small pieces of wood within the body, glued vertically to the ribs between belly and back to strengthen the instrument.—A hammer in the piano *"blocks"* when it remains against the string after striking, instead of recoiling, thus *"blocking"* (deadening) the tone.

Bluegrass. Folk music of the Kentucky countryside characterized by an unaffected rhythmic quality and played on string instruments, principally the banjo.

Blue note. The lowered third and seventh degree in a major scale, as *B* flat and *E* flat in the *C* major scale; the blue note is characteristic in melodies of the blues and jazz.

Blues. A somewhat wistful American ballad of black origins. It is in 4/4 time, has a melody characterized by lowered third and seventh ("blue") notes, and has a stereotyped, 12-measure harmonic pattern.

B moll (Ger., bā mŏhl′). *B* flat minor.

Boat song. Barcarole; Gondoliera.

Bob. A term in change-ringing applied to the various sets of changes which may be rung on 6 bells (bob minor), 8 bells (bob major), 10 bells (bob royal), or 12 bells (bob maximus).

Bocca (It., bŏhk′kăh). Mouth . . . (*Con*) *bocca chiusa* [kew′-săh], with closed mouth; humming. See BRUMMSTIMMEN.

Bocedisation. A medieval system of Solmization, with the notes of the scale named bo-ce-di, etc., instead of do-re-mi.

Body. 1. The resonance-box of a stringed instrument.—2. That part of a wind-instrument remaining when mouthpiece, crooks and bell are removed.—3. The tube of an organ-pipe above its mouth.—4. A tone is said to have "body" when it is full and sonorous; the resonance of a tone is also called the "body."

Boehm system. A system of playing the flute with keys replacing the holes in the old instruments, making it more convenient to play. Named after the 19th-century German inventor Theobald Boehm.

Bogen (Ger., boh′gen). 1. A bow.—2. A slur, or a tie.

Bois (Fr., bwăh). "Wood"—the woodwinds.

Bolero (Sp., bŏh-leh′rŏh). 1. A Spanish national dance in 3/4 time and lively tempo (allegretto), the dancer accompanying his steps with castanets.—2. A composition in bolero style.

Bombard. 1. A large kind of oboe, or shawm, now obsolete.—2. A 16′ reed stop in the organ.

Bombarde (Fr., bŏhn-bar′d). A bombard. Also see Posaune.

Bombardon. A large bass trumpet; as now made, a bass saxhorn.—Also a deep-toned organ stop.

Bones. A primitive rhythm instrument of 2 bones clicked together by the fingers; used in American Negro minstrel shows.

Bongos. Paired, hand-held Cuban drums, struck by the fingertips.

Boogie-woogie. Type of jazz with ostinato bass figures.

Bop. Shortened name for Bebop.

Boston. A form of slow waltz, also called the "hesitation waltz," popular in the 1910's–1920's.

Bossa nova. Popular Brazilian dance music influenced by American jazz. The name means "new voice" in Portuguese.

Bouche (Fr., boosh). Mouth . . . *À bouche fermée,* same as *Bocca chiusa.*

Bouffe (Fr., boof). Comic, burlesque . . . *Opéra bouffe,* comic opera.

Bourdon (Fr., boor-dŏhn′). 1. An organ stop of 16′ or 32′ pitch, having stopped wooden pipes, sometimes with metallic tops; French organs also have open bourdons of 8′ and 4′ pitch.—2. A great bell, as the bourdon of Notre-Dame.—3. The lowest string of the 'cello and double bass.

Bourrée (Fr., boo-rā′). 1. A dance of French or Spanish origin, in rapid tempo, having 2 sections of 8 measures each, and in 2/4 or 4/4 time.—2. A movement in the earlier Suites, in *alla breve* time.

Boutade (Fr., boo-tăhd′). 1. A short, impromptu ballet.—2. An instrumental impromptu or fantasia.

Bouts. The incurvations on either side of the violin, etc., which form the "waist."

Bow. The implement used in playing instruments of the violin type. The *hair* is attached to the *stick* by a bent *point* or *head,* and drawn into proper tension by the sliding *nut,* which is worked by the *screw* . . . *Bow-arm* or *-hand,* the right arm or hand . . . *Bow-guitar,* a kind of violin with a guitar-shaped body . . . *Bow-instrument,* one played with a bow . . . *Bow-zither,* see ZITHER.

Bow (verb). To execute with a bow; also to mark a piece with signs indicating the bowing.

Bowing. The art of handling the bow; a player's method or style; also, the signs for, and manner of, executing any given passage.

Braccio (It., brah'cho). "Arm"; instruments held in the arms were designated *da braccio,* "of the arm."

Brace. 1. The character { which connects two or more staves indicating that the parts on these staves are to be played simultaneously.—2. The group of staves so connected, as the *upper brace.*

Branle, Bransle (Fr., brahn'l'). A Brangle or Brawl; an old French dance in 4/4 time, in which several persons joined hands and took the lead in turn.

Brass band. Differs from full military band by omission of reed instruments.

Bratsche (Ger., brah'chĕ). The viola.

Brautlied (Ger., browt'-lēt). Bridal or wedding song.

Bravo. A shout of acclaim for the performer, commonly used to hail an opera singer. The feminine form is *brava.*

Bravour (Ger., brăh-voor). Bravura . . . *Bravourarie,* aria di bravura . . . *Bravourstück,* a vocal or instrumental piece of a brilliant and difficult character.

Bravoure (Fr., brăh-voor). Bravura . . . *Valse de bravoure,* an instrumental waltz in brilliant, showy style.

Bravura (It., bräh-voo′räh). Boldness, spirit, dash, brilliancy . . . *Aria di bravura,* a vocal solo consisting of difficult runs and passages, designed to show off the singer's voice or skill . . . *Con bravura,* with boldness, etc.

Brawl. See BRANLE.

Break. 1. The point where one register of a voice or instrument passes over into another; in the voice, the junction of the head and chest registers; in the clarinet, between the notes . . . *Breaking of the voice,* see MUTATION.—2. A false or imperfect tone produced by incorrect lipping of a horn or trumpet; or by some difficulty with the reed of the clarinet (this "break" is called "the goose"); or, in singing, by some defect in the vocal organs.—3. In an organ stop, when playing up the scale, the sudden return to the lower octave (caused by an incomplete set of pipes); also, in compound stops, any point in their scale where the relative pitch of the pipes changes.

Breath bands. The vocal cords.

Breathing mark. A sign inserted in a vocal part to show that the singer may (or must) take breath at that point; written variously (′, *, √, v, ″).

Breit (Ger., brīt). Broadly.

Breve (brēv). A note equal to 2 whole notes or semibreves; the longest used in modern notation; written:

Breve (It., brâ′vĕh). Short.

Brevemente (It., brĕh-vĕh-men′tĕh). Short, abruptly.

Bridge. In bowed instruments, a thin, arching piece of wood set upright on the belly to raise and stretch the strings above the resonance-box, to which the bridge communicates the vibrations of the strings.—In the piano, and other stringed instruments, a rail of wood or steel over which the strings are stretched.

Brillante (It., brēl-lähn'tĕh). Brilliant, showy, sparkling.

Brindisi (It., brēn-dē'-zē). A drinking song.

Brio, con (It., kŏhn brē'ŏh).
Brioso (It., brē-oh'sŏh).
"With noise" and gusto; spiritedly.

Brisé (Fr., brē-zā'; "broken"). In violin playing, short, detached strokes of the bow.

Broken cadence. See CADENCE ... *Broken chords,* chords whose tones are sounded in succession instead of together (see ARPEGGIO). *Broken octaves,* series of octaves in which the higher tones alternate with the lower:

Broken music. An old description of a consort having both strings and wind instruments; the expression *Broken music* is found in Shakespeare as contrasted with a *Whole consort,* where all the instruments were of the same kind.

Brummstimmen (Ger., brŏŏm'shtim'men). "Humming voices," production of the tone without words, through the nose, with closed mouth (BOCCA CHIUSA).

Bruscamente (It., brŏŏ-skäh-men'tĕh). Brusquely or forcibly accented.

Brusco (It., brŏŏ'skŏh). Rough, harsh.

Buffo,-a (It., bŏŏf'fŏh,-fäh). Comic, burlesque; hence, *Buffo, Buffo-singer,* a comic actor (singer) in an opera ... *Aria buffa,* a comic air or aria ... *Opera buffa,* comic or burlesque opera.

Buffonescamente (It., bŏŏf-fŏh-nĕ-skäh-men'tĕh). Comically, drolly.

Buffonesco,-a (It., bŏŏf-fŏh-nĕ'skŏh,-skäh). Comic, droll, burlesque.

Bugle. 1. A wind-instrument of brass or copper, with cupped mouthpiece, used for infantry calls and signals.—2. The

key-bugle, with 6 keys, and a compass of over 2 octaves.—3. The valve-bugle. See SAXHORN.

Bühne (Ger., bü′-ne). Stage.

Bühnenfestspiel (Ger., bü′-nen-fĕst-spēl). Stage festival
play.

Bühnenmusik (Ger., bü′-nen-moo-zĭk′). Incidental music
for plays or music performed on the stage.

Burden. 1. A chorus or refrain repeated after each stanza of a
song.—2. The drone of a bagpipe.—3. The bass part.—4. A
dance accompaniment sung without instruments.

Burla (It., boor′läh). A jest; raillery.

Burlando (It., bŏŏr-lähn′dŏh). Joking, jesting, romping.

Burlescamente (It., bŏŏr-lĕ-skäh-men′tĕh). In burlesque
style.

Burlesco,-a (It., bŏŏr-lĕ′skŏh, -skäh). Comic, farcical.

Burlesque (bur-lesk′). A dramatic extravaganza, or farcical
travesty of some serious subject, with more or less music.

Burletta. A burlesque; a musical farce.

Busain, Busaun, Buzain. A reed stop on the organ pedal,
usually of 16′ tone.

C

C. 1. (Ger. *C*; Fr. *ut*; It. *do*). The first tone and degree in the
typical diatonic scale of C major.—2. In musical theory,
capital *C* designates the *C*-major triad, small *c* the *c*-minor
triad.—3. Middle-*C* is the note c^1 on the piano keyboard :

 Tenor-*C* is the lowest note
in the tenor voice, *c*:

Cabaletta (It., käh-bäh-let′tah). In late Italian opera, the
concluding section of an aria, forming a summary in rapid
tempo.

Caccia (It., căht′chăh). The chase; a hunt . . . *Alla caccia,* in hunting style, that is, accompanied by horns.

Cachucha (Sp., că-choo′chăh). A dance much like the *Bolero.*

Cacophony. A raucous conglomeration of sound.

Cadence. 1. A CADENZA.—2. Rhythm.—3. The closing strains of a melody or harmonized movement; the Close or ending of a phrase, section, or movement . . . *Amen cadence,* a popular term for *Plagal cadence* (to which the word "Amen" is often sung) . . . *Authentic c.,* a cadence in which the penultimate chord is the dominant, and the final chord is the tonic. . . . *Avoided, Broken, Deceptive, Evaded,* or *False cadence,* a cadence that settles on an unexpected chord. . . . *Full cadence,* a Perfect cadence . . . *Half cadence* (Half close), or *Imperfect c.,* a cadence on any chord other than the tonic. . . . *Interrupted* or *Irregular cadence,* an unexpected progression avoiding some regular cadence . . . *Mixed cadence,* a close with dom., subdominant, dominant, and tonic chords in succession (this is also an authentic cadence) . . . *Perfect cadence,* an authentic cadence in which both dominant and tonic chords are in root position, and the last chord has the root in the highest voice as well as the tonic chord; the "authentic cadence" of the church modes . . . *Plagal cadence,* the subdominant chord followed by the tonic . . . *Radical cadence,* a close, either partial or complete, formed with two fundamental chords . . . *Surprise cadence,* an Interrupted cadence . . . *Whole cadence,* a Perfect cadence. Many of these categories overlap.

Perfect Authentic   Plagal   Interrupted, Deceptive, etc.

Mixed

Cadenza (It., kăh-den′dzăh). 1. In a vocal solo, a brilliant passage, usually at the end.—2. An elaborate passage or fantasia at the end of the first or last movement of a concerto, and played by the solo instrument (piano, violin, etc.).

Cæsura. See CESURA.

Caisse (Fr., kăss). Drum.

Caisse claire (Fr., kăss klâr). Snare drum.

Caisse, grosse (Fr., grōs kăss). Bass drum.

Caisse roulante (Fr., kăss roo-lăhn′t). Side drum.

Caisse sourde. Tenor drum.

Cakewalk. An American Negro folk dance in ragtime rhythm.

Calando (It., kăh-lăhn′dŏh). "Decreasing"; growing softer and (usually) slower.

Calcando (It., kăhl-kăhn′dŏh). "Pressing"; hastening the tempo.

Calliope (cal-li′o-pe). A steam organ; a pipe organ whose harsh tone is produced by steam, instead of wind, under pressure.

Callithumpian concert. A boisterous serenade given to some person who has become an object of popular hostility or ridicule; characterized by the blowing of horns, beating on tin pans, derisive cries, hoots, groans, cat-calls, etc.

Calma, con (It., kŏhn kăhl′măh). See CALMATO.

Calmando(si) (It., kăhl-măhn′dŏh[-sē]). Growing calm, becoming tranquil.

Calmato (It., kăhl-mah′tŏh). With calm; calmly, tranquilly.

Calore, con (It., kŏn kăh-loh′rĕh).⎱
Caloroso (It., kăh-lŏh-roh′sŏh). ⎰
   With warmth, passion; passionately.

Calypso. Popular music of the West Indies, much influenced by American jazz, with lyrics often reflecting topical subjects.

Cambiata (It., kăhm-byăh′tah). In Italian, "changed"; *nota cambiata,* a CHANGING NOTE.

Camera (It., kah′mĕh-răh). Chamber, room, small hall . . . *Alla camera,* in the style of chamber music . . . *Musica da camera,* chamber music.

Camminando (It., kăhm-mē-năhn′dŏh). "Walking"; a flowing movement, like Andante.

Campagnuolo,-a (It., kăhm-păhn-yô′lŏh). Pastoral, idyllic; rustic.

Campana (It., kăhm-pah′năh). A bell.

Campanellino (It., —nel-lē′nŏh).⎱
Campanello (It., —nel′lŏh).   ⎰
   A small bell.

Campestre (It., kăhm-pĕ′strĕh). Pastoral, rural, idyllic.

Canarie. A dance in triple time, supposedly imitating the rhythms of the native music of the Canary Islands.

Cancan. A fast French vaudeville dance in 2/4 time, once regarded as naughty.

Cancel. The Natural, ♮.

Canción (Sp., kăhn′-thē-ŏn). Song.

Cancrizans (Latin). Retrogressive; moving backward.

Canon. The strictest form of musical imitation, in which 2 or more parts take up, in succession, the given subject note for note.

Canonical Hours. Of the Roman Catholic Church are established times for daily prayer: *matins* (including *nocturns* and *lauds*), *prime, terce, sext, nones, vespers,* and *complin.*

Canonic imitation. Strict imitation of one part by another.

Cantabile (It., kăhn-tah′bē-lĕh). "Singable"; in a singing or vocal style.

Cantando (It., kăhn-tăhn′dŏh). ⎫
Cantante (It., kăhn-tăhn′teh). ⎭
Singing; smooth and flowing.

Cantata (It., kăhn-tah′tăh.). A vocal work with instrumental accompaniment, consisting of choruses and solos, recitative, duets, etc., shorter than an oratorio. Cantatas may be *sacred* or *secular.*

Cantato (It., kăhn-tah′tŏh). "Sung"; singingly.

Canterellando (It., kăhn-tĕh-rel-lăhn′dŏh). Singing softly.

Canticchiando (It., kăhn-tik-yăhn′dŏh). Singing softly; humming.

Canticle. One of the nonmetrical hymns of praise and jubilation in the Bible; or a sacred chant similar to it.

Cantilation. Chanting in a simple manner without accompaniment; usually applied to Jewish liturgy.

Cantilena (It., kăhn-tē-lâ′năh). ⎫
Cantilene (Ger., kăhn-tē-lā′nĕ). ⎬
Cantilène (Fr., kăhn-tē-län′). ⎭
"A little song"; a ballad or light popular song; a flowing, song-like passage on an instrument.

Canto (It., kăhn′tŏh). A melody, song, chant; the soprano (highest vocal or instrumental part) . . . *Col canto,* "with the melody," a direction to accompanists to follow the solo part in tempo and expression . . . *Canto fermo,* a Cantus firmus.

Cantor. The leading singer in German, Protestant church services or in Jewish synagogues.

Cantus firmus (Latin). A fixed or given melody: (*a*) Plainsong; (*b*) in counterpoint, a given melody, like a plainsong tune, to which other parts are to be set according to rule.

Canzone (It., kähn-tsoh′něh). A song, folksong; also, a part-song in madrigal style.

Canzonet. A little air or song; a short part-song; a madrigal.

Capo (It., kah′pŏh). Head, beginning . . . *Da capo,* from the beginning . . . *Da capo al segno,* from the beginning to the sign (𝄋 or 𝄉).

Capo d'astro. [An English corruption of *capotasto.*] The "capo d'astro bar" in the piano is a metallic bar fixed across the strings near the wrestplank, bearing down on the 3 highest octaves (more or less).

Capotasto (It., kah-pŏh-täh′stŏh). 1. The nut of stringed instruments having a fingerboard.—2. A piece of wood or ivory which can be set across a fretted fingerboard to raise the pitch of all the strings at once.

Cappella (It., kähp-pel′läh). [Wrongly spelled *capella.*] A choir; an orchestra; both together. . . . *A* (or *alla*) *cappella,* vocal chorus without instrumental accompaniment.

Capriccio (It., käh-prit′chŏh). An instrumental piece of free form, distinguished by originality in harmony and rhythm; a Caprice . . . *A capriccio,* at pleasure.

Capricciosamente (It., käh-prit-chŏh-säh-men′těh). ⎱
Capriccioso (It., käh-prit-chŏh′sŏh).   ⎰
    In a capricious, fanciful, fantastic style.

Caressant (Fr., käh-rěs-sähn′).   ⎱
Carezzando (It., käh-ret-sähn′dŏh).   ⎬
Carezzevole (It., käh-ret-sä′vŏh-lěh).   ⎰
    Caressingly, soothingly.

Carillon (Fr., käh-rē-yŏhn′). 1. A Glockenspiel, or set of fixed bells played from a keyboard or by a barrel-mechanism; also a tune played on these bells, or an instrumental piece imitating their effect.—2. A piano with bells instead of strings.—3. A mixture stop in the organ.

Carità, con (It., kŏhn kăh-rē-tah′). With tender expression.

Carol. To sing joyously; hence, a joyous Christmas song of praise.

Cassa (It., kăh′săh). Drum.

Cassa, gran (It., grăhn′ kăh′săh). Bass drum.

Cassation. 18th-century instrumental suite, similar to the *Divertimento* and *Serenade.*

Castanets. A pair of small concave pieces of wood or ivory, attached by a cord to a dancer's thumb and forefinger, and struck together in time with the music.

Castrato (It., kăh-strah′tŏh). An adult male singer with soprano or alto voice.

Catch. A round or canon for 3 or more voices, each singer having to "catch" or take up his part at the right instant. Modern catches are generally humorous.

Catgut. Popular name for gut strings.

Cavallina (It., kăh-văhl-lē′năh). A forced, jerky delivery (coloratura).

Cavatina (It., kăh-văh-tē′năh). A song; particularly, a short aria without second section or *Da capo.*

C clef. A clef written ‖ ‖ ‖ ‖ etc. See "The Clefs," p. ix.

C dur (Ger., tsā door′). *C* major.

Cedendo (It., chā-den′dŏh). Growing slower.

Cédez (Fr., sā-dā′). Go slower.

Celere (It., chěh′lěh-rěh). Rapid, swift.

Celerità, con (It., kŏhn chěh-lěh-rē-tah′). With celerity, rapidly.

Celesta. Percussion instrument invented by Mustel in Paris,

1886, consisting of tuned steel bars connected to a keyboard.

Céleste (Fr., sā-lest'). Celestial.

'Cello (It., chel'lŏh). Abbreviation of Violoncello.

Cembalo (It., chĕm'băh-lŏh). Harpsichord, pianoforte; in old times, a dulcimer . . . *A cembalo,* for piano (or harpsichord).

Ces (Ger., tsĕss). *C* flat.

Ces dur (Ger., tsiss door). C flat major.

Ceses (Ger., tsĕss'ĕss). *C* double flat.

Cesura, Cæsura. The dividing line between two melodic and rhythmical phrases within a period called *masculine* or *feminine* according as it occurs after a strong or weak beat.

Cha-cha. Latin American dance in an insistent binary rhythm; sometimes it is called more emphatically Cha-cha-cha.

Chaconne (Fr., shăh-kŏhn'). A Spanish dance. Also, an instrumental piece consisting of a series of variations above a ground bass not over 8 measures in length, in 3/4 time and slow tempo.

Chalumeau (Fr., shăh-lü-moh'). An old wind instrument having 9 finger holes and a beating reed. See CLARINET.

Chamber music. Vocal or instrumental music suitable for performance in a room or small hall; especially, quartets and similar concerted pieces for solo instruments.

Chamber orchestra. A small orchestra.

Chamber opera. An opera suitable for performance in a small hall, with a limited number of performers and accompanied by a chamber orchestra.

Chamber symphony. A symphony for chamber orchestra.

Chance music. See ALEATORY.

Change. 1. In harmony, MODULATION.—2. In the voice,

MUTATION.—3. Any melodic phrase or figure played on a chime of bells.

Change-ringing. The art and practice of ringing a peal of bells in varying and systematic order.

Changing note. A dissonant note (tone) entering on the strong beat, and passing by a step to a consonance, or by a skip to a chord note or a note belonging to another chord.

Chanson (Fr., shăhn-sŏhn′). A song.

Chansonnette (Fr., shăhn-sŏhn-net′). A short song of a light nature.

Chant. A short sacred song.—1. The Anglican chant, adapted to the Canticles and Psalms, consists of 7 measures, harmonized, the time-value of the single note constituting the first and fourth measures being lengthened or shortened to fit the words, whereas the others are sung in strict time. Each of its 2 divisions (of 3 and 4 measures respectively) begins on a reciting-note and ends with a cadence.—2. The Gregorian chant is a Gregorian melody repeated with the several verses of biblical prose text; it has 5 divisions, (1) the intonation, (2) the first dominant, or reciting-note, (3) the mediation, (4) the 2d dominant, or reciting-note, and (5) the cadence.

Chant (Fr., shăhn). Song; singing; melody; tune. Also, voice (the vocal part as distinguished from the accompaniment).

Chanter. The melody-pipe of the bagpipe.

Chanterelle (Fr., shăhn-t′-rel′). The highest string on a violin, lute, etc.

Chanty. A unison song sung by workmen in time with their motions; also spelled *Shanty*.

Chapel. A company of musicians attached to the establishment of any distinguished personage.

Characteristic piece. A character-piece; one depicting a definite mood, impression, scene, or event.

Characteristic tone. 1. The leading tone.—2. That tone in any key which specially distinguishes it from nearly related keys; like *F♯* in *G* major, distinguishing it from *C* major.

Characters. Musical signs in general.

Charme, avec (Fr., ăh-vek′ sharm). With charm; gracefully.

Che (It., kā). Than; that.

Chef d'orchestre (Fr., shef dor-kes′tr). Conductor of an orchestra.

Chest of viols. Old English description of a set of string instruments of various sizes, in olden times kept in a specially constructed chest.

Chest register. The lower register of the male or female voice, the tones of which produce sympathetic vibration in the chest.

Chest tone. }
Chest voice. }
Vocal tone possessing the quality of the chest register.

Chiaramente (It., k'yăh-răh-men′tĕh). }
Chiarezza, con (It., kŏhn k'yăh-ret′săh). }
Clearly, distinctly, limpidly.

Chiaro,-a (It., k'yah′rŏh, -răh). Clear, pure.

Chiesa (It., kee-eh′sah). Church; used in definitions such as *sonata da chiesa,* a sonata suitable for church performance.

Chime. 1. A set of from 5 to 12 bells tuned to the scale, and played by swinging either the bells themselves or clappers hung within them. Also, a tune so played.—2. A set of bells and hammers played by a keyboard; a Carillon.

Chinese blocks. Resonant wood blocks struck with a drumstick or mallet.

Chin rest. An oval plate of ebony attached to the edge of the violin to the left of the tailpiece.

Chitarra (It., kē-tar′răh). A guitar.

Chitarrone (It., kee-tar-roh'neh). A large lute.

Chitarrata (It., kē-tar-rah'täh). A piano piece imitating the guitar.

Chiuso,-a (It., kew'sŏh, -säh). Closed . . . *A bocca chiusa,* with closed mouth; humming.

Choeur (Fr., kühr). Chorus.

Choir. 1. A company of singers, especially in a church.—2. A choral society.—3. In the Anglican Church, the singers of the daily choral service, who sit divided on the *decani* and *cantoris* sides of the chancel.—4. A subdivision of a chorus; for example, the 1st and 2d choirs in 8-part music.

Choirmaster. Leader (leading singer) of a choir.

Choir organ. See ORGAN.

Choral. Relating or pertaining to a chorus, or to vocal concerted music . . . *Choral notes,* the square notes used for writing plain song . . . *Choral service,* a church service with music by the choir.

Chorale (kŏh-rahl'). A hymn tune of the German Protestant Church, or one similar in style.

Chorale prelude. An instrumental composition based on a chorale or hymn tune.

Choralmässig (Ger., kŏh-rahl'mä'sīyh). In the style of a chorale.

Chord. 1. A harmony of 2 or more tones.—2. A harmony of from 3 to 5 tones, forming an ascending series of diatonic thirds (see "Chords," pp. xv-xvi).—3. A *"flat"* or *"solid"* chord is one whose tones are produced simultaneously, opposed to *broken.*—4. A string.

Choreography. The dancing scenario in a ballet.

Chôros. A Brazilian folk dance, or a work written in a Brazilian folk style.

Chorus. A company of singers; hence, a composition, most often in 4 parts, each sung by several or many singers; a double chorus has 8 parts. Also, the refrain or burden of a song.

Chorus master. A choirmaster; also the conductor of a chorus.

Christe eleison (Gk., crēs′tä ā-lā′ē-sohn, "Christ, have mercy"). Part of the Kyrie. See MASS.

Chromatic. Relating to tones foreign to a given key (scale) or chord; opposed to diatonic. *Chromatic signs,* the sharp (♯), flat (♭), natural (♮), double sharp (×), and double flat (♭♭).

Church modes. The octave scales employed in medieval church music.

Ciaccona (It., chăk-koh′năh). A Chaconne.

Cimbalo (It., chĭm′băh-lŏh). A cymbal; a harpsichord; a tambourine.

Cimbalom. A large dulcimer, typical of Hungarian Gypsy bands.

Cinelli (It., chĭn-nĕl′lē). Cymbals.

Cinque-pace (sink′pās). An old dance, probably French, with a five-step movement.

Cipher. A tone is said to "cipher" on the organ when, owing to some derangement of the action, it persists in sounding.

Circle of Fifths. A series of fifths tuned (as on the piano) in equal temperament, so that the *twelfth* fifth in the series has the same letter name as the first tone. See "The Keys," pp. xiv–xv.

Circular canon. A canon closing in the key a semitone above that in which it begins; 12 repetitions would thus carry it through the "circle" of 12 keys.

Cis (Ger., tsiss). *C* sharp.

Cis dur (Ger., tsiss door). In German, *C* sharp major.

Cis moll (Ger., mohl). *C* sharp minor.

Cisis (Ger., tsiss′iss). *C* double sharp.

Cither (sith′er), **Cithern**, **Cittern** (sit′-). A kind of lute or guitar, strung with wire and played with a pick; used in the 16th and 17th centuries.

Civetteria, con (It., kŏhn chē-vet-teh-rē′äh). With coquetry; in a coquettish, trifling style.

Clang (Ger. *Klang*). A fundamental tone with its harmonics; *Clang-color, Clang-tint,* "tone color," timbre.

Claque. Hired groups of people paid to applaud an opera singer or some other performer; practiced until recently.

Clarabella. An organ stop having open wooden pipes of 8′ pitch and soft, mellow tone.

Claribel-flute. A 4′ Clarabella.

Clarinet. A transposing wind instrument derived from the Chalumeau. It has a cylindrical wooden or metal tube pierced by 18 holes, 13 being closed by keys, yielding a chromatic series of 19 prime tones (*e* to *b*[1]♭). Its compass comprises 3 octaves in 4 different registers; the Low register ("chalumeau"), Medium register, High register ("clarinetto"), and Super-acute register.

Clarinet stop. See KRUMMHORN.

Clarinetto (It., kläh-rē-net′tŏh). Clarinet.

Clarion. 1. A small, shrill-toned trumpet.—2. In the organ, a 4′ reed stop of shrill, piercing tone.

Clarionet. 1. A Clarinet.—2. In the organ, an 8′ reed stop.

Clarionet flute. A flue stop with perforated cover.

Classical music. 1. European music from about 1770 to 1830.—2. Colloquially, any serious music, as opposed to popular music.

Classical suite. An instrumental suite of dance forms, also called the *Baroque Suite.* It has 4 principal movements: Allemande, Courante, Sarabande, and Gigue. Lighter dance movements, such as the Minuet, Bourrée, and Gavotte, are often interpolated between the Sarabande and the Gigue.

Clavecin (Fr., klăh-v'-săn').

Clavicembalo (It., klăh-vē-chem'băh-lŏh).
A harpsichord.

Claves. Hardwood sticks used in Latin American rhythm bands, which produce a sharp sound when clicked together.

Clavichord. A precursor of the pianoforte, differing in action from the latter in having, instead of hammers, upright metal wedges called tangents on the rear end of the keys; on pressing a key, the tangent strikes the wire and remains pressed against it till the finger is lifted, causing only one section of the string to vibrate.

Clavier (klă-vēr'). A keyboard. See KLAVIER.

Clavier (Fr., klăh-v'yā'). A keyboard; a manual. . . . *Clavier de récit,* swell manual.

Clef. A character set at the head of the staff to fix the pitch or position of one note, and thus of the rest. See "The Clefs," p. ix.

Cloches (Fr., klŏsh). Chimes.

Close (klōz). A cadence ending a section, movement, or piece.

Close harmony. In regular 4-voice settings, the 3 upper voices are placed within an octave in close harmony.

C moll (Ger., tsā mohl). *C* minor.

Coda (It., koh'dăh). A "tail"; hence, a passage ending a movement.

Codetta (It., kŏh-det'tăh). A short coda.

Cogli (kŏhl'yē), **Col, Coll', Colla, Colle, Collo** (It.). With the.

Color. 1. Timbre.—2. In 14th and 15th century isorhythmic music, a repeated pitch pattern.

Coloratura (It., kŏh-lŏh-răh-too'răh). Vocal runs, passages, trills, etc., enhancing the brilliancy of a composition and displaying the singer's skill. (Also used for instrumental ornaments.)

Coloris (Fr., kŏh-lŏh-rē′). The changes in vocal or instrumental "tone-color," or in the instrumentation or registration, employed for obtaining special effects; the "color-scheme" of a composition.

Colpo (It., kŏhl′pŏh). A blow; *di colpo,* suddenly.

Combination pedal. A metal foot-lever above the organ pedals; the *forte pedal* draws all the stops of its keyboard; the *mezzo pedal,* the chief 8- and 4-foot stops of its keyboard; the *piano pedal* pushes in all but a few of the softest stops.

Combo. A jazz ensemble; the word is short for combination.

Come (It., kô′měh). As, like.

Come prima (It., kô′měh prē′măh). As before, as at first (that is, "resume the previous tempo").

Come retro (It., kô′měh rā′trŏh). As before.

Come sopra (It., kô′měh soh′präh). As above.

Come sta (It., kô′měh stah). As it stands, as written.

Comes (L, coh′mās). Answer to the subject in a fugue. Literally, "companion."

Comic opera. Opera with a comic subject; but in French Opéra Comique, it means an opera with the inclusion of spoken dialogue.

Comma. The Greek term for the minute interval that represents the difference between a perfect fifth in tempered pitch and the pure interval formed in the natural harmonic series.

Commodo (It.). See COMODO.

Common chord. A major or minor triad . . . *Common hallelujah metre,* or *Common long metre,* see METRE . . . *Common measure,* common time . . . *Common metre, Double common metre, Common particular metre,* see METRE. *Common time,* a measure containing 2 (or 4) half notes, or 4 quarter notes, with 2 or 4 beats respectively; duple or quadruple time. (Ordinarily, common time is understood to mean 4 quarter notes, and as many beats, to the measure.)

Comodamente (It., kŏh-mŏh-däh-men′tĕh). See COMODO.

Comodetto (It., kŏh-mŏh-det′tŏh). Rather easy or leisurely.

Comodo (It., kô′mŏh-dŏh). Easy, leisurely, at a convenient pace.

Compass. The range of a voice or instrument; the scale of all the tones it can produce, from the lowest to the highest.

Compiacevole (It., kŏhm-p'yäh-chä′vŏh-lĕh). }
Compiacevolmente (—chä-vohl-men′tĕh).   }
Pleasing(ly), charming(ly).

Complement, Complementary interval. An interval which, added to any given interval not wider than an octave, completes the octave; a fourth is the complement of a fifth, a minor third of a major sixth, etc.

Complete stop. See STOP.

Complin(e). A short evening service, completing the 7 Canonical Hours.

Composed through. This term is applied to songs with different settings for each stanza of the poem.

Composer. A man or woman who writes music professionally.

Composition. The broadest term for writing music in any form for any instruments or voices.

Composition pedal. In the organ, a pedal which draws out or pushes in several stops at once.

Compound meter. A measure with a number of beats composed of 2 or more different simple meters such as 5/4 (2/4 + 3/4) or 7/4 (4/4 + 3/4).

Compound. An organ stop having more than one rank of pipes.

Compressed score. A short score.

Con (It., kŏhn). With; in a style expressive of.

(For definitions of phrases beginning with "con," see the second word in the given phrase.)

Concave pedals. Radiating pedals.

Concentrando (It., kŏhn-chen-trăhn′dŏh). "Concentrating"; an expression mark in vocal music calling for an intensified effect of tone.

Concert. A musical performance requiring the coöperation of several musicians.

Concertante (It., kŏhn-châr-tăhn′tĕh). 1. A concert piece.—2. A composition for 2 or more solo voices or instruments with accompaniment by orchestra or organ, in which each solo part is in turn brought into prominence.—3. A composition for 2 or more unaccompanied solo instruments in orchestral music . . . *Concertante style,* a style of composition admitting of a brilliant display of skill on the soloist's part.

Concerted music. Music written in parts for several instruments or voices, like trios, quartets, etc.

Concertina. The improved accordion invented by Wheatstone in 1829.

Concert grand. A grand piano.

Concertino. 1. A small concerto, scored for a small ensemble.—2. The group of soloists in a CONCERTO GROSSO.

Concertmaster. The leader of the first violin section in the orchestra.

Concertmeister. See KONZERTMEISTER.

Concerto (It., kŏhn-châr′tŏh). An extended composition for a solo instrument, usually with orchestral accompaniment, and in (modified) sonata form.

Concerto grosso (It., kŏhn-châr′tŏh′ grô′sŏh). An instrumental composition employing a small group of solo instruments against a larger group or full orchestra. See CONCERTINO.

Concerto for orchestra. A symphonic work in which the orchestral instruments play the role of soloists.

Concert overture. An overture for full orchestra, performed as an independent composition at a symphony concert.

Concert pitch. The actual sound produced by an instrument, as distinct from a written note in transposing instruments. Thus in the *B* flat clarinet, the written note *C* sounds *B* flat which is the concert pitch.

Concertstück (Ger., kŏhn-tsârt'shtük). Concert-piece; concerto.

Concitato (It., kŏhn-chē-tah'tŏh). Moved, excited, agitated.

Concord. Euphony; harmony; consonance.

Concrete music. An experimental technique of composition making use of recorded sounds and incidental noises analogous with the collage in painting. Often referred to in French as *Musique concrète,* since it originated in Paris.

Conduct. The "leading" of a part.

Conductor. Director of an orchestra or chorus.

Conductus. A contrapuntal part combined with a given original melody in polyphonic music of the Middle Ages.

Cone-gamba. Bell-gamba.

Conical mouthpiece. See CUPPED . . . *Conical tube,* one tapering very gradually; a *cylindrical tube* does not taper.

Conjunct degree. The nearest degree in the scale (chromatic or diatonic) to the given degree . . . *Conjunct motion,* progression by conjunct degrees or intervals.

Consecutive intervals. Intervals of the same kind following each other in immediate succession; "consecutives" are progressions of parallel fifths or octaves, forbidden in strict harmony.

Consequent. In a canon, the Follower; the part imitating the antecedent or Leader.

Conservatoire (Fr., kŏhn-sâr-văh-twar′). ⎫
Conservatorium (L.).
Conservatory. ⎬
A public institution for providing practical and theoretical instruction in music.

Consolante (It., kŏhn-sŏh-lăhn′tĕh). Consoling, soothing.

Console. The organ's keyboard, stops, and pedals.

Consonance. A combination of two or more tones, harmonious and pleasing in itself, and requiring no further progression to make it satisfactory . . . *Imperfect consonances,* the major and minor Thirds and Sixths . . . *Perfect consonances,* the Octave, Fifth, and Fourth.

Consonant chord. One containing no dissonant interval . . . *Consonant interval,* a consonance of two tones.

Consort. An old English term for an instrumental ensemble; a *whole consort* consisted of all wind or all string instruments while a *broken consort* was a mixed group.

Contano (It., kŏhn′tăh-nŏh). "They count"; in a score, parts so marked are to pause.

Continued bass. ⎫
Continuo (It., kŏhn-tē′nŏŏ-ŏh). See BASSO CONTINUO. ⎬

Contra (L.; It.). "Against"; prefixed to names of instruments, it means "an octave below."

Contrabass. A double bass.

Contrabasso (It., kŏhn-trăhb-băhs′sŏh). Double bass.

Contradanza (It., kŏhn-trăh-dahn′tzăh). Italian name for the English Country Dance.

Contrafagotto (It., kŏhn-trăhf-făh-gŏht′tŏh). 1. Double-bassoon.—2. A reed stop in the organ.

Contraltino (It., kŏhn-trăhl-tē′nŏh). A high, light tenor voice of fluent delivery.

Contralto (It., kŏhn-trăhl'tŏh). See ALTO 1.

Contra-octave. The octave below the Great Octave.

Contrapuntal. Pertaining to the art or practice of counterpoint.

Contrapuntist. One versed in the theory and practice of counterpoint.

Contrary motion. Parts progress in contrary motion when one moves up while the other moves down.

Contre (Fr., kŏhn'tr). "Against"; contra-, counter-... *Contredanse,* the Quadrille.

Contredanse (Fr., kŏhn-truh-dahns'). French name for the Country Dance.

Cool. An American JAZZ style of the 1950's, characterized by a less frenetic ("hot") atmosphere than earlier styles, use of "nonjazz" instruments (flute, French horn), and adoption of "classical" techniques (fugue).

Coperto (It., kŏh-pâr'tŏh). Covered, muffled.

Cor (Fr., kor). A horn... *Cor anglais* (ăhn-glä'), the English horn.

Coranto (It., kŏh-răhn'tŏh). 1. Courante.—2. Country dance.

Corda (It., kôr'dăh). A string. [Plural *corde* (kôr'-dĕh.)] ... *Sopra una corda,* play "on one string" ... *Una corda,* or *U. C.,* take soft pedal of piano ... *Due corde,* release soft pedal; or (when the soft pedal shifts the keyboard), "play with soft pedal pressed halfway down" ... In violin playing, *due corde* means "play the note on two strings." ... *Tutte* (*le*) *corde,* "all the strings"; that is, "release the soft pedal." *Corda vuota,* open string.

Cornemuse. French word for bagpipe.

Cornet. A brass instrument of the trumpet family (*cornet à pistons*), with conical tube and cupped mouthpiece; improved from the old post-horn by the addition of 3 valves;

medium compass 2 octaves and 3 tones; it is a transposing instrument:

Notation   Actual pitch

this being for the ordinary cornet in B♭.—The old cornet was a wooden instrument with finger holes.—On the organ there are various cornet stops: (*a*) Reed stops of 2′, 4′, 8′, and 16′ pitch; (*b*) the German *Kornett,* of 2′ or 4′ pitch, on the pedal; (*c*) a compound stop having from 3 to 5 ranks; (*d*) the *Echo-cornet,* a soft-toned cornet stop enclosed in a wooden box; (*e*) the *Mounted cornet,* mounted on a separate soundboard to render its tone louder.

Cornet à pistons (Fr., kôr-nä′ ăh pēs-tŏhn′). The ordinary valve-cornet.

Corno (It., kôr′nŏh). A horn (plural *corni*).

Cornon (Fr., kor-nŏhn′). 1. A cornet stop.—2. A brass wind instrument of broad scale, invented in 1844.

Cornopean (kor-nŏ′pe-an). 1. Cornet à pistons.—2. An organ stop on the swell manual.

Corrente (It., kŏhr-ren′tĕh). Courante.

Corto,-a (It., kohr′tŏh, -tăh). Short . . . *La cadenza sia corta,* let the cadenza be short.

Cotillion (Fr., *cotillon* [kŏh-tē-yŏhn′]). A French dance, the same as the German, to quadrille music.

Cottage organ. The ordinary portable parlor organ (reed organ).

Cottage piano. 1. A small style of upright piano.—2. A small grand piano in upright form, invented by Wilhelm Kress, of Vienna, in 1891.

Coulé (Fr., koo-lā′). *Legato,* slurred; also, a harpsichord GRACE NOTE.

Count. An accent, beat, or pulse of a measure. . . . *Counting,* the marking of the successive beats by counting.

Counter. Any vocal part set to contrast with the principal part or melody; specifically, the *counter-tenor* (high tenor, or alto) ... *Bass counter,* a second bass part ... *Counter-exposition,* reëntrance of a fugue-subject ... *Counter-sub-ject,* a fugal theme following the subject in the same part ... *Counter-tenor,* a voice usually developed from the headtones and falsetto of a bass-voice; compass from *g* to *c²* ... *Counter-tenor clef,* the *C*-clef on the 2d line (obsolete).

Counterpoint. 1. The art of polyphonic composition.—2. Composition with 2 or more simultaneous melodies ... *Double Counterpoint* is written so that the upper part can become the lower part, and vice versa ... in *triple* and *quadruple counterpoint,* 3 and 4 parts are written so that they can be mutually exchanged.

Country dance. A dance in 2/4 or 3/4 time, in which the partners form two opposing lines, which advance and retreat, the couples also dancing down the lines and returning to their places.

Country/Western. A term that covers a variety of American rural and cowboy styles.

Coup de glotte (Fr., koo dŭh glaht). A highly dramatic way of interrupted breath in singing which was very popular among Italian singers, but is now regarded as somewhat exaggerated. The French phrase can be translated as "stroke of the glottis."

Coupler. A mechanical organ stop acting to connect two manuals, or pedal with manual, so that when one is played on, the other is combined with it. A *Coupler-pedal* is a coupler worked by the foot.

Couplet. 1. Two successive lines forming a pair, usually rhymed.—2. In triple times, 2 equal notes occupying the time of 3 such notes in the regular rhythm, thus:

Courante (Fr., koo-rähn′t). A Courant, or old French dance in 3/2 time; hence, the instrumental piece so called.

Covered. See OCTAVE ... *Covered strings,* strings of silk, wire, or gut, covered with spiral turns of fine silver or copper wire.

Crab canon. A canon performed backwards.

Crab movement. Backwards movement of a melody.

Cracovienne (Fr., kräh-kŏh-v′yen′). A Polish dance for a large company, the music in duple time with frequent syncopations; rhythm:

Credo (L., crā′doh). "I believe"; part of the Mass.

Crescendo (It., krĕh-shen′dŏh). Swelling, increasing in loudness.

Crescendo pedal. A pedal mechanism drawing all stops successively up to "full organ" ... Also, the swell-pedal.

Crescent; also Chinese crescent, or **Pavilion.** An instrument of Turkish origin, used in military music; it has crescent shaped brass plates hung around a staff and surmounted by a cap or pavilion; around the plates little bells are hung, which are jingled in time with the music.

Crescente (It., krĕh-shen′tĕh). Same as CRESCENDO.

Croche (Fr., krohsh). An Eighth note.

Cromorne (Fr., kroh-mahrn′). KRUMMHORN.

Crook. A short tube, bent or straight, which can be fitted to the main tube of a horn or trumpet to lower the pitch.

Crooner. A popular singer who intones his songs in a soft, seductive manner.

Cross flute. One held *across* the mouth, and blown from the side.

Cross relation. Same as FALSE RELATION.

Crotchet. A quarter-note ... *Crotchet-rest,* a quarter-rest.

Crucifixus (L., kroo-chĕ-fĕx'oos). Part of the Mass, in the Credo section.

Crwth (krŭth). An ancient Welsh or Irish bow instrument, probably the oldest European instrument of its class. Its square body was terminated by 2 parallel arms joined at the end by a crossbar, the center of which supported the fingerboard; it had originally 3, in modern times 6, strings. Also spelled *Crouth* or *Crouch.*

Csárdás (Hungarian, char'dahsh). A national Hungarian dance, distinguished by its passionate character and changing tempo.

Cue. A phrase, from a vocal or instrumental part, occurring near the end of a long pause in another part, and inserted in small notes *in the latter* to serve as a guide in timing its reëntrance.

Cuivré (Fr., kyuh-eev-ray'). With a brassy tone, as played particularly on the French horn.

Cupo,-a (It., koo'pŏh, -păh). Dark, deep, obscure; reserved ... *Con voce cupa,* with a veiled, intense tone.

Cupped mouthpiece. The shallower, cup-shaped form of mouthpiece for brass wind instruments; the *conical* (cone-shaped) mouthpiece is the deeper form.

Cut time. See ALLA BREVE.

Cyclical forms of composition embrace a cycle or set of movements; like the old Suite or Partita, or the Sonata, Symphony, and Concerto.

Cymbal. In the organ, a mixture stop of very high pitch.

Cymbals. The orchestral cymbals are 2 concave plates of brass or bronze, with broad, flat rims, and holes for the straps by which they are held; used to make strong accents, or to produce peculiar effects.

Czárdás. A common, but incorrect, spelling of Csárdás.

D

D (Ger. *D*; Fr. *ré*: It. *re*). The 2d tone and degree in the typical diatonic scale of C major.—In musical theory, capital *D* designates the *D*-major triad, small *d* the *d*-minor triad.—*D.* also stands for *Da* (D. C. = *Da capo*) and *Dal* (D. S. = *Dal segno*).

Da (It., dah). By, from, for, of ... *Da capo,* from the beginning ... *Da capo al fine,* repeat from beginning to end (that is, to the word *Fine,* or to a hold) ... *Da capo al segno,* from the beginning to the sign (   ) ... *D. C. al segno, poi (segue) la coda,* from the beginning to the sign, then play the coda ... *D. C. dal segno,* repeat from the sign. ... *D. C. senza replica* (or *senza ripetizione*), play through from the beginning without noticing the repeats ... *Da eseguirsi,* to be executed.

Dactyl(e) (L., *dactylus,* a finger).   A metrical foot with syllables arranged like the finger-joints, one long and two short; the accent on the first: $-\smile\smile$.

Dactylion. An apparatus for finger-gymnastics; invented by Henri Herz in 1835.

Dagli (dähl′yē), **dai** (dah′ē), **dal, dall′, dalla, dalle, dallo** (It.). To the, by the, for the, from the, etc.

Dal segno (It., dähl sān′yŏh). From the sign ... *Dal segno al fine,* from the sign to the end.

Damenisation. Graun's system of sol-faing with the syllables da, me, ni, po, tu, la, be.

Damper. 1. A mechanical device for checking the vibration of the piano-string ... *Damper-pedal,* the right, or loud, pedal.—2. The *mute* of a brass instrument.

Dämpfer (Ger., däm′pfĕr). A damper or mute.

Dance band. An instrumental ensemble accompanying ballroom dancing and composed of saxophones, trumpets, trombones, and percussion.

Danse champêtre (Fr., dahns shan-petr′). A peasant dance in an open field.

Danza. Italian and Spanish word for *dance.*

D dur (Ger., dā door). *D* major.

Deaconing. A practice in early American Protestant churches of reading aloud a line of a hymn before singing it.

Debile (It., dā′bē-lĕh). ⎫
Debole (It., dā′bŏh-lĕh). ⎭
    Feeble, weak.

Début (Fr., dā-bü′). A first appearance.

Débutant (Fr., dā-bü-tăn′; *masculine*). ⎫
Débutante (Fr., dā-bü-tăhn′t′; *feminine*). ⎭
    A performer or singer who appears for the first time.

Deceptive cadence. A cadence leading to the chord of the sixth degree of the scale instead of the expected tonic chord. Sometimes called *interrupted cadence.*

Decibel. A scientific unit for the measurement of loudness or intensity of sound.

Decima (L., dehs′ĭ-mŭ). 1. The interval of a tenth.—2. An organ stop pitched a tenth higher than the 8′ stops.

Decisione, con (It., kŏhn dā-chē-zē-oh′nĕh). With decision.

Deciso (It., dā-chē′zŏh). Decided, energetic, with decision.

Declamando (It., dā-kläh-măhn′dŏh). "Declaiming"; in declamatory style.

Declamatión. In vocal music, clear and correct enunciation of the words.

Declamato (It., dā-kläh-mah′tŏh). "Declaimed"; in declamatory style.

Decrescendo (It., dā-crĕh-shen′dŏh). Decreasing in loudness.

Decuplet. A group of 10 equal notes executed in the time

proper to 8 notes of like value, or to 4 notes of the next
highest value, in the regular rhythm; marked by a slur and
a figure 10.

Deficiendo (It., dā-fē-ts'yen′dŏh). Dying away.

Degli (It., dāl′yē). Of the; than the.

Degree. 1. One of the 8 consecutive tones in a major or minor
diatonic scale. Degrees are counted upward from the keynote.—2. A line or space on the staff.—3. A step.

Dehnen (Ger., dā′nen). To prolong.

Dehors, en (Fr., än dĕ-or). "Outside"—with emphasis.

Dei (It., dā′ē). Of the; than the.

Del, dell', della, delle, dello (It.). Of the; than the.

Delayed resolution. See RESOLUTION.

Deliberamente (It., dĕh-lē-bĕh-răh-men′tĕh).⎫
Deliberato (It., dĕh-lē-bĕh-rah′tŏh). ⎬
Deliberately. ⎭

Delicatamente (It., dĕh-lē-kăh-tăh-men′tĕh). Delicately.

Delicatezza, con (It., kŏhn dĕh-lē-kăh-tet′săh). With deli-
cacy.

Delicato (It., dĕh-lē-kah′tŏh). Delicately; in a delicate, refined style.

Delirante (It., dĕh-lē-răhn′tĕh). ⎫
Delirio, con (It., kŏhn dĕh-lē′rē-ŏh). ⎬
Raving; deliriously, frenziedly. ⎭

Demiquaver. A sixteenth note.

Demisemiquaver. A thirty-second note.

Depress. To lower (as by a ♭ or ♭♭) . . . *Depression,* chromatic
lowering of a tone.

Derivative. 1. Same as *derivative chord,* that is, the inversion
of a fundamental chord.—2. The root of a chord.

Des (Ger., dess). *D* flat.

Descant. Same as DISCANT.

Des dur (Ger., dess door). *D* flat major.

Deses (Ger., dess'ess). *D* double flat.

Desiderio, con (It., kŏhn dĕh-sē-dâ′rē-ŏh). With desire; longingly, yearningly.

Desto (It., dĕh′stŏh). Sprightly.

Destra (It., dĕh′străh). Right ... *Mano destra* (*destra mano, colla destra*), "play with the right hand." (Abbreviated *m. d.*)

Détaché (Fr., dā-tăh-shā′). In violin playing, "detached," that is, playing successive notes with downbow and upbow in alteration, but not staccato ... *Grand détaché,* a whole stroke of the bow to each note.

Determinato (It., dĕh-târ-mē-nah′tŏh). Determined, resolute.

Deux (Fr., dö). Two ... *À deux mains,* for 2 hands ... *Deux temps,* or *Valse à deux temps,* a "two-step" waltz.

Development. The working out or evolution (elaboration) of a theme by presenting it in varied melodic, harmonic, or rhythmic treatment.

Devozione, con (kŏhn dĕh-vŏh-tsē-oh′nĕh). In a devotional style; devoutly.

D flute. The orchestral or German flute.

Di (It., dē). Of, from, to, by; than.

Diapason. 1. An octave.—2. Either of the 2 principal foundation-stops of the organ, both of 8′ pitch; (*a*) the *open diapason,* with metal pipes open at the top, and (*b*) the *stopped diapason,* with wooden pipes closed at the top with wooden plugs. *Pedal* diapasons are usually 16′ stops.—3. Compass of a voice or instrument (in poetical usage).—4. A fixed pitch; the "normal diapason" is an accepted standard of pitch.

Diapason tone. Same as ORGAN TONE.

Diaphony. Literally, "sounding through"; a form of medieval counterpoint allowing certain liberties in crossing of parts and in using passing dissonances.

Diatonic. By, through, with, within, or embracing the tones of the standard major or minor scale . . . *Diatonic harmony* or *melody,* that employing the tones of but one scale . . . *Diatonic instrument,* one yielding only the tones of that scale of which its fundamental tone is the key-note . . . *Diatonic interval,* one formed by 2 tones of the same scale . . . *Diatonic modulation,* see MODULATION . . . *Diatonic progression,* stepwise progression within one scale . . . *Diatonic scale,* see SCALE.

Di colta (It., dē kôl′tăh). Suddenly, at once.

Diesis (It., dē-ā-sĭs). ⎫
Dièse (Fr., dē-ez). ⎭
Sharp; the sign ♯.

Differential tone. A tone produced by the difference of the frequencies of vibration between 2 notes when played loudly on a string instrument; such a tone lies well beneath the original 2 sounds, and produces a jarring effect; sometimes it is called "wolf tone."

Difficile (It., dēf-fē′chē-lĕh). ⎫
Difficile (Fr., dē-fē-sēl′). ⎭
Difficult.

Di gala (It., dē gäh′läh). Gaily, merrily.

Digital (dĭ′jĭ-tăl). A key on the keyboard of the piano, organ, etc.

Dignità, con (It., kŏhn dēn-ye-tah′). With dignity.

Dilettante (It., dē-let-tăhn′tĕh). An amateur.

Diligenza, con (kŏhn dē-lē-jen′dzăh). "With diligence"; carefully.

Diluendo (It., dē-loo-en′dŏh). Growing softer, dying away.

Diminished interval. A perfect or minor interval contracted by a chromatic semitone . . . *Diminished chord,* one whose highest and lowest tones form a diminished interval . . . *Diminished subject* or *theme,* one repeated or imitated in diminution . . . *Diminished triad,* a root with minor Third and diminished Fifth.

Diminished seventh chord. A chord consisting of 3 conjunct minor thirds, forming the interval of the diminished seventh between the top and bottom notes.

Diminuendo (It., dē-mē-noo-en′dŏh). Diminishing in loudness . . . *Diminuendo pedal,* a pedal-mechanism for gradually pushing in the stops (organ).

Diminution. The repetition or imitation of a theme in notes of smaller time value ($\frac{1}{2}$, $\frac{1}{3}$, or $\frac{1}{4}$ that of the original).

Di molto (It., dē mŏhl′tŏh). Very, extremely; *allegro di molto,* extremely fast.

Di nuovo (It., dē nô′vŏh). Anew; over again.

Direct. The sign ⌇ or ∨ set at the end of a staff to show the position of the first note on the next staff.

Direct motion, resolution, turn. See the nouns.

Dirge. A funeral hymn, or vocal or instrumental composition written in commemoration of the dead.

Diritto,-a (It., dē-rit′tŏh, -tăh). Direct, straight . . . *Alla diritta,* in direct motion.

Dis (Ger., dĭs). *D* sharp.

Discant. 1. The first attempts at polyphony with contrary motion in the parts (12th century); opposed to the *or-′ganum,* in which parallel motion was the rule.—2. Treble or soprano voice; the highest part in part-music.

Discord. Dissonance.

Discotheque. A gathering place where people dance to the sounds of amplified recordings.

Discretezza, con (It., kŏhn dē-skrĕh-tet′săh).}

Discrezione, con (It., kŏhn dē-skrĕh-tsē-oh′nĕh).}
 "With discretion"; discreetly, cautiously.

Discreto (It., dē-skrā′tŏh). Discreet; comparatively subdued.

Disinvolto (It., dē-zin-vŏhl′tŏh). Free, easy, graceful.

Disinvoltura, con (It., kŏhn dē-zin-vŏhl-too′rah). With ease, grace; flowingly.

Disis (Ger., dĭs′ĭs). *D* double sharp.

Disjunct motion. Progression by leaps.

Disk. Phonograph record.

Dis moll (Ger., dĭs mohl). *D* sharp minor.

Disperato (It., dē-spĕh-rah′tŏh). Desperate, hopeless.

Disperazione, con (It., kŏhn dē-spĕh-rắh-tsē-oh′nĕh). In a style expressive of desperation or despair.

Dispersed harmony. See HARMONY.

Dissonance. A combination of 2 or more tones requiring resolution.

Dissonant interval. Two tones forming a dissonance. The dissonant intervals are the seconds, sevenths, and all diminished and augmented intervals ... *Dissonant chord,* one containing one or more dissonant intervals.

Distance. Interval. [Seldom used.]

Distanza (It., dē-stähn′tsăh). Interval; distance ... *In distanza,* at a distance, marking music to be performed as if far away.

Distintamente (It., dē-stin-tăh-men′tĕh). Distinctly.

Distinto (It., dē-stin′tŏh). Distinct, clear.

Dital (dĭt′al). A key which, on pressure by the finger or thumb, raises the pitch of a guitar string or lute string by a semitone ... *Dital harp,* a guitar-shaped lute with 12 to 18 strings, each having a dital to raise its pitch a semitone; invented by Light in 1798.

Divertimento (It., dē-vâr-tē-men′tŏh). }
Divertissement (Fr., dē-vâr-tēs-măhn′). }

A light and easy piece of instrumental music. Also, an instrumental composition in 6 or 7 movements, like a Serenade. Also, an *entr'acte* in an opera, in the form of a short ballet, etc.

Divide. To play Divisions.

Divisi (It., dē-vē′zē). "Divided." Signifies that 2 parts written on one staff are not to be played as double stops, but by the division into 2 bodies of the instruments playing from that staff. *Divise* (dē-vē′zĕh) is the feminine form.

Division. A "dividing up" of a melodic series of tones into a rapid coloratura passage; if for voice, the passage was to be sung in one breath. (Obsolete.)—*To run a division,* to execute such a passage . . . *Division-viol,* the Viola da gamba.

Division mark. The slur or bracket written for triplets, quadruplets, etc., with a figure 3, 4, etc.

Dixieland. An American JAZZ style which began around 1915 and became prominent in the 1920's. It is ensemble music—the instruments are typically trumpet (or cornet), clarinet, piano, banjo, and drums—and is characterized by collective improvisation, dotted rhythms, and syncopation.

D moll (Ger., deh mohl). *D* minor.

Do (It., doh). 1. The note *C.*—2. In solmisation, the usual syllable name for the 1st degree of the scale. In the *fixed Do* method of teaching, Do is the name for all notes bearing the letter-name *C,* whether keynotes or not; in the *movable Do* method, Do is always the keynote.

Dodecuplet. A group of 12 equal notes, to be performed in the time of 8 notes of the same kind in the regular rhythm.

Dodecaphony. Technique of composition developed by Schoenberg and others about 1925, in which the basic theme of a given composition contains 12 different notes; the name is derived from the Greek words *dodeca,* "twelve," and *phone,* "sound." In dodecaphonic writing the key signature is abolished and the concept of tonality undergoes a radical change; furthermore, dissonances are emancipated and are used on a par with consonant combinations.

Doh stands for *Do* in Tonic Sol-fa.

Doigté (Fr., doo-ah-teh′). Fingering.

Dolce (It., dŏhl′chĕh). 1. Sweet, soft, suave.—2. A sweet toned organ stop.

Dolcemente (It., dŏhl-chā-men′tĕh). ⎫
Dolcezza, con (It., kŏhn dŏhl-chet′säh). ⎭
Sweetly, softly.

Dolcian (Ger., dŏhl-tsiahn′). ⎫
Dolciana (It., dŏhl-chah′näh). ⎬
Dolciano (It., dŏhl-chah′nŏh). ⎭
An early kind of bassoon; now, an 8′ or 16′ reed stop in the organ; a Fagotto.

Dolciato (It., dŏhl-chah′tŏh). Softer, calmer.

Dolcissimo (It., dŏhl-chis′sē-mŏh). Very sweetly, softly; also, a very soft toned 8′ flute stop in the organ.

Dolendo (It., dŏh-len′dŏh). ⎫
Dolente (It., dŏh-len′tĕh). ⎭
Doleful, plaintive, sad.

Dolentemente (It., dŏh-len-tĕh-men′tĕh). Dolefully, plaintively.

Dolore, con (It., kŏhn dŏh-loh′rĕh). ⎫
Dolorosamente (It., dŏh-lŏh-rôh-säh-men′tĕh). ⎬
Doloroso (It., dŏh-lŏh-roh′sŏh). ⎭
In a style expressive of pain or grief; pathetically.

Dolzflöte (Ger., dŏhlts′flö′tĕ). An 8′ open flute stop (organ).

Dominant. The fifth tone in the major or minor scale ... *Dom. chord,* (*a*) the dominant triad; (*b*) the dom. chord of the 7th ... *Dom. section* of a movement, a section written in the key of the dominant, lying between and contrasting with two others in the key of the tonic ... *Dom. triad,* that having the dominant as root.

Domra. A Russian balalaika.

Dopo (It., doh′pŏh). After.

Doppel (Ger., dŏhp′pĕl). Double.

Doppelfuge. See DOUBLE FUGUE.

Doppelgriff (Ger., dŏhp′pel-grēf). Double stop (violin); *Doppelgriffe,* Thirds, Sixths, etc., played with one hand (piano).

Doppelkreuz (Ger., dŏhp′pel-kroytz). Double sharp.

Doppio (It., dô′pī-ŏh). Double . . . *Doppio movimento,* twice as fast . . . *Doppio note* or *doppio valore,* twice as slow (that is, the absolute time value of the notes is doubled) . . . *Doppio pedale,* pedal part in octaves.

Dorian mode. A church mode which corresponds to the scale from *D* to *D* played on white keys of the piano.

Dot. A dot set after a note prolongs its time value by half

(𝅘𝅥𝅭 = 𝅘𝅥 𝅘𝅥𝅮); a second or third dot prolongs the time value

of the dot immediately preceding it by half

(𝅗𝅥𝅭𝅭 = 𝅘𝅥 𝅘𝅥𝅮 𝅘𝅥𝅯).

Double. 1. A variation.—2. Repetition of words in a song.—3. In organ playing, a 16′ stop (accompanying the 8′) stops in the lower octave).—4. A substitute singer.—5. In change-ringing, changes on 5 bells.—6 (*adjective*). "Producing a tone an octave lower"; as double-bassoon, double-bourdon, etc.—7 (*verb*). To add the higher or lower octave (to any tone or tones of a melody or harmony).

Double bar. The 2 vertical lines drawn through the staff at the end of a section, movement, or piece.

Double bass. The largest and deepest-toned instrument of the violin family, with either 3 strings (G_1-*D-A* being the Italian, A_1-*D-G* the English tuning), or 4 strings (E_1-A_1-*D-G*). See VIOLIN.

Double chorus. One for 2 choirs, or divided choir, usually in 8 parts.

Double counterpoint. The type of counterpoint in which the upper and the lower voices are inverted so that the low voice becomes the top voice and vice versa. See COUNTERPOINT.

Double croche (Fr., doo-ble crosh′). A sixteenth note.

Double flat. The sign ♭♭.

Double fugue. One with 2 themes.

Double note. A breve; ‖𝗈‖ —a note twice the length of a whole note.

Double octave. A 15th, or the interval of 2 octaves.

Double quartet. A quartet for 2 sets of 4 solo voices, or of 4 solo instruments.

Double reed. The reed used for instruments of the oboe family; 2 separate pieces of cane bound together to produce a characteristic vibration.

Double sharp. The sign ✕.

Double stop. In violin playing, to stop 2 strings together, thus obtaining 2-part harmony.

Double tongue. In playing the flute, and certain brass instruments, the application of the tongue in rapid alternation to the upper front teeth and the palate, to obtain a clear-cut and brilliant staccato.

Doublette (Fr., doo-blet′). A 2′ organ stop, octave of the Principal.

Douce (Fr., doos). ⎫
Doux (Fr., doo). ⎬
Soft, sweet, suave.

Doucement (Fr., doos-măhn′). Softly, sweetly, suavely.

Downbeat. 1. The downward stroke of the hand in beating time, which marks the primary or first accent in each measure.—2. Hence, the accent itself (strong beat, thesis).

Down-bow. In violin playing, the downward stroke of the bow from nut to point; on the 'cello and double bass, the stroke from nut to point. Usual sign ⊓.

Doxology. A song of praise to God in Roman Catholic liturgy, and also used in a modified form in Protestant church services. The word comes from the Greek *Doxa,* "glory," and *Logos,* "saying."

Drabant. A ceremonial Polish dance of the 18th century.

Dramatic music. 1. Program music.—2. Music accompanying and illustrating an actual drama on the stage.

Drame lyrique (Fr., drăhm lē-rēk′). French designation for opera.

Dramma per musica (It., drahm-măh pĕr moo′zē-kăh). Literally, "drama by music"; a designation used at the birth of opera in Italy about 1600.

Drammaticamente (It., drăhm-măh-tē-kăh-men′tĕh).⎫
Drammatico (It., drăhm-măh′tē-kŏh). ⎭
 Dramatically; in a vivid, dramatic style.

Drängend (Ger., dreng′ent). Pressing, hastening; *stringendo.*

Draw stop. Any organ stop drawn by hand.

Drei (Ger., drī). Three.

Dreifach (Ger., drī′-făyh). Triple.

Drohend (Ger., drŏh′ent). Menacing.

Dröhnend (Ger., drö′nent). Thundering; *tonando.*

Droit (Fr., drwăh). ⎫
Droite (Fr., drwăh′t). ⎭
 Right; *main droite,* right hand.

Drone. In the bagpipe, a continuously sounding pipe of constant pitch; a drone-pipe ... *Drone-bass,* a bass on the tonic, or tonic and dominant, which is persistent throughout a movement or piece, as in the Musette 2.

Drum. An instrument of percussion, consisting of a cylindrical, hollow *body* of wood or metal, over one or both ends of which a membrane (the *head*), is stretched tightly by means of a *hoop,* to which is attached an endless *cord* tightened by leathern *braces,* or by rods and screws. *Rhythmical* drums (side drum, snare drum, bass drum) do not vary in pitch; *musical* drums (the Kettledrum) produce musical tones distinct in pitch.

D string. The 3d string on the violin; 2d on the viola, 'cello and double bass.

Due (It., doo'ĕh). Two . . . *A due,* (*a*) for 2; as *a due voci,* for 2 parts or voices; (*b*) both together (after *Divisi*) . . . *Due corde,* see CORDA. . .*Due volte,* twice. . .*I due pedali,* both (piano-) pedals at once.

Duet. 1. A composition for 2 voices or instruments.—2. A composition for 2 performers on one instrument, as the piano.—3. A composition for the organ, in 2 parts, each to be played on a separate manual.

Duetto (It., doo-et'tŏh). Duet.

Dulciana. 1. An organ stop, having metal pipes of a some-what sharp, thin tone.—2. A small reed stop of delicate tone.—3. A small bassoon.

Dulcimer. An ancient stringed instrument, having wire strings stretched over a soundboard or resonance-box, and struck with mallets or hammers. The modern dulcimer has from 2 to 3 octaves' compass (see PANTALON); it was a precursor of the pianoforte.

Dumb piano. A small keyboard instrument resembling a piano, but without hammers and strings; intended for silent finger practice.

Dumka (Polish, dŏŏm'kăh). A sort of vocal or instrumental Romance, of a melancholy cast, a lament or elegy.

Dummy pipes. Pipes which do not speak, displayed in the front of the organ.

Duo (It., doo'ŏh). A duet.—*Duo* is sometimes distinguished from *Duet* by applying the former term to a 2-part composition for 2 voices or instruments of *different* kinds, and the latter to a 2-part composition for 2 voices or instruments of the *same* kind.—Also, a composition in 2 parts for *one* instrument; for example, a violin-*duo,* in contradistinction to a violin-*duet* for *two* violins.

Duodecima (It., doo-ŏh-dä′chē-mäh). 1. The interval of a Twelfth.—2. The Twelfth (organ stop).

Duodrama. A kind of melodrama, or spoken dialogue accompanied by music.

Duolo, con (It., kŏhn dŏŏ-ô′lŏh). Dolefully, grievingly.

Duple. Double ... *Duple rhythm,* rhythm of 2 beats to a measure ... *Duple time.* See Time.

Dur (Ger., door). Major, as in *C dur* (*C* major), *F dur* (*F* major), etc.

Dur(e) (Fr., dür). Harsh, unpleasing in tone.

Duramente (It., doo-räh-men′tĕh). ⎫
Durezza, con (It., kŏhn doo-ret′säh). ⎭
Sternly, harshly.

Durchkomponiert (Ger., doorh-kom-poh-neert′). A description of song form in which every subsequent stanza has a different musical setting.

Durchführung (Ger., doorh′für-ŏŏngᵏ). "Through leading."—1. The development section in sonata form.—2. The exposition in a fugue.

Duro (It., doo′rŏh, -räh). Hard, harsh.

Düster (Ger., dü′ster). Gloomy, mournful.

Dutch concert. The singing of an entire company in which each person sings whatever he pleases; or the persons present sing in alternation any verse that comes into their heads, the refrain by the whole company being a regular repetition of some popular verse.

Dux. The subject in a fugue; literally, "leader" in Latin.

Dynamics. The varying and contrasting degrees of intensity or loudness in musical tones.

E

E (Ger. *E*: Fr. and It. *mi*). The 3d tone or degree in the typical diatonic scale of *C* major.

E (It., ā). And.—When preceding a word beginning with "e," it should be written *ed*; before other vowels, either *e* or *ed* may be used; before consonants, only *e*.

Ebollimento (It., ā-bŏhl-lē-men'tŏh).
Ebollizione (It., ā-bŏhl-lē-tsē-oh'nĕh).
Ebullition; a sudden and passionate expression of feeling.

Eccheggiare (It., ā-kĕd-jē-āh'rĕh). To echo.

Eccitato (It., et-chē-tah'tŏh). Excited.

Ecclesiastical modes. The octave scales employed in medieval church music.

Ecco (It., ek'kŏh). Echo. (Better written *Eco.*)

Echo. 1. A subdued repetition of a strain or phrase.—2. An echo stop.

Echo organ. A separate set of pipes, either enclosed in a box within the organ, or placed at a distance from the latter, to produce the effect of an echo.

Echo stop. One producing an echo-like effect.

Eco (It., ĕh'kŏh). Echo.

Écossaise (Fr., ā-kŏh-säz'). Originally, a Scotch round dance in 3/2 or 3/4 time; now, a lively contredanse in 2/4 time. Compare SCHOTTISCHE.

Ed (It., ed). And. See E.

Edel (Ger., ā'del). Noble; refined, chaste.

E dur (Ger., eh door). *E* major.

Effetto (It., ef-fet'tŏh). Effect, impression.

Effusione, con (It., kŏhn ef-foo-zē-oh'nĕh). With effusion; with warmth.

Eguaglianza, con (It., kŏhn ā-guāhl-yähn'tsäh).
Egualmente (It., ā-guāhl-men'tĕh).

Evenly, smoothly; *con molta eguaglianza,* very smoothly, evenly.

Eguale (It., ā-guah′lĕh). Equal; even, smooth.

Eighteenth. Interval of 2 octaves and a fourth.

Eighth. 1. An octave.—2. An eighth note. See ELEMENTS OF NOTATION, p. viii.

Eilen (Ger., ī′len). To hasten, accelerate, go faster.

Eilend (Ger., ī′lent). Hastening; *stringendo.*

Eilig (Ger., ī′lĭyh). Hasty, hurriedly; rapid, swift.

Ein, Eins (Ger., īn, īns). One.

Einfach (Ger., īn′fäh). Simple; simply; *semplice.*

Eingang (Ger., īn′gähng^k). Introduction.

Einklang (Ger., īn′klähng^k). Unison, consonance.

Einlage (Ger., īn′lähge). An interpolation or inserted piece.

Einleitung (Ger., īn′lī-toong^k). Introduction.

Einsatz (Ger., īn′sähtz). 1. An attack.—2. An entrance of a vocal or instrumental part.

Einstimmig (Ger., īn′shtĭm-mĭyh). Monophonic, one-voiced.

Eis (Ger., ā′iss). *E* sharp.

Élan, avec (Fr., ăh-vek′ ā-lähn′). With dash; *con islancio.*

Élargissez (Fr., ā-lar-zhē-sē′). *Allargate.*

Electric guitar. Electronically amplified guitar, widely used in modern rock groups.

Electronic music. A new resourceful method of tone production by electronic means. The earliest electronic instrument was demonstrated by the Russian inventor Theremin in 1920; a few years later the French composer Martenot introduced a keyboard electronic instrument known as *Ondes musicales* (musical waves). The most advanced electronic instruments are the Synthesizers, capable of generating any desired pitch, any scale, any rhythm, any tone color, and any degree of loudness.

Electronic organ. A powerful modern electronic organ activated not by pipes but by electrical devices and capable of unlimited tone production.

Elegante (It., ā-lā-gähn′tĕh).

Elegantemente (It., —gähn-tā-men′tĕh).

Eleganza, con (It., kŏhn ā-lā-gähn′tsäh).
In an elegant, graceful, refined style.

Elegie (Ger., ā-lā-zhe′).

Élégie (Fr., ā-lā-zhe′).

Elegy.
A vocal or instrumental composition of a melancholy cast, having no fixed form.

Elevato (It., ā-lā-vah′tōh). Elevated, lofty, sublime.

Elevazione, con (It., kŏhn ā-lā-văh-tsē-oh′nĕh). In a lofty, elevated style.

Embellishment. See GRACE.

Embouchure (Fr., ähn-boo-shür′). The mouthpiece of a wind instrument, also the manipulation of the lips and tongue in playing a wind instrument.

E moll (Ger., eh mohl). *E* minor.

Emozione (It., ā-mŏh-tsē-oh′nĕh). Emotion.

Empfindung, mit (Ger., mit em-pfin′dŏŏng^k).

Empfindungsvoll (Ger., em-pfin′dŏŏngs-fŏhl).
With emotion, feelingly, full of feeling.

Emphase, avec (Fr., ăh-vek′ ähn-fahz′).

Emphase, mit (Ger., mit em-fah′zĕ).
With emphasis.

Enchaînez (Fr., ähn-shä-nā′). "Go on directly"; *attaccate.*

Encore (Fr., ähn-kor′). "Again!" (so used in English when recalling an actor or singer; the French cry "bis!").—Also, a recall on the stage; or, the piece or performance repeated or added.

En dehors (Fr., ahn de-or'). "Outside"; to emphasize, or bring out the melody.

En élargissant (Fr., ăhn ā-lar-zhē-săhn'). *Allargando.*

Energia, con (It., kŏhn ā-nâr-jē'ăh).

Energicamente (It., ā-nâr-jē-käh-men'tĕh).

Energico (It., ā-nâr'jē-kŏh).

Énergie, avec (Fr., ăh-vek' ā-nâr-zhi').

Energisch (Ger., ā-nâr'gish).

With energy and decision, energetically. A passage so marked is to be vigorously accented and distinctly phrased.

Enfasi, con (It., kŏhn en'fäh-zē).

Enfatico (It., en-fäh'tē-kŏh).

With emphasis, emphatic.

English horn. An instrument of the oboe family, which transposes a fifth below the written note.

Enharmonic tones. Tones derived from different degrees, but practically identical in pitch; like $c\sharp$ *and* $d\flat$ on the piano or organ . . . *Enharmonic chords* are chords differing in notation but alike in sound; such chords are called "enharmonically changed," and passing from one to the other is an "enharmonic modulation" . . . *Enharmonic interval,* one formed between 2 enharmonic tones.

En mesure (Fr., ăhn mŭ-zür'). See MISURATO.

Ensemble (Fr., ăhn-săhn'bl'). 1. General effect (of a composition).—2. Style of performance (of a body of musicians) . . . *Morceau d'ensemble,* concerted piece.

Entr'acte (Fr., ăhn-trăhkt'). "Interval between acts"; hence, a light instrumental composition or short ballet, for performance between acts.

Entrata (It., en-trah'tăh).

Entrée (Fr., ăhn-trā').

1. The orchestral prelude to a ballet, following the overture.—2. A division in a ballet like a "scene" in a play.—3. An old dance like a Polonaise, usually in 4/4 time.

Entschlossen (Ger., ent-shlŏshs′sen). Resolutely, in a deter-mined manner.

Entusiasmo, con (It., kŏhn en-too-zē-ăhz′mŏh). With en-thusiasm.

Episode (ep′ĭ-sōd). An intermediate or incidental section; in the fugue, a digression from the principal theme, interpo-lated between the developments of the latter.

Epithalamium. A wedding hymn.

Equabile (It., ā-kwah′bē-lĕh). Equable; even, uniform.

Equabilmente (It., ā-kwăh-bēl-men′tĕh). Evenly, smoothly.

Equal counterpoint. Counterpoint in equal notes.

Equal temperament. See TEMPERAMENT.

Equal voices. Voices of the same class; that is, either women's and boy's (soprano and alto), or men's (tenor and bass).

Equivocal chord. A dissonant chord of uncertain resolution, like the diminished 7th.

Ergriffen (Ger., âr-grif′fen). Affected, stirred.

Ergriffenheit (Ger., âr-grif′fen-hīt). Emotion, agitation.

Erhaben (Ger., âr-hah′ben). Lofty, exalted.

Erhabenheit (Ger., âr-hah′ben-hīt). Loftiness, sublimity.

Erklingen (Ger., âr-kling′en). To resound.

Ermattet (Ger., âr-măht′tet). Exhausted, wearied.

Ernst (Ger., ârnst). Earnest, grave.

Eroico,-a (It., ā-rôh′ē-kŏh, -kăh). Heroic; strong and digni-fied.

Erschüttert (Ger., âr-shüt′tert). Shaken, agitated.

Erzählung (Ger., âr-tsä′lŏŏng^k). Story, tale, narration.

Es (Ger., ess). *E* flat.

Esaltazione, con (It., kŏhn ā-zăhl-tăh-tsē-oh′nĕh). With ex-altation; in a lofty, fervent style.

Esclamato (It., ĕh-sklăh-mah′tŏh). "Exclaimed"; forcibly declaimed.

Es dur (Ger., ess door). *E* flat major.

Eses (Ger., ess'ess). *E* double flat.

Es moll (Ger., ess mohl). *E* flat minor.

Espandendosi (It., ĕh-spähn-den'dŏh-sē). Growing broader and fuller; with growing intensity.

Espansione, con (It., kŏhn ĕh-spähn-sē-oh'nĕh).⎫
Espansivo (It., ĕh-spähn-sē'vŏh). ⎭
With intense feeling.

Espirando (It., ĕh-spē-rähn'dŏh). Dying away, expiring.

Espressione, con (It., kŏhn ĕh-spres-sē-oh'nĕh).⎫
Espressivo (It., ĕh-spres-sē-vŏh). ⎭
With expression, expressively . . . *Con molta* (or *molt'*) *espressione,* very expressively.

Esquisse (Fr., es-keese'). A sketch.

Essential. Any ♯ or ♭ belonging to a key-signature.

Essential harmony. See HARMONY . . . *Essential note,* chord-note, or melody-note . . . *Essential seventh,* the leading-tone; also, the dominant 7th chord.

Estinguendo (It., ĕh-stin-gwen'dŏh). Extinguishing; dying away.

Estinto (It., ĕh-stin'tŏh). Barely audible; the extreme of *pianissimo.*

Estremamente (It., ĕh-strā-mǎh-men'tĕh). Extremely.

Estro poetico (It., â'strŏh pŏh-â'te-kŏh). Poetic fervor.

Étude (Fr., ā-tüd'). A study; especially, one affording practice in some particular technical difficulty. *Étude de concert,* one designed for public performance.

Etwas (Ger., et'vähss). Rather, somewhat.

Euphone (u-fō'ne). In the organ, a 16' free-reed stop, with a soft, sweet tone like the clarinet.

Euphonium. 1. An instrument invented by Chladni in 1790, consisting of graduated glass tubes made to sound by the moistened fingers, and connected with steel rods.—2. The bass saxhorn.

Eurhythmics. A system of musical training introduced by Jaques-Dalcroze in 1910 in which the pupils were taught to represent complex rhythmic movement with their entire bodies, to the accompaniment of specially composed music.

Evening song, Evensong. In the Anglican Church, a form of worship appointed to be said or sung at evening; known as Vespers in the Roman Catholic Church.

Execution. 1. Style, manner of performance.—2. Technical ability.

Exercise. A short technical study for training the fingers (or vocal organs) to overcome some special difficulty.—Also, a short study in composition.

Exposition. 1. The opening of a sonata movement, in which the principal themes are presented for the first time.—2. Sections of a fugue which present the subject.

Expressionism. A modern movement in music, beginning around 1910, giving expression to the inner state of a composer's mind and emotion; the term itself originated in painting. Expressionism reflects anxious moods characteristic of modern life in a musical idiom using atonally constructed melodies and spasmodic, restless rhythms.

Expression mark. A written direction (either a sign, word, or phrase) for the performance of a piece.

Expression stop. In the harmonium, a stop which closes the escape-valve of the bellows, so that wind pressure and intensity of tone are partly controlled by the pedals.

Expressive organ. The harmonium.

Extemporize. To perform spontaneously in the manner of improvisation.

Extended compass. Tones beyond the usual range of a voice or instrument.

Extended harmony, interval. See HARMONY; INTERVAL.

Extension pedal. The loud (right) piano pedal.

Extravaganza. A stage show with music marked by exaggerated comic effects.

Extreme interval. Augmented interval.—The *chord of the extreme sixth* has a major Third and sharp Sixth, and occurs on the 6th degree in minor in 3 principal forms. See AUGMENTED SIXTH.

Extreme parts. In part music, the outer parts.

F

F (Ger. *F*; Fr. and It. *fa*). The 4th tone and degree in the typical diatonic scale of *C* major ... *f* = *forte; ff* or *fff* = *fortissimo.*

Fa. 1. In solmisation, the usual name for the 4th degree of the scale.—2. Name of the tone *F* in Italy, France, Spain, and Russia.

Faburden. Old English term describing a progression in consecutive 6/3 chords, similar but not identical to Fauxbourdon.

Facile (It., fah′chē-lĕh).
Facile (Fr., făh-sēl′).
    Facile, easy, fluent.

Fackeltanz (Ger., făhkl′-tants). Torch dance.

Fado. A popular Portuguese song.

Fagott (Ger., făh-gŏht′). Bassoon.—Also, a reed stop in the organ.

Fagotto (It., făh-gŏht′tŏh). Bassoon.

Fah. In Tonic Sol-fa, it stands for Fa.

False relation. The chromatic contradiction of a tone in one part by another part; it consists in sounding, either together or in succession, a tone and its chromatically altered octave.

Falsetto. The highest of the vocal registers.

Fancy. Type of 17th-century English instrumental music. See FANTASIE.

Fandango (Sp.). A lively dance in triple time, for 2 dancers of opposite sex, who accompany it with castanets or tambourine.

Fanfare (fan′fâr). A flourish of trumpets or trumpet-call.

Fantaisie (Fr., fähn-tä-zē′).
Fantasia (It., fähn-täh-zē′äh).
Fantasie (Ger., fähn-täh-zē).
  1. An improvisation.—2. An instrumental piece in free imitation (17th and 18th centuries).—3. A composition free in form and more or less fantastic in character; a Fantasy.—4. A potpourri or paraphrase.

Fantasia, con (It.). Fancifully, spiritedly.

Fantastico (It., fähn-täh′stē-kŏh). Fantastic, fanciful.

Farandola (It., fäh-**r**ähn-doh′läh).
Farandole (Fr., fäh-**r**ähn-dŏhl′).
  A circle-dance in 6/8 time and very rapid tempo.

Farce. A one-act opera or operetta of ultracomical or burlesque character.

Fastosamente (It., fäh-stŏh-säh-men′tĕh). Pompously; in a stately style.

Fastoso (It., fäh-stoh′sŏh). Pompous, stately.

Fauxbourdon (Fr., foh-boor-dŭn). A contrapuntal technique of the 15th century, marked by parallel progressions in thirds and sixths. This practice eventually led to the use of consecutive 6/3 chords, common in classical usage. The reason for the name, "false drone," is probably owed to the introduction of the "false bass," which was not the tonic of the chord, but its mediant.

F clef. The bass clef: 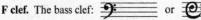 or

F dur (Ger., ĕff door). *F* major.

Feierlich (Ger., fī′er-līyh). Ceremonial, solemn, grave.

Fermamente (It., fâr-măh-men′tĕh). Firmly, with decision.

Fermata (It., fâr-mah′tăh). ⎱
Fermate (Ger., fâr-mah′tĕ). ⎰
A hold: ⌒; a pause or interruption. See HOLD.

Fermezza, con (It., kŏhn fâr-met′săh). In a firm, decided, energetic style.

Fermo (It., fâr′mŏh). Firm, decided; fixed, unchanged . . . *Canto fermo,* same as CANTUS FIRMUS.

Ferne (Ger., fâr′nĕ). Distance . . . *Wie aus der Ferne,* as from a distance.

Fernflöte (Ger., fârn′flö′tĕ). A covered 8′ organ stop of very soft tone.

Feroce (It., fā-roh′chēh). ⎫
Ferocemente (It., fā-rŏh-chĕh-men′teh). ⎬
Ferocità, con (It., kŏhn fā-rŏh-chē-tah′). ⎭
Wildly, fiercely, vehemently.

Fervente (It., fâr-ven′tĕh). ⎱
Fervore, con (It., kŏhn fâr-voh′rĕh). ⎰
Fervently, ardently, passionately.

Fes (Ger., fess). *F* flat.

Festivamente (It., fĕh-stē-văh-men′tĕh). ⎱
Festività, con (kŏhn fĕh-stē-vē-tah′). ⎰
In a gay, festive style.

Festivo (It., fĕh-stē′vŏh). ⎫
Festlich (Ger., fest′līyh). ⎬
Festoso (It., fĕh-stoh′sŏh). ⎭
Festive, festal.

Festschrift (Ger., fĕst′shrĭft). An offering in honor of a musical scholar or composer on the occasion of a birthday or retirement, in the form of a published volume of collected articles by his students and colleagues.

Festspiel (Ger., fĕst′shpēl). German term for a stage play in which music is included.

Feuer, mit (Ger., mit fahü′er). }
Feuerig (Ger., fahü′ĕ-rīyh). }
With fire; fiery, impetuous.

F holes. The 2 *f*-shaped sound-holes in the belly of the violin, etc.

Fiacco (It., fē-ăhk′kŏh). Languishing, feeble.

Fiato (It., fē-äh′tŏh). "Breath"; *stromenti a fiato* are wind instruments.

Fiddle. A violin ... *Fiddle-bow, Fiddlestick,* see Bow.

Fieramente (It., fē-ĕh-răh-men′tĕh). }
Fierezza, con (kŏhn fē-ĕh-ret′săh). }
Wildly, boldly.

Fiero,-a (It., fē-â′rŏh, -răh). Wild, fierce; bold, vigorous.

Fife. An octave cross flute with 6 holes and without keys; compass d^2 to d^4.—Also, a piccolo-stop.

Fifteenth. A double octave.—Also, an organ stop of 2′ pitch.

Fifth. An interval of 5 diatonic degrees (see INTERVAL).— Also, the 5th degree in any diatonic scale; the Dominant ... *False Fifth,* a diminished fifth.

Figuration. Rapid figures or phrases, containing passing and changing notes.

Figure. A group of notes in a melody.

Figured bass. One of the most important methods of indicating the harmony to be used in the keyboard part in Baroque music, in which the bass line alone is given, annotated with numbers which indicate the intervals to be used from the bass up, and thus determining the harmony. Numerous elaborations were also in use, sucn as flats or sharps after the figures, etc. The practice of figured bass disappeared in the 19th century. Figured bass is also called throughbass, thoroughbass or BASSO CONTINUO.

Filar la voce (It., fē-lar′ lăh voh′chĕh).⎫
Filer la voix (Fr., fē-lā′ lăh vwăh). ⎭

To prolong a tone, slowly swelling and diminishing.

Filato (It., fē-lah′tŏh). Long, drawn out.

Filo di voce (It., fē′lŏh dē voh′chĕh). The very softest and lightest vocal tone.

Finale (It., fē-nah′lĕh). The last movement in a sonata or symphony; the closing number (s) of an act (opera) or Part (oratorio).

Fine (It., fē′nĕh). End; close; indicates either the end of a "repeat" (after the *Da capo* or *Dal segno*), or the end of a piece.

Fingering. 1. The method of applying the fingers to the keys, holes, strings, etc., of musical instruments.—2. The marks guiding the performer in placing his fingers.... *English fingering* (for the piano), that in which notes taken by the thumb are marked ×, with 1,2,3,4 for the fingers... *German* (or *Continental*) *fingering,* the thumb marked 1, and the fingers 2,3,4, 5.

Fingersatz (Ger., fin′ger-sähts). Fingering.

Fino (It., fē′nŏh). Till, up to, as far as.

Fioritura (It., fē-ŏh-rē-too′räh). An embellishment; an ornamental turn, flourish, or phrase, introduced into a melody. (Plural *fioriture.*)

Fipple flute. Obsolete vertical flute, blown from the end; the word is derived from fipple, a plug in the mouthpiece.

First. Of voices or instruments of the same class, the highest; as *1st soprano, 1st violin.*—In the staff, the lowest; as *first line, first space.*—The *first string* of an instrument is the highest.

Fis (Ger., fiss). *F* sharp.

Fis dur (Ger., fiss door). *F* sharp major.

Fisis (Ger., fiss'iss). *F* double sharp.

Fis moll (Ger., fiss mohl). *F* sharp minor.

Fistel, Fistelstimme (Ger., fis'tel-shtim'mĕ). Falsetto.

Fixed Do. In the fixed Do system of solmisation the tone *C,* and all its chromatic derivatives (*C♯, C♭, C✕, C♭♭*), are called Do, *D* and its derivatives are called Re, etc., in whatever key or harmony they may appear.

Fixed-tone instrument. One (like the piano or organ) the pitch of whose tones cannot be modified at the player's pleasure, like (for example) the tones of the violin. Such an instrument is said to have "fixed intonation."

Flag. A hook (♪) on the stem of a note.

Flageolet. A small direct flute, a wind instrument of the whistle family. The French flageolet has a compass of 2 octaves and 3 semitones, from g^1 to $b^3♭$.—Also, a small flute stop in the organ, of 1′ or 2′ pitch. . . . *Flageolet-tones,* Harmonics.

Flamenco. A typical dance of the Andalusian gypsies and Spanish dancers elsewhere. It is characterized by vigorous heel stamping and passionate gesticulation.

Flat. The character ♭, which lowers the pitch of the note before which it is set by a semitone; the Double flat ♭♭ lowers its note by 2 semitones . . . *Flat chord,* one whose tones are performed simultaneously; a *solid* chord; opposed to *broken* . . . *Flat fifth,* diminished fifth.

Flatterzunge (Ger., flăht-ter-tsoon'gheh). Literally, "flutter-tongue." A special effect on the flute and occasionally other wind instruments, consisting of the rapid insertion of the tongue in the keyhole resulting in a sort of stuttering sound. Double tonguing and triple tonguing are further varieties of Flatterzunge.

Flautando (It., flăh-ŏŏ-tăhn'dŏh). ⎫
Flautato (It., flăh-ŏŏ-tah'tŏh). ⎬

A direction in violin music to play near the fingerboard, so as to produce a somewhat "fluty" tone.

Flauto (It., flah′ŏŏ-tŏh). Flute; also as the name of organ stops, as *Flauto amabile*, etc. . . . *Flauto traverso*, cross-flute.

Flebile (It., flâ′bē-lĕh). Tearful; plaintive, mournful.

Flehend (Ger., flā′hent). Pleading.

Flexatone. A primitive instrument consisting of a metal plate attached to a piece of wood. It produces a twanging sound when the metal plate is plucked.

Fliessend (Ger., flē′sent). Flowing, smooth; *scorrendo*.

Fling. A Scotch dance resembling the Reel, in quadruple time.

Florid. Embellished with runs, passages, figures, graces, etc.

Flourish. A trumpet fanfare.

Flüchtig (Ger., flü̆yh′tĭyh). Flightily, hastily; lightly, airily.

Flue pipe. See Pipe.

Flügel (Ger., flü̆′gel). "Wing." The grand pianoforte or harpsichord so-called because of its winged shape.

Flügelhorn. A brass instrument similar to but larger than the cornet.

Flute. The orchestral flute (*Boehm flute*) has a wooden or metal tube of cylindrical bore, with 14 ventages closed by keys; it is blown through an oval orifice near the upper end. Compass from c^1 to c^4. This is the so-called *Cross flute,* being held across the mouth; the *Direct flute* is blown from the end, like a whistle.

Flute à bec. Recorder.

Flute stop. A flue stop with flute tone.

Flute work. In the organ, all flue stops not belonging to the *Principal-work* or *Gedacktwork*.

Flutter-tongue. A special effect in flute playing, done by moving the tongue rapidly in and out of the keyhole. Same as FLATTERZUNGE.

F moll (Ger., ef mohl). *F* minor.

Foco (It., fô′kŏh). Fire. See FUOCO.

Folgend (Ger., fŏhl′ghent). "Following"; *colla parte* or *voce.*

Folia (Sp., fŏh-lē′äh). ⎫
Follia (It., fŏhl-lē′äh). ⎬
⎭
A Spanish dance for one person, in slow tempo and 3/4 time.

Folk song. A song of the people, tinged by the musical peculiarities of the nation, and usually in simple, unaffected ballad form.

Follower. A Consequent.

Foot. 1. A group of syllables having one accent like a simple measure in music.—2. That part of an organ pipe below the mouth.—3. The unit of measure in designating the pitch of organ stops, and of the several octaves in the musical scale. An 8′ stop is one whose longest pipe produces the tone *C* and is about 8 feet in length, that is, a stop whose pipes produce tones corresponding in pitch to the keys touched; 4′ stop is an octave stop; a 16′ stop yields tones an octave lower than indicated by the keys touched.—The 8′ octave embraces the tones from *C* upwards. See ABSOLUTE PITCH.

Footing. The method of applying the heels and toes to the organ pedals.

Foreign chords or **tones.** Those that do not belong to a given key.

Forlana (It., fohr-lah′năh). ⎫
Forlane (Fr., fohr-lähn′). ⎬
⎭
A lively Italian dance in 6/8 or 6/4 time.

Form. In music, a concept of organization governing the order, character, meter, and key of a composition. The most elementary form is binary, in which only 2 elements are presented. Ternary form evolves from binary by the interpolation of a middle section. In a large work, such as a sonata or a symphony, formal elements often intermingle and are distinguished by their similarities or contrasts.

Fort (Ger., fort). Off (organ music).

Forte (It., fôhr′těh). Loud, strong; usually written *f*; *piu forte,* louder; *piano forte* (*pf*), begin softly and swell rapidly; *poco forte,* rather loud; *forte piano* (*fp*), accent strongly, instantly diminishing to piano; *fortemente* (for-těh-měn′ těh), loudly, forcibly; *forte possible* (pŏhs-sě′be-lěh), as loud as possible.... *Forte-stop* (harmonium), a slide opened by a draw stop or knee-lever, to produce a *forte* effect ... *Forte generale,* the full organ combination stop.

Fortepiano. A term used for the 18th-century piano, to distinguish it from the modern instrument.

Fortissimo (It., fohr-tis′sē-mŏh). Extremely loud (usually written *ff,* or *fff*).

Forza, con (It., kŏhn fôr′tsăh). With force, forcibly.

Forzando (It., fohr-tsăhn′dŏh). ⎫
Forzato (It., fohr-tsah′tŏh). ⎭
With force, energy; means that the note or chord is to be strongly accented; usually written *fz.*

Foundation stop. See STOP.

Four-hand piano. Pieces written for 2 piano players, one playing the treble parts and the other the bass. Once very popular for piano pupils, 4-hand music has unfortunately all but disappeared from piano teaching.

Fourniture (Fr., foor-nē-tür′). Mixture stop.

Fourth. An interval embracing 4 degrees.—Also, the 4th degree in the diatonic scale; the subdominant.

Fox trot. A popular duple/quadruple metered ballroom dance that originated in the 1920's. Once considered a jazz dance.

Française (Fr., frähn-säz′). A dance in triple time, resembling the country-dance.

Francamente (It., frähn-käh-men′tĕh). ⎤
Franchezza, con (kŏhn frähn-ket′säh). ⎦
Free in delivery; boldly; frankly, ingenuously.

Frase larga (It., frah′zĕh lar′gäh). "Broad phrase"; *largamente*.

Freddamente (It., fred-däh-men′tĕh). ⎤
Freddezza, con (kŏhn fred-det′säh). ⎦
Coldly; coolly, indifferently.

Freddo (It., fred′dŏh). Cold; indifferent.

Free fugue. One written with more or less disregard of strict rules.

Free jazz. A Jazz style of the 1960's and 1970's, linked to the "black power" and black ethnic pride movements. It is characterized by collective improvisation without reference to preset harmonic or formal structures.

Free part. One added to a canon or fugue to complete the harmony.

Free style (of composition). That in which the rules of strict counterpoint are relaxed.

Frei (Ger., frī). Free . . . *Frei im Vortrag*, free in style (delivery).

Fremente (It., frä-men′tĕh). Furiously.

French horn. Brass instrument in the shape of spiral with a tunnel-shaped opening. The modern French horn possesses a mellow tone capable of great expressive power.

French sixth. This is the common name for a chord containing the augmented sixth between the bottom and the top notes, other intervals from the bottom being a major third and an augmented fourth, as in *A* flat, *C, D,* and *F* sharp. See AUGMENTED SIXTH.

French overture. A type of overture developed in France in the 18th century, consisting of 3 sections: The first in slow tempo, the second, rather quick, and the third, again slow.

Fret. One of the narrow ridges of wood, metal, or ivory, crossing the fingerboard of the mandolin, guitar, zither, etc., on which the strings are "stopped."

Fretta, con (It., kŏhn fret'tâh).

Frettolosamente (It., fret-tŏh-lŏh-săh-men'tĕh).

Frettoloso (It., fret-tŏh-loh'sŏh).
Hastily, hurriedly.

Freude (Ger., froy'-deh). Joy.

Freudig (Ger., froy'diyh). Joyous.

Frisch (Ger., frish). Brisk, vigorous; *brioso*.

Friss. The rapid section of the Hungarian dance Csárdás.

Frog. Wrong translation of *Frosch,* "nut."

Fröhlich (Ger., frö'lĭyh). Gay, glad, joyous.

Frosch (Ger., frŏsh). Nut (of a bow).

Frottola (It., froht'toh-lah). A type of choral madrigal popular in Italy in the 16th century.

Frühlingslied (Ger., frü'lings-lēt). Spring song.

F-Schlüssel (Ger., shlüsel). The Bass or F clef.

Fuga (L. and It., foo'găh). A fugue.

Fugara. An organ stop having metal flue pipes of 8' or 4' pitch; tone sharp and "stringy."

Fugato (It., fŏŏ-gah'tŏh; "in fugue style"). A passage or movement consisting of fugal imitations, but not worked out as a regular fugue.

Fuge (Ger., foo'gĕ). Fugue.

Fughetta (It., fŏŏ-get'tăh). A short fugue; a fugue exposition.

Fuging tune. A choral hymn with an imitative, though not truly fugal, section. Very popular in late 18th-century New England.

Fugue (fewg). The most highly developed form of contra-puntal imitation, based on the principle of the equality of the parts, a theme proposed by one part being taken up successively by all participating parts, thus bringing each in turn into special prominence.—The elements essential to every fugue are (1) the Subject, (2) the Answer, (3) Coun-tersubject, (4) Stretto; to these are commonly added (5) Episodes, (6) an Organ point, (7) a Coda.—In a *Real Fugue* the answer is an exact transposition of the subject, in a *Tonal Fugue,* the subject is modified in the answer in order to lead back to the original key.

Fugued, Fuguing. Written like a fugue, either strict or free.

Fuguing tune. Alternate spelling for FUGING TUNE.

Full anthem. One for chorus without soli ... *Full band,* a military band, or an orchestra, having all the customary instruments ... *Full cadence,* a perfect cadence ... *Full Choir* (Great, Swell), draw all stops of Choir (Great, Swell) organ ... *Full chord,* a chord having one or more of its original 3 or 4 tones doubled in the octave ... *Full orches-tra,* compare FULL BAND ... *Full organ,* with all stops and couplers drawn ... *Full score,* see SCORE. *Full to Fifteenth,* draw all stops but mixtures and reeds.

Fundamental. 1. The root of a chord.—2. A tone which pro-duces a series of harmonics; a generator (or fundamental bass [note, tone]) ... *Fundamental chord,* triad (see "Chords," pp. xv–xvi). ... *Fundamental position,* any ar-rangement of chord-notes in which the root remains the lowest.

Funèbre (Fr., fu-nä′br).

Funebre (It., fŏŏ′nâ-brĕh).

Funerale (It., fŏŏ-nĕh-rah′lĕh).

 Funereal, mournful, dirge-like.

Funeral march. A march in slow 4/4 time in a minor key, sometimes used as a part of a larger work. The most famous funeral march is the slow movement from Chopin's piano sonata in *B* flat minor, often played at funerals of important persons.

Funky. A JAZZ style of the 1950's and 1960's which returns to the relative simplicities of BLUES; a reaction against the complexities and sophistication of BEBOP and COOL.

Fuoco, con (It., kŏhn fŏŏ-ô′kŏh).⎤
Fuocoso (It., fŏŏ-ŏh-koh′sŏh). ⎦
    With fire, fiery, spirited.

Furia, con (It., kŏhn foo′rē-äh).
Furibondo (It., foo-rē-bŏhn′dŏh).
Furiosamente (It., foo-rē-ŏh-säh-men′tĕh).
Furioso (It., foo-rē-oh′sŏh).
    Furiously, wildly.

Furiant, Furie. A rapid Bohemian dance, with alternating rhythms and changing accentuation.

Furlana (It., foor-lah′näh). See FORLANA.

Furniture stop. A mixture stop.

Furore (It., foo-roh′rĕh). Fury, passion; also a rage, mania (for anything) . . . *Con furore,* passionately.

Futurism. A literary and musical modern movement which originated in Italy early in the 20th century. It declared a rebellion against traditional art of all kinds, and preached the use of noises in musical composition.

G

G. The fifth tone and degree in the typical diatonic scale of *C* major . . . G. stands for *gauche* in *m. g.* (*main gauche,* left hand); G. O. (or simply G), for *Grand-orgue* (Great organ).

Gagliarda (It., gähl-yar′däh). ⎤
Gagliarde (Ger., gähl-yar′dĕ). ⎦
    A galliard.

Gai (Fr., gä). Gay, lively, brisk.

Gaiamente (It., găh-yah-men'tĕh).
Gaiement (Fr., gä-măhn').
Gaily, briskly.

Gaillarde (Fr., găh-yard'). A galliard.

Gala, di (It., dē găh'lăh). Gaily, merrily.

Galant (Fr., gah-lan'). Gallant; *Style galant* was the description of the light style of composition popular in France in late 18th century.

Galanter stil (Ger., găh-lant'er shtēl). The German term for the French *Style galant,* characteristic of harpsichord music in the 18th century.

Galanterien (Ger., găh-lan-ter-ē'ehn). The movements in the Classical suite that are placed before the last movement, principally the Minuet, Gavotte, Bourrée, Polonaise, and Air.

Galliard. An old French dance for 2 dancers, gay and spirited, but not rapid, and in 3/4 time.

Galop (Fr., găh-lŏh').
Galopp (Ger., găh-lŏhp').
A lively round dance in 2/4 time.

Gamba (It., gahm'băh). 1. A viola da gamba.—2. An organ stop similar in tone.

Gamelan. A typical instrumental orchestra of Indonesia, which includes woodwind instruments, some indigenous string, and a number of percussion instruments.

Gamme (Fr., găhm). A scale.

Gamut. 1. The scale.—2. The staff.

Ganz (Ger., găhnts). 1. Whole; *ganze Note,* whole note.—2. Very; *ganz langsam,* very slowly.

Garbamente (It., gar-băh-men'tĕh).
Garbato (gar-bah'tŏh).
Garbo, con (kŏhn gar'bŏh).

Gracefully, elegantly; in a refined style.

Gathering note. In chanting, a hold on the last syllable of the recitation.

Gato. One of the most popular country dances of Argentina, in 6/8 and 3/4 time.

Gauche (Fr., gohsh). Left.

Gaudioso (It., găh-ŏŏ-dē-oh′sŏh). Joyous, jubilant.

Gavotta (It., găh-vôht′tăh). ⎫
Gavotte (Fr., găh-vŏht). ⎭
A Gavot; an old French dance in strongly marked duple time (*alla breve*), beginning on the upbeat.

G clef. See "The Clefs," p. ix.

G dur (Ger., ḡa door). *G* major.

Gebrauchsmusik (Ger., gĕ-browhs′moo-zĭk). "Utility music," music for amateur or home use.

Gebunden (Ger., gĕ-bŏŏn′den). Tied; *legato.*

Gedackt (Ger., gĕ-dăhkt′). Stopped (of organ pipes).

Gedämpft (Ger., gĕ-dempft′). Damped; muffled; muted.

Gedehnt (Ger., gĕ-dānt′). Sustained, prolonged; slow, stately; *largamente; steso.*

Gefallen, nach (Ger., năh gĕ-făhl′len). Ad libitum.

Gefällig (Ger., gĕ-fel′lĭyh). Pleasing, graceful.

Gefühl, mit (Ger., mit gĕ-fül′). ⎫
Gefühlvoll (Ger., gĕ-fül′fŏhl). ⎭
With feeling, expressively.

Gehalten (Ger., gĕ-hăhl′ten). Held, sustained.

Gehaucht (Ger., gĕ-howht′). "Sighed"; very softly and lightly sung or played.

Geheimnisvoll (Ger., gĕ-hīm′nĭs-fŏhl). Mysterious.

Gehend (Ger., ḡa′ent). Andante.

Geige (Ger., gī′gĕ). Violin . . . *Geigenprinzipal,* violin-diapason (stop).

Geist (Ger., gīst). Spirit, soul; essence.

Gelassen (Ger., gĕ-lähs′sĕn). Calm, placid, easy.

Geläufig (Ger., gĕ-lähü′fīyh). Fluent, easy . . . *Geläufigkeit* (gĕ-lähü′fīyh-kīt), fluency, velocity.

Gemächlich (Ger., gĕ-mĕyh′lĭyh). Easy, comfortable; *comodo.*

Gemässigt (Ger., gĕ-mä′sĭyht). Moderate (in tempo).

Gemendo (It., jä-men′dŏh). Moaning.

Gemessen (Ger., gĕ-mes′sen). Measured(ly), moderate(ly); *moderato.*

Gemischte Stimmen (Ger., gĕ-mĭsh′te shtĭ′mmen). Mixed voices.

Gemshorn (Ger., gems′horn). A flute stop of 8′, 4′, or 2′ pitch on the manuals, and 16′ on the pedals, with mellow, horn-like tone.

Gemüt(h), mit (Ger., mit ge-müt′). With feeling; soulfully.

Gemüt(h)lich (Ger., gĕ-müt′lĭyh). Easily and cheerily; *disin-volto; comodo* (of tempo).

Generalbass (Ger., gĕh-nĕh-rahl′băhs). Basso continuo.

Generalpause (Ger., gĕh-nĕh-rahl′pow′-zŭ). A rest for an entire orchestra.

Generator. 1. A root, or fundamental tone.—2. A tone which produces a series of harmonics.

Generoso (It., jĕh-nĕh-roh′sŏh). Free, ample.

Gentile (It., jen-tē′lĕh).

Gentilezza, con (köhn jĕn-tē-let′säh).

Gentilmente (It., jen-tēl-men′tĕh).

In a graceful, refined style.

German flute. The cross flute.

German sixth. A chord of the augmented sixth between the bottom and the top notes. Other intervals from the bottom are a major third and a perfect fifth, as in *A* flat, *C, E* flat, *F* sharp. See Augmented sixth.

Ges (Ger., gess). *G* flat.

Gesang (Ger., gĕ-zăhng^{k′}). Singing, song; a song; melody; voice (vocal part).

Gesangreich (Ger., gĕ-zăhng^{k′}rīyh). Very singingly; *cantabile*.

Geschleift (Ger., gĕ-shlīft′). Slurred; *legato*.

Geschmackvoll (Ger., gĕ-shmăhk′fõhl). Tastefully.

Geschwindt (Ger., gĕ-shvint′). Swift(ly), rapid(ly).

Ges dur (Ger., gĕs door). *G* flat major.

Geses (Ger., gess′ess). *G* double flat.

Gesteigert (Ger., gĕ-shtī′gert). Intensified; *rinforzato*.

Gestopft (Ger., gĕ-shtŏ′pft). Stopped. The modification of the tone of a horn caused by inserting the hand into the bell of the instrument; it raises the tone a half step.

Gestossen (Ger., gĕ-shtŏh′sen). 1. Staccato.—2. Détaché.

Geteilt (Ger., gĕ-tīl′t). Divided.

Getragen (Ger., gĕ-trah′gen). Sustained, *sostenuto*.

Gezogen (Ger., gĕ-tsoh′gen). Drawn out; *largamente, sostenuto, steso*.

Ghiribizzoso (It., gē-rē-bid-zoh′sŏh). Whimsical.

Giga (It., jē′găh). ⎫
Gigue (Fr., zhig). ⎭
   A Jig.

Giochevole (It., jŏh-kā′vŏh-lĕh). ⎫
Gioco, con (It., kŏhn jô′kŏh). ⎭
   Playfully, sportively, merrily.

Giocondo,-a (It., jŏh-kŏhn′dŏh). ⎫
Giocondamente (It., jŏh-kŏhn-dăh-men′tĕh). ⎭
   In a jucond, joyous style.

Giocosamente (It., jŏh-kŏh-săh-men′tĕh). ⎫
Giocoso,-a (It., jŏh-koh′sŏh). ⎭
   Playfully, sportively, merrily.

Gioia, con (It., kŏhn jô′yäh).

Gioiante (It., jŏh-yähn′tĕh).

Gioiosamente (It., jŏh-yŏh-säh-men′tĕh).

Gioioso (It., jŏh-yŏh-′sŏh).
    Joyfully, joyously, gaily, merrily.

Gioja, etc. See GIOIA.

Gioviale (It., jŏh-vē-ah′lĕh). Jovial, cheerful.

Giovialità, con (It., kŏhn jŏh-vē-äh-lē-tah′). Jovially, cheerfully.

Gis (Ger., giss). *G* sharp.

Gisis (Ger., gĭss′ĭs). *G* double sharp.

Gis moll (Ger., mohl). *G* sharp minor.

Giubilante (It., joo-bē-lähn′tĕh). Jubilant.

Giubilazione (It., joo-bē-läh-tsē-oh′nĕh).

Giubilio (It., joo-bē-lē′ŏh).

Giubilo (It., joo′bē-lŏh).
    Joy, rejoicing, jubilation.

Giuoco, etc. See GIOCO.

Giustamente (It., jŏŏ-stäh-men′tĕh).

Giustezza, con (It., kŏhn jŏŏ-stet′säh).
    Exactly, with precision.

Giusto (It., jŏŏ′stŏh). Strict, appropriate, proper (*tempo giusto*), exact, correct.—*Allegro giusto,* moderately fast.

Glass harmonica. A set of glasses of different sizes which are rubbed on the rim with wet fingers producing a gentle ethereal sound. It was so popular in the 18th century that Mozart wrote a piece for it. Developed by Benjamin Franklin.

Glee. A secular composition for 3 or more unaccompanied solo voices, peculiar to England. Serious "glees" are written as well as merry ones.

Gli (It., l′yē). The (masculine plural).

Glissando (It., glis-sähn′dŏh). 1. On bow instruments, (*a*) demands a flowing, unaccented execution of a passage; (*b*) same as PORTAMENTO.—2. On the piano, a rapid scale effect obtained by sliding the thumb, or thumb and one finger, over the keys. Also *Glissato, Glissicando, Glissicato.*

Glocke (Ger., glŏh'kĕ). A bell.

Glockenspiel (Ger., glŏh'ken-shpēl'). 1. See CARILLON 1.—2. A set of bells or steel bars, tuned diatonically and struck with a small hammer.—3. An organ stop having bells instead of pipes.

Glottis. The aperture between the vocal cords when they are drawn together in singing.

G moll (Ger., gä mohl). *G* minor.

Gondellied (Ger., gŏhn'del-lēt').
Gondoliera (It., gŏhn-dŏh-lē-â'räh).
A BARCAROLE.

Gong. A suspended circular metal plate, struck with a mallet and producing a sustained reverberation.

Goose. A harsh break in the tone of the clarinet, oboe, or bassoon.

Gopak. A Ukrainian folk dance in rapid 2/4 time. Same as HOPAK.

Gospel song. A Protestant church hymn.

G. P. Abbreviation for GENERALPAUSE.

Grace. A vocal or instrumental ornament or embellishment not essential to the melody or harmony of a composition.

Grace note. A note of embellishment, usually written small.

Gracile (It., grah'tsē-lĕh). Graceful, delicate.

Gradatamente (It., grä-däh-täh-men'tĕh). By degrees, gradually.

Gradevole (It., grä-dā'vŏh-lĕh).
Gradevolmente (It., grä-dā-vŏhl-men'tĕh).
Pleasingly, agreeably.

Gradual. 1. An antiphon following the epistle.—2. A book of

chants containing the graduals, introits, and other antiphons of the Roman Catholic Mass.

Gramophone. A trademark commonly used in England for
the phonograph.

Gran (It., grähn).   ⎫
Grand' (It., grähnd).   ⎬
Grande (It., grähn′děh).   ⎭
Large, great, full, complete. (*Grande* is the regular form,
used after nouns; it is abbreviated to *grand'* before vowels,
and to *gran* before consonants.)

Gran cassa (It., grahn cah′säh). Bass drum; literally, "big
box."

Grand. Technical term for Grand Pianoforte.

Grand (Fr., grähn). Large, great; full ... *Grand barré,* a stop
of over 3 notes ... *Grand bourdon,* double-bourdon ...
Grand chœur, full organ ... *Grand jeu,* (*a*) full organ; (*b*) an
harmonium stop for full power ... *À grand orchestre,* for
full orchestra ... *Grand-orgue,* (*a*) full organ; (*b*) Great
organ; (*c*) pipe organ.

Grandezza, con (It., kŏhn grähn-det′säh).   ⎫
Grandiosità, con (It., kŏhn grähn-dē-ŏh-sē-tah′).   ⎬
Grandioso (It., grähn-dē-oh′sŏh).   ⎭
With grandeur; majestically, pompously, loftily.

Grandisonante (It., grähn-dē-sŏh-năhn′těh). Loud or long
sounding, sonorous; pompous, affected.

Grand opera. A type of opera, usually in 5 acts, treating a
heroic, mythological, or historical subject, sumptuously
costumed, and produced in a large opera house.

Granulato (It., grăh-nŏŏ-lah′tŏh). Non legato.

Grave (It., grah′věh). 1. Grave or low in pitch.—2. Heavy,
slow, ponderous in movement.—3. Serious.

Gravemente (It., grăh-věh-men′těh).   ⎫
Gravità, con (kŏhn grăh-vē-tah′).   ⎬
Slowly, ponderously; seriously, gravely.

Gravicembalo (It., gräh-vē-chĕm-bahl'oh). Harpsichord.

Grazia, con (It., kŏhn grah'tsē-äh).

Graziosamente (It., grä-tsē-oh-säh-men'tĕh).

Grazioso,-a (It., grä-tsē-oh'sŏh, -säh).
 Gracefully, elegantly.

Great octave. Common name for the octave beginning on *C*, two leger lines below the staff of the bass clef. See "Table of Clefs," p. xi.

Great organ. The chief manual of an organ, and the pipes controlled by it.

Gregorian chant. Plainchant, as revised and established by Pope Gregory I (d. 604).

Grido (It., grē'dŏh). Cry, shout.

Grob-gedacht (Ger., grŏb-ge-da'ht). Large diapason organ stop.

Gross-gedacht (Ger., grōs-ge-da'ht). 16′ double diapason organ stop.

Grosso (It., grô'sŏh). Great, grand; full, heavy.

Grottesco (It., grŏht-tĕh'skŏh). Grotesque, comic.

Ground bass. A continually repeated bass phrase of 4 or 8 measures; a *basso ostinato*.

Group. 1. A short series of rapid notes, especially when sung to one syllable.—2. A section of the orchestra (or score) embracing instruments of one class: *e.g.,* the strings.

Gruppetto (It., grŏŏp-pet'tŏh). Formerly, a trill; now, a turn; also, any "group" of grace notes.

Gruppo (It., grŏŏp'pŏh). Same as GRUPPETTO.

G string. The lowest string on the violin. On the viola and cello it is the second string above the lowest string; on the double bass it is the highest string.

Guaracha (Sp., gwäh-rah'chäh). Lively Spanish dance, part in 3/4 or 3/8, part in 2/4 time.

Guerriero (It., gwĕr-rē-â'rŏh). Martial, war-like.

Guide. A Direct; also, a subject or antecedent.

Guitar. An instrument of the lute family. The modern Spanish guitar has 6 strings, and a compass of 3 octaves and a Fourth, from E to a^2. The music is written an octave higher than it sounds, in the G clef.

Gusli. An ancient Russian zither-type instrument.

Gusto (It., gŏō'stŏh). Taste.

Gut (Ger., goot). Good.

Gymel. A type of "twin" singing (gymel comes from the Latin word *gemellus,* "a twin") common during the Middle Ages, harmonized in thirds.

H

H. In scores, H stands for *Horn;* in organ music, for *Heel;* in music for piano (organ), for *Hand* (*r.h., l.h.*).

H (Ger., hah). The note *B.*

Habanera (Sp., hăh-băh-nâ'răh). A Cuban dance, in duple meter, characterized by dotted or syncopated rhythms.

Halb (Ger., hăhlp). Half.

Half note. A note one-half the value of a whole note and represented by a white circle with a stem. (♩)

Half step. A semitone.

Hallelujah (Hebr.). "Praise ye the Lord!"

Halling. A national Norwegian dance in 2/4 time.

Hammerclavier (Ger., hăhm'mer-klăh-vēr'). Old name for the Pianoforte.

Hanacca. A Moravian dance in 3/4 time, like the Polonaise, but quicker.

Handle piano. A mechanical pianoforte on the principle of the barrel organ.

Hand organ. A portable barrel organ.

Harfe (Ger., har'fĕ). Harp.

Harmonic. 1. (*adjective*). Pertaining to chords (either consonant or dissonant), and to the theory and practice of harmony ... *Harmonic curve,* the curved figure described by a vibrating string ... *H. figuration,* broken chords ... *H. flute,* see H. STOP ... *H. mark,* in music for violin, etc., a sign (°) over a note, calling for an harmonic tone ... *H. note,* see H. TONE ... *H. reed,* see H. STOP ... *H. scale,* (*a*) the succession of harmonic tones; (*b*) minor scale with minor Sixth and major Seventh ... *H. stop,* an organ stop having pipes double the ordinary length, and pierced midway, so that a 16′ pipe yields an 8′ tone ... *H. tone,* or *Flageolet-tone,* see HARMONIC 2 (*b*).

Harmonic. 2. (*noun*). (*a*) One of the series of tones (the so-called *partial tones*) which usually accompany, more or less faintly, the prime tone (*generator*) produced by a string, an organ pipe, the human voice, etc. The *prime tone* (*fundamental,* or *generator*) is the strong tone produced by the vibration of the whole string, or the entire column of air in the pipe; the *partial* tones are produced by the vibration of fractional parts of that string or air column. (*b*) These same harmonics (harmonic tones) are obtained, on any stringed instrument which is stopped (violin, zither), by lightly touching a nodal point of a string.

Harmonica. Also called mouth harmonica or mouth organ. A set of graduated metal reeds mounted in a narrow frame, blown by the mouth, and producing different tones on expiration and inspiration.

Harmonic mark. The sign ° set over notes to be touched (not stopped).

Harmonicon. 1. A mouth harmonica.—2. An orchestrion.—3. A keyed harmonica combined with a flue stop or stops.

Harmonie. French term for wind instruments.

Harmonic series. A natural series of overtones, sounding an octave above the fundamental tone, then a fifth higher than that, a fourth higher, a major third higher, a minor third higher, etc. The first 6 members of the natural harmonic series form the harmony of the major triad, fundamental to all acoustical phenomena.

Harmonisch (Ger., har-moh′nish). Harmonic (*adj.*); harmonious.

Harmonium. A popular portable organ, activated by 2 pedals with both feet operating one after another to pump the air. It used to be very popular at home and in small churches as a substitute for the organ.

Harmony. 1. A musical combination of tones or chords.—2. A chord, either consonant or dissonant.—3. The harmonic texture of a piece; as 2-part, 3-part harmony ... *Chromatic harmony* has chromatic tones and modulations ... *Close harmony* (in 4-part writing) has the 3 highest parts within the compass of an octave ... *Compound harmony* has 2 or more essential chord-tones doubled ... *Dispersed, Extended harmony,* see OPEN HARMONY ... *Essential harmony,* (*a*) the fundamental triads of a key; (*b*) the harmonic frame of a composition minus all figuration and ornaments ... *False harmony,* (*a*) the inharmonic relation; (*b*) discord produced by imperfect preparation or resolution; (*c*) discord produced by wrong notes or chords ... *Figured harmony* varies the simple chords by figuration of all kinds ... *Open harmony* (in 4-part writing) spreads the 3 highest parts beyond the compass of an octave ... *Pure harmony,* music performed with pure (not tempered) intonation, as by a string quartet, or unaccompanied chorus ... *Spread harmony,* open harmony ... *Strict harmony,* composition according to strict rules for the preparation and resolution of dissonances ... *Tempered harmony,* music performed with tempered intonation, as on the organ or piano.

Harp. A stringed instrument of ancient origin. The modern orchestral harp (Erard's double-action harp) has a nearly 3-cornered wooden *frame,* the *foot* of which is formed by an upright *pillar* meeting the hollow *back* (the upper side of which bears the *soundboard*) in the *pedestal*; the upper ends of pillar and back are united by the curving *neck*. The gut strings are 46 (or 47) in number. Compass, $6\frac{1}{2}$ octaves, from $C_1\flat$ to $f^4\flat$ (or $g^4\flat$).

Harpsichord. A keyboard stringed instrument in which the strings are twanged by quills or bits of hard leather. See Pianoforte.

Haupt (Ger., howpt). Head; chief, principal . . . *Hauptmanual,* Great-organ manual . . . *Haupt-prinzipal,* 8′ diapason (on manual), 16′ (on pedal) . . . *Hauptsatz,* principal movement or theme.

Hautbois (Fr., ŏh-bwăh′). Oboe or hautboy.

Hautboy (Engl., hoh′boy). Oboe.

Havanaise (Fr., ăh-văh-năz′). A Habanera.

H dur (Ger., hah door). *B* major.

Head. 1. Point (of bow).—2. In the violin, etc., the part comprising peg-box and scroll.—3. In the drum, the membrane stretched over one or both ends.—4. In a note, the oval (or square) part which determines its place on the staff.

Head tones, Head voice. The vocal tones of the head register.

Heckelphone. A baritone oboe with a range an octave below the oboe; invented by Heckel. It is used in some modern scores.

Heftig (Ger., hef′tĭyh). Vehement, impetuous, passionate.

Heftigkeit, mit (Ger., mit hef′tĭyh-kīt). Vehemently, etc.

Heimlich (Ger., hīm′lĭyh). Secret, mysterious; *misterioso*; furtive, stealthy.

Heiter (Ger., hī′ter). Serene; cheerful, glad; *gioioso*.

Heldentenor. In German, "heroic tenor," requiring a robust voice for difficult operatic parts, particularly in Wagner's music dramas.

Helicon. A brass wind instrument, used chiefly in military music as a bass; its tube is bent in a circle, and it is carried over the shoulder.

Hell (Ger., hel). Clear, bright.

Helper. An octave-pipe (organ) set beside and sounding with another of 8′ pitch, for the sake of brilliancy.

Hemidemisemiquaver. A sixty-fourth note ... *H.-rest,* a sixty-fourth rest.

Hemiola. In mensural notation of the Middle Ages, the use of 3 notes of equal duration in a bar alternating with 2 notes of equal value, in the same bar length, so that the longer notes equal 1½ shorter ones (the word comes from the Greek, meaning "one-and-a-half"). In modern notation the hemiola is represented by a succession of bars in 6/8 and 3/4.

Hervorgehoben (Ger., hâr-fŏhr′gĕ-hō′ben). Emphasized.

Hervortretend (Ger., hâr-fŏhr′trā-tent). A term indicating that the voice or part to which it is applied is to be brought to the fore, in contrast to the other parts which are accompanying.

Herzig (Ger., hâr′tsīyh). Hearty, heartily; tenderly.

Hexachord. The 6 tones *ut re mi fa sol la* in Solmisation.

Hidden fifths, octaves. Progressions of intervals leading towards an open fifth, or an octave, from the same direction, forbidden in strict harmony.

Hillbilly music. A description used for American country music, particularly that cultivated by the rustic inhabitants of the hill country of Kentucky.

His (Ger., hiss). *B* sharp.

H moll (Ger., hĭss mohl). *B* minor.

Hochzeitlied (Ger., hōh′-tsīt-lēt). Wedding song.

Hocket. A curious contrapuntal device much in vogue in the Middle Ages, in which one voice stops and another voice comes in, sometimes in the middle of a word, creating the effect of hiccuping (*hocket* is an old word for *hiccup*).

Hohlflöte (Ger., hohl′flö′tĕ). In the organ, an open flue stop whose dark, mellow tone is rather hollow (whence its name); usually of 8′ or 4′ pitch ... The *Hohlquinte* is a mutation stop in the fifth.

Hold. [In England, usually called *Pause.*] The sign ⌒ over, or ⌣ under, a note or rest, indicating the prolongation of its time value at the performer's discretion.—Placed over a bar, the hold indicates a slight pause or breathing-spell before attacking what follows. See FERMATA.

Holding note. A note sustained in one part while the other parts are in motion.

Homophonic. Alike in sound or pitch.—In modern music, a style in which one melody or part, supported to a greater or less extent by chords or chordal combinations (that is, an *accompanied melody*), predominates, is called homophonic; opposed to *polyphonic.*

Homophony. Homophonic music; the homophonic style; opposed to *antiphony* and *polyphony.*

Hook. A stroke attached to the stems of eighth notes, sixteenth notes, etc.

Hopak. Ukrainian pronunciation of GOPAK.

Hoquet (Fr., oh-keh′). Hocket.

Horn. The orchestral horn is a brass wind instrument, having a conical tube variously bent upon itself (the smallest horn generally used, in high $B\flat$, has a tube nearly 9 feet long; that an octave lower, nearly 18 feet); wide and flaring bell; the tone rich, mellow, and sonorous. The old *natural* or *French horn* yields only the natural tones supplemented by stopped tones and crooks, giving a total possible compass of $3\frac{1}{2}$ octaves, from $B_1\flat$ to *f.*—The modern *Valve-horn*, played like a cornet, is much easier to handle.—The horn is a transposing instrument. Also called *French Horn.*

Horn band. A band of trumpeters.—*Russian horn band,* a band of performers on hunting horns, each of which produces but one tone.

Hörner (Ger., hör′ner). Horns (*corni*).

Hornpipe. An old English dance in lively tempo, the earlier ones in 3/2 time, the later in 4/4 time.

Holz-flöte (Ger., hŏlts′-flöte). "Wood flute," an organ stop.

Humoresque. A light, whimsical instrumental piece, often for piano.

Hurdy-gurdy. A stringed instrument having 2 melody-strings, and from 2 to 4 drones. The melody-strings are "stopped" by keys touched by the left hand; the right hand turns a crank which revolves a rosined wheel, the latter scraping the strings and producing the rough musical tones.

Hurtig (Ger., hŏŏr′tĭyh). Swift, headlong.

Hydraulic organ. A small kind of organ invented by Ktesibios of Alexandria (180 B.C.), in which the wind pressure was regulated by water.

Hymn. A religious or sacred song; usually, a metrical poem to be sung by a congregation.—In foreign usage, a national song of lofty character, like the *Marseillaise*.

Hypo-. In the system of church modes, the prefix *hypo-* indicates the starting point of a mode a fourth below its tonic; therefore, if the Dorian mode begins on *D,* then the Hypodorian mode will begin on *A,* a fourth below. A similar relationship exists for other modes.

I

I (It., ē; *masculine plural*). The.

Iambus. A metrical foot of 2 syllables, one short and one long, with the accent on the long: ◡–.

Ictus. A separation mark in Gregorian chant before and after an important note in the melody; in poetic usage, *ictus* means a "stress."

Idée fixe. In French, "fixed idea"; a term used by Berlioz in his *Fantastic Symphony* for the recurrent theme in the work.

Idyl. A composition of a pastoral or tenderly romantic character, without set form.

Idillio (It., ē-dil′lē-ŏh).
Idylle (Fr., ē-dil′).
Idylle (Ger., ē-dil′lĕ).
An Idyl.

Il (It., ēl; *masculine singular*). The ... *Il più,* the most.

Im (Ger., im). In the ... *Im Tempo,* in the regular tempo; *a tempo.*

Imbroglio (It., em-broh′lyo). Literally, "confusion"; a term used to describe scenes in opera where several groups of singers or instrumental ensembles perform together, but each serving a different purpose dramatically.

Imitando (It., ē-mē-tăhn′dŏh). Imitating.

Imitation. The repetition of a motive, phrase, or theme proposed by one part (the antecedent) in another part (the consequent), with or without modification ... *Canonic imitation,* strict imitation ... *Free imitation,* that in which changes of the antecedent are permitted in the consequent ... *Strict imitation,* that in which the consequent answers the antecedent note for note and interval for interval.

Immer (Ger., im′mer). Always; continuously ... *Immer stärker werdend,* continually growing louder; *immer langsamer,* slower and slower; *immer langsam,* slowly throughout.

Impaziente (It., im-păh-tsē-en′tĕh).
Impazientemente (It., —tĕh-men′tĕh).
Impatient, impatiently.

Imperfect cadence, consonance, interval, stop. See the nouns.

Imperioso (It., im-pĕh-rē-ŏh′sŏh). Imperious, haughty, lofty.

Impeto, con (It., kŏhn im′pĕh-tŏh).

Impetuosamente (It., im-pĕh-tŏŏ-ŏh-säh-men′tĕh).

Impetuosità, con (It., kŏhn im-pĕh-tŏŏ-oh-sē-tah′).

Impetuoso (It., im-pĕh-tŏŏ-oh′sŏh).
Impetuously, impetuous, vehemently.

Imponente (It., im-pŏh-nen′tĕh). Imposing, impressive.

Impresario (It., im-prĕh-sah′rē-ōh). The agent or manager of an opera or concert company.

Impressionism. A term used to describe modern French composition of the early 20th century, in which subtle impressions rather than programmatic descriptions are conveyed through the use of ethereal harmonies in free modulation and colorful instrumentation.

Impromptu. 1. An improvisation.—2. A composition of loose and extemporaneous form and slight development; a Fantasia.

Improvisation. Offhand musical performance; extemporizing.

In alt, altissimo. See ALT; ALTISSIMO.

Incalzando (It., in-kähl-tsähn′dŏh). "Pursuing hotly"; growing more vehement ... *Incalzando e stringendo,* growing more vehement and rapid.

Incarnatus, Et. See MASS.

Incidental music. Music supplementary to a spoken drama; such as an overture, interludes, songs, etc.

Inciso (It., in-chē′sŏh). Incisive; sharply marked ... *Incise,* "mark the notes sharply."

Incomplete stop. A half stop.

Indeciso (It., in-dĕh-chē′sŏh). Irresolute, undecided.

Independent chord, harmony, triad. One which is consonant (contains no dissonance), and is, therefore, not obliged to change to another chord by progression or resolution.

Indifferente (It., in-dif-fĕh-ren'tĕh). ⎫
Indifferentemente (It., —tĕh-men'tĕh). ⎬
Indifferenza, con (It., kŏhn in-dif-fĕh-ren'tsăh). ⎭
  Indifferently, carelessly.

Indirect resolution. See Resolution.

Infernale (It., in-fâr-nah'lĕh). Infernal.

Infinite canon. One without a closing cadence, that may be repeated at pleasure.

Infino (It., in-fē'nŏh). Up to, as far as, till you reach.

Ingenuamente (It., in-jĕh-nŏŏ-ăh-men'tĕh). Naturally, ingenuously.

Inharmonic relation. See False relation.

Iniziale (It., ē-nē-tsē-ah'lĕh). Initial; the first.

Inner parts. Parts in harmony lying between the highest and lowest.

Inner pedal. A pedal point on an inner part.

Innig (Ger., in'nĭyh). Heartfelt, sincere, fervent, intense; *intimo, con affetto*.

Innigkeit, mit (Ger., mit in'nĭyh-kīt). ⎫
Inniglich (Ger., in'nĭyh-lĭyh). ⎬
  With deep emotion, fervently.

Innocente (It., in-nŏh-chen'tĕh). Innocent, unaffected.

Innocentemente (It., in-nŏh-chen-tĕh-men'tĕh). ⎫
Innocenza, con (It., kŏhn in-nŏh-chen'tsăh). ⎬
  Innocently, artlessly.

Inquieto (It., in-kwē-ēh'tŏh). Unrestful, uneasy.

Insensibile (It., in-sen-sē'bē-lĕh). Imperceptible.

Insensibilmente (It., in-sen-sē-bēl-men'tĕh). Insensibly.

Insistendo (It., in-sē-sten'dŏh). ⎫
Insistenza, con (It., kŏhn in-sē-sten'tsăh). ⎬
  Urgently.

Inständig (Ger., in'shten'dih). }
Instante (It., in-stähn'těh). }
　Urgent, pressing.

Instantemente (It., in-stähn-těh-men'těh). Urgently.

Instrumentation. The theory and practice of composing, arranging, or adapting music for a body of instruments of different kinds, especially for orchestra.

Intenzionato (It., in-ten-tsē-ŏh-nah'tŏh). }
Intenzione, con (It., kŏhn in-ten-tsē-oh'neh). }
　With stess, emphasis.

Interlude. 1. An intermezzo.—2. An instrumental strain or passage connecting the lines or stanzas of a hymn, etc.—3. An instrumental piece played between certain portions of the church service (*Interludium*).

Intermezzo (—med'zŏh). 1. A light musical entertainment alternating with the acts of the early Italian tragedies.—2. Incidental music in modern dramas.—3. A short movement connecting the main divisions of a symphony.—4. Many instrumental compositions take the name Intermezzo for want of a better, not being "characteristic" pieces.

Interruzione, senza (It., sen'tsäh in-těr-rŏŏ-tsē-oh'něh). Without interruption.

Interval. The difference in pitch between two tones. Intervals are regularly measured from the lower tone to the higher. *An interval is:*—*Augmented,* when wider by a chromatic semitone than major or perfect . . . *Chromatic,* when augmented or diminished (except augm. fourth, and dim. fifth and seventh) . . . *Compound,* when wider than an octave . . . *Consonant,* when not requiring resolution . . . *Diatonic,* when occurring between 2 tones belonging to the same key (except the augmented second and fifth of the harmonic minor scale) . . . *Diminished,* when a chromatic semitone narrower than major or perfect . . . *Dissonant,*

when requiring resolution . . . *Enharmonic,* see ENHAR-
MONIC TONES . . . *Extended,* or *Extreme,* when augmented
. . . *Flat,* when diminished . . . *Harmonic,* when both tones
are sounded together . . . *Imperfect,* when diminished . . .
Inverted, when the higher tone is lowered, or the lower
tone raised, by an octave . . . *Major,* when equal to the
standard second, third, sixth, and seventh of the major
scale . . . *Melodic,* when the two tones are sounded in succession . . . *Minor,* when a chromatic semitone narrower
than major or perfect . . . *Parallel* (with an interval preceding), when its two tones progress in the same direction and
at the same interval . . . *Perfect* (or *Perfect major*), when
equal to the standard prime, fourth, fifth, and octave of
the major scale . . . *Redundant,* when augmented . . . *Simple,* when not wider than an octave . . . *Standard,* when
measured upward from the keynote . . . *Superfluous,* when
augmented.

Intimissimo (It., in-tē-mis′sē-mŏh). Very tenderly, warmly.

Intimo (It., in′tē-mŏh). Heartfelt, fervent.

Intonation. 1. The production of tone, either vocal or instrumental.—2. The method of chanting employed in Plainchant.—3. The opening notes leading up to the reciting
tone of a chant . . . *Fixed intonation,* see FIXED-TONE IN-
STRUMENT.

Intoning. The chanting by the minister, in monotone, of
parts of the Anglican church service.

Intrada (It., in-trăh′dăh). A short introduction or prelude.

Intrepidamente (It., in-trâ-pē-dăh-men′tĕh).⎫
Intrepidezza, con (It., kŏhn in-trâ-pē-det′săh). ⎭
Boldly, daringly, dashingly.

Intrepido,-a (It., in-trâ′pē-dŏh, -dăh). Intrepid, bold.

Introduction. A phrase or division preliminary to and pre-
paratory of a composition or movement.

Introit (L., ĭn-trō′ĭt, "entrance"). An antiphon sung while

the priest is approaching the altar to celebrate the
Mass.—In the modern Anglican Church, an anthem or
psalm, sung as the minister approaches the Communion
table.

Invention. A short piece in free contrapuntal style, develop-
ing one motive in an impromptu fashion.

Inversion. The transposition of the notes of an interval or
chord. (*a*) In a simple interval the higher note is set an
octave lower, or the lower note an octave higher. (*b*) A
chord is *inverted* when its lowest note is not the root. See
"Chords," p. xvi. (*c*) In double counterpoint, the transposition of 2 parts, the higher being set below the lower, or
vice versa; this inversion may be by an octave or some
other interval, and is called "inversion in the octave," "in
the tenth," "in the fifth," etc. (*d*) An organ point is *inverted*
when in some other part than the lowest. (*e*) A melody is
inverted when ascending intervals are made to descend by
the same degree, and vice versa. The melody is therefore
turned upside down.

Invertible counterpoint. A type of polyphonic writing in
which contrapuntal parts could be inverted and placed in
different voices without forming forbidden discords. Also
called DOUBLE COUNTERPOINT.

Ionian mode. An ecclesiastical mode corresponding to a
major scale.

Ira, con (It., kŏhn ē′răh). ⎫
Irato (It., ē-rah′tŏh).   ⎬
    Wrathfully, passionately.

Irlandais,-e (Fr., ēr-lăhn-dä′, däz′). Hibernian, Irish.

Ironia, con (It., kŏhn ē-rŏh-nē′ăh).   ⎫
Ironicamente (It., ē-rŏh-nē-kăh-men′tĕh). ⎬
    Ironically.

Ironico (It., ē-rô′nē-kŏh). Ironical.

Irregular cadence. See CADENCE.

Irresoluto (It., ir-rĕh-sŏh-loo'tŏh). Irresolute, undecided, vacillating.

Islancio, con (It., kŏhn ē-zlăhn'chŏh). Vehemently, impetuously, with dash.

Isorhythm. In the 14th and 15th centuries, a technique using a repeated pitch pattern (COLOR) and a rcpcatcd rhythmic pattern (TALEA). The color and talea do not necessarily coincide, so that the repeated pitches are presented in different rhythms and phrases.

Istesso (It., ē-stes'sŏh). Same . . . *L'istesso tempo,* "the same tempo" (or "time"); signifies (*a*) that the tempo of either the measure or measure note remains the same after a change of time signature; or (*b*) that a movement previously interrupted is to be resumed.

Italian overture. An overture current in the 17th and 18th centuries consisting of 3 sections—quick, slow, and quick—in contradistinction to the French overture in which the sections are slow, quick, and slow.

Italian sixth. A chord of three notes, containing the augmented sixth from bottom to top and a major third from bottom to the middle note, as in *A* flat, *C,* and *F* sharp. See AUGMENTED SIXTH.

Ite, missa est. "Go, ye are dismissed." The final words of the Mass.

J

Jack. 1. In the harpsichord and clavichord, an upright slip of wood on the rear end of the key lever, carrying (in the former) a bit of crow-quill or hard leather set at a right angle so as to pluck or twang the string, or (in the latter) a metallic tangent.—2. In the pianoforte, the escapement lever, or hopper.

Jagdhorn (Ger., yăht'horn). Hunting horn.

Jagdstück (Ger., yăh'shtük). Hunting piece.

Jägerchor (Ger., yă′ger-kohr′). Hunters' chorus.

Jaleo (Sp., hăh-lä′ŏh). A Spanish dance for one performer, in 3/8 time and moderate tempo.

Jam session. A free improvisation by a jazz group.

Janizary music. Shrill and noisy military music, with drums, cymbals, etc., predominating.

Jankò keyboard. A piano keyboard invented by Paul von Jankò of Totis, Hungary, in 1882. It has 6 rows of keys so arranged that any given tone can be struck in 3 different places, that is, on every other row.

Jarábe (Sp., hăh-răh′bĕ). Type of Mexican dance of Spanish origin.

Jazz. A term covering a variety of styles of black American origin: RAGTIME, BLUES, DIXIELAND, SWING, BEBOP, COOL, THIRD STREAM, FREE JAZZ, FUNKY, JAZZ-ROCK, and other styles less amenable to specific categorization. Most are characterized by improvisation and a "swinging beat" composed of a steady, prominent meter and dotted or syncopated rhythms.

Jazz-rock. A style of the late 1960's–1970's which merges the electric amplification and heavy beat of ROCK with some of the more sophisticated improvisatory features of JAZZ.

Jeu (Fr., zhö). 1. Style of playing.—2. A stop of an organ, etc. ... *Grand jeu,* or *Plein jeu,* full organ, full power ... *Demi-jeu,* half power.

Jew's harp. A small instrument with rigid iron frame, having a thin vibratile metal tongue; the frame is held between the teeth, and the metallic tongue plucked with the finger.

Jig. A kind of country dance, with many modifications of step and gesture, in triple or compound time, and rapid tempo.—In the Suite, the *Gigue* is usually the last movement.

Jingling Johnny. A noise-making exotic instrument, consisting of a stick overhung with jingles and bells. It is also known as a Turkish Crescent or Chinese Pavilion, indicating its supposed outlandish provenance.

Jodel. See Yodel.

Jongleur (Fr., zhon-glör′). A medieval minstrel employed by royalty and aristocracy to provide light entertainment; the word itself corresponds to the English juggler, implying that such a minstrel also performed acrobatic acts.

Jota (Sp., hoh′täh). A national dance of northern Spain, danced by couples, in triple time and rapid movement, something like a waltz.

Just intonation. Singing or playing music precisely true to pitch; opposed to tempered intonation.

K

Kammer (Ger., kähm′mer). "Chamber"; "court"; *Kammermusik,* chamber music; *Kammermusiker,* court musician; *Kammerkantate,* chamber cantata.

Kantate (Ger., kähn-tah′tĕ). Cantata.

Kantele. National Finnish instrument, plucked with fingers like a zither.

Kapelle (Ger., käh-pel′lĕ). 1. A private band or choir.—2. An orchestra.

Kapellmeister (Ger., käh-pel′mīs′ter). 1. Conductor of an orchestra.—2. Choirmaster.

Kavatine (Ger., käh-väh-tĕ′nĕ). Cavatina.

Kazoo. A toy-like instrument consisting of a short tube with membranes at each end, into which the player hums, producing a curiously nasal tone. It is also known as Mirliton; in the 17th century it was called a *flûte-eunuque* ("eunuch flute").

Keck (Ger., kek). Bold, confident; pert.

Keckheit, mit (Ger., mit kek′hīt). Boldly, confidently.

Keraulophon. An 8′ partial flue stop, having metal pipes surmounted by adjustable rings, and with a hole bored near the top of each pipe. Tone soft and "reedy."

Kettledrum. An orchestral drum consisting of a hollow brass or copper hemisphere (the kettle) resting on a tripod, with a head of vellum stretched by means of an iron ring and tightened by a set of screws, or by cords and braces. It is generally played in pairs, the larger drum yielding any tone from F to c, and the smaller from $B\flat$ to f. Music now written at actual pitch.

Key (1). The series of tones forming any given major or minor scale, considered with reference to their harmonic relations, particularly the relation of the other tones to the tonic or keynote … *Attendant keys,* see ATTENDANT … *Chromatic key,* one having sharps or flats in the signature … *Extreme key,* a remote key … *Major key,* one having a major Third and Sixth … *Minor key,* one having a minor Third and Sixth … *Natural key,* one with neither sharps nor flats in the signature … *Parallel key,* (*a*) a minor key with the same keynote as the given major key, or vice versa, (*b*) a *Relative key* (see RELATIVE) … *Remote key,* an indirectly related key.

Key (2). (*a*) A digital or finger lever in the keyboard of a piano or organ.—(*b*) A pedal or foot key in the organ or pedal piano.

Key (3). A flat padded disk attached to a lever worked by the finger or thumb, closing the sound-holes of various wind instruments.

Key (4). A wrest, or tuning key.

Key action. In the keyboard of a piano or organ, the keys and the entire mechanism connected with and set in action by them.

Keyboard. The range of keys on an organ or piano.

Key bugle. See BUGLE.

Key chord. The tonic triad.

Key harp. An instrument formed like a piano, but having tuning forks in lieu of strings. Invented in 1819 by Dietz and Second.

Keynote. The first note of a key or scale.

Key signature. The sharps or flats at the head of the staff.

Key stop. A key attached to the fingerboard of a violin so as to replace the fingers in stopping the strings; the instrument is called a key-stop or keyed-stop violin.

Key trumpet. A trumpet provided with keys.

Kindlich (Ger., kint′lĭyh). Childlike, artless.

Kirchenmusik (Ger., kĭryh′en-moo-zĭk). Church music.

Kit. The small violin used by dancing masters, about 16 inches long, and tuned c^1-g^1-d^2.

Kithara. An ancient Greek instrument of the lyre family, with several strings stretched over the soundbox.

Klagend (Ger., klah′ghent). Mournfully, plaintively.

Klang (Ger., klăng^k). 1. A sound.—2. A composite musical tone (a fundamental tone with its harmonics).—3. A chord, as in *Dreiklang*—triad.

Klangfarbe (Ger., klăng^k′far-bĕ). Tone color.

Klangfarbenmelodie (Ger., klăng^k-fahr-bĕn-mel′oh-dē). A technique of the 20th-century Viennese school in which melodies have wide and dissonant skips and changing tone colors.

Klappe (Ger., klăhp′pĕ). A key (3) ... *Klappenhorn,* key bugle.

Klarinette (Ger., klăh-rē-net′tĕ). Clarinet.

Klavier (Ger., klăh-vēr′). 1. A keyboard.—2. A keyboard stringed instrument; in the 18th century, a clavichord; now, a pianoforte of any kind.

Klavierauszug (Ger., klăh-vēr′ows′tsŏŏh). Piano arrangement.

Klaviermässig (Ger., klăh-vēr′mä′siyh). Suitable for the piano; in piano style.

Kleingedackt (Ger., klīn′gĕ-dăhkt′). Flute (organ stop).

Knabenstimme (Ger., knăh′bĕn-shtĭ′mĕ). A boy's voice.

Knee stop. A knee lever under the manual of the reed organ. There are 3, used (*a*) to control the wind supply, (*b*) to open and shut the swell-box, (*c*) to draw all the stops.

Kniegeige (Ger., knē′gī-gŭh). *Viola da gamba;* literally, "knee violin."

Konzert (Ger., kŏhn-tsârt′). 1. Concerto.—2. Concert.

Konzertmeister (Ger., kŏhn-sârt′mī-ster). CONCERTMASTER.

Konzertstück (Ger., kŏhn-tsârt′shtük). 1. A concert piece.—2. A short concerto in 1 movement and free form.

Koppel (Ger., kŏhp′pel). Coupler . . . *Koppel ab,* off coupler . . . *Koppel an,* draw coupler, couple.

Koto. Japanese string instrument similar to a zither.

Kraft, mit (Ger., mit krăhft). ⎱
Kräftig (Ger., kref′tĭyh).   ⎰
Forceful, vigorous, energetic; *con forza.*

Krakowiak. A Cracovienne.

Krebsgang (Ger., krĕps′gähng). Literally, "crab walk"; a retrograde motion of a given theme or passage.

Kreuz (Ger., kroytz). The sharp sign (♯).

Krummhorn (Ger., krŏŏm′horn). An obsolete woodwind instrument with double reed. Hence, an organ stop of similar tone (mournful).

Kujawiak. A Polish dance in the rhythm of a mazurka, but at a faster tempo.

Kurz (Ger., kŏŏrts). Short . . . *Kurz und bestimmt,* short and decided.

Kyrie (Gk., kü′rē-ĕh). "Lord"; the first word in the opening division of the Mass.

L

L. Stands for *left* (or *links,* Ger.) in the direction *l.h.* (left hand).

La. 1. The 6th Aretinian syllable.—2. The note *A* in French and Italian.—3. (It., läh). The.

Lacrimosa (L., läh-crē-mŏh'zäh). A part of the Requiem Mass.

Lage (Ger., lah'gĕ). Position (of a chord); position, shift (in violin playing) . . . *Enge* (*weite*) *Lage,* close (open) position or harmony.

Lagrimando (It., läh-grē-mähn'dŏh). Complainingly, plaintively.

Lagrime, con (It., kŏhn lah'grē-mēh).⎱
Lagrimoso (It., läh-grē-moh'sŏh).⎰
   "Tearful," plaintive, like a lament.

Lah stands for *La* in Tonic Sol-fa.

Lamentabile (It., läh-men-tah'bē-lĕh).
Lamentabilmente (It., —täh-bēl-men'tĕh).
Lamentando (It., —tähn'dŏh).
Lamentevole (It., —tā'vŏh-lĕh).
Lamentevolmente (It., —tĕh-vŏhl-men'tĕh).
Lamentoso (It., —toh'sŏh).
   Lamentingly, plaintively, mournfully.

Lamentazione (It., läh-men-täh-tsē-oh'nĕh).⎱
Lamento (It., läh-men'tŏh).⎰
   A lament, complaint.

Ländler (Ger., lent'ler). A slow waltz of South Germany and the Tyrol (whence the French name *Tyrolienne*), in 3/4 or 3/8 time, and the rhythm

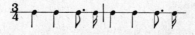

Langsam (Ger., lăhng$^{k'}$zähm). Slow ... *Langsamer,* slower.

Languendo (It., lăhn-gwen'dŏh). ⎫
Languente (It., lăhn-gwen'tĕh). ⎭
Languishing, plaintive.

Languidamente (It., lăhn-gwē-dăh-men'tĕh). ⎫
Languido (It., lăhn'gwē-dŏh). ⎬
Languore, con (It., kŏhn lăhn-gô'rĕh). ⎭
Languidly, languishingly.

Largamente (It., lar-găh-men'tĕh). Largely, broadly; in a manner characterized by a vigorous and sustained tone and general breadth of style, without change of tempo.

Largando (It., lar-găhn'dŏh). "Growing broader"; that is, slower and more marked; generally a *crescendo* is implied.

Large. A Plainchant note equal to 2 (or 3) longs.

Larghetto (It., lar-get'tŏh). The diminutive of *Largo,* and demands a somewhat more rapid tempo, nearly *Andantino.*

Larghezza, con (It., kŏhn lar-get'säh). Same as *Largamente.*

Largo (It., lar'gŏh). Large, broad; the slowest tempo-mark, calling for a slow and stately movement with ample breadth of style ... *Largo assai,* very slowly and broadly (also *Largo di molto, Molto largo,* or *Larghissimo*) ... *Poco largo,* "with some breath"; can occur even during an Allegro.

Larigot (Fr., lăh-rē-gŏh'). Originally, a kind of flageolet; now, an organ stop of $1\frac{1}{3}'$ pitch.

Lassú. The slow section of the Csárdás.

Lauda (Latin). A laud (hymn or song of praise) ... *Laudes,* lauds; together with matins, the first of the 7 Canonical Hours.

Laudamus te. "We praise Thee"—part of the Gloria of the Mass.

Laudi spirituali. Medieval songs of devotion.

Launig (Ger., low'nĭyh). 1. With light, gay humor.—2. With facile, characteristic expression.

Laute (Ger., low'tĕ). Lute.

Lavolta. A dance of Italian origin (properly *la volta*, "a turn") popular in Shakespeare's time in England.

Lay. A melody or tune.

Le (It., lā; Fr., lŭ). The.

Lead. 1. The giving-out or proposition of a theme by one part.—2. A cue.

Leader. 1. Conductor, director.—2. In the orchestra, the 1st violin; in a band, the 1st cornet; in a mixed chorus, the 1st soprano.—3. An antecedent.

Leading. 1. (*noun*). The melodic progression or conduct of any part.—2. (*adjective*). Principal, chief; guiding, directing ... *Leading* chord, the dominant seventh chord ... *Leading melody,* principal melody or theme ... *Leading motive,* see LEITMOTIV ... *Leading note, tone,* the 7th degree of the major and harmonic minor scales.

Leaning note. Appoggiatura.

Leap. 1. In piano playing, a spring from one note or chord to another.—2. In harmony, a skip.

Lebendig (Ger., lĕh-ben'dĭyh). ⎫
Lebhaft (Ger., lāb'hăhft). ⎭
Lively, animated. ... *Lebhaft, aber nicht zu sehr,* lively, but not too much so.

Lebhaftigkeit (Ger., lāb'hăhf-tĭyh-kīt). Animation; *mit Lebhaftigkeit und durchaus mit Empfindung und Ausdruck,* with animation, and with feeling and expression throughout.

Ledger line. A Leger line.

Legando (It., lĕh-gähn'dŏh). "Binding." 1. Legato.—2. An expression mark calling for the smooth execution of two or more consecutive tones by a single "stroke of the glottis" (vocal), in one bow (violin, etc.), by a single stroke of the tongue (wind instruments), or *legatissimo* (on organ or piano).

Legate (It., lĕh-gah′tĕh). Slurred; played or sung smoothly and evenly.

Legatissimo (It., lĕh-găh-tĭs′sē-mŏh). Very smoothly and evenly. On the piano, in passages marked *legatissimo,* each finger is to hold its note as long as possible.

Legato (It., lĕh-gah′tŏh). Bound, slurred; a direction to perform the passage in a smooth and connected manner, with no break between the tones; also indicated by the "legato mark," a curving line under or over notes to be so executed.

Legend (lē- or lĕj′end).
Legende (Ger., lĕh-gen′dĕ).
Légende (Fr., lā-zhahnd′).
A vocal or instrumental composition depicting the course of a short tale of legendary character.

Legendenton, im (Ger., im lĕh-gen′den-tohn). In the tone (style) of a legend.

Leger line. A short line used for writing notes which lie above or below the staff ... *Leger space,* a space bounded on either side or both sides by a leger line. (Pronounced, and often written, *Led′ger.*)

Leggeramente (It., led-jĕh-răh-men′tĕh).
Leggerezza, con (kŏhn led-jĕh-ret′săh).
Leggermente (It., led-jâr-men′tĕh).
Lightly, briskly.

Leggero (It., led-jâ′roh). Light, airy.

Leggiadramente (It., led-jâh-drăh-men′tĕh). Neatly, elegantly, gracefully.

Leggiadro (It., led-jah′drŏh). Neat, elegant, graceful.

Leggiero, etc. (It., led-jâ′rŏh). See LEGGERO.

Legno, col (It., kŏhl lān′yŏh). "With the stick"; let the stick of the bow fall on the strings.

Leicht (Ger., līyht). Light, brisk; easy, facile ... *Leicht bewegt,* lightly and swiftly; with slight agitation.

Leichtlich (Ger., līyht′lïyh). Lightly, easily.

Leidenschaft, mit (Ger., mit lī′den-shähft).⎫
Leidenschaftlich (Ger., lī′den-shähft′lïyh). ⎭
With passion; passionately.

Leidvoll (Ger., līt′fōhl). Sorrowful, mournful.

Leise (Ger., lī′zĕ). Low, soft; *piano.*

Leiser (Ger., lī′zer). Softer; *immer leiser,* softer and softer.

Leitmotiv (Ger., līt′mŏh-tēf′). Leading motive; any striking musical motive (theme, phrase) characterizing or accompanying one of the actors in a drama, or some particular idea, emotion, or situation in the latter.

Lenezza, con (It., kŏhn lĕh-net′säh). Faintly, gently, quietly.

Leno (It., lā′nŏh). Faint, gentle, quiet.

Lentamente (It., len-täh-men′tĕh). Slowly.

Lentando (It., len-tähn′dŏh). Growing slower.

Lentezza, con (It., kŏhn len-tet′säh). Slowly.

Lento (It., len′tŏh). Slow; calls for a tempo between *andante* and *largo* ... *Adagio non lento,* slowly, but not dragging.

Lesson. English instrumental piece of the 17th and 18th centuries composed for the harpsichord or organ.

Lesto (It., lâ′stŏh). Gay, lively, brisk.

Liberamente (It., lē-bĕh-räh-men′tĕh). Freely, boldly.

Libretto (It., lē-bret′tŏh). A "booklet"; the words of an opera, oratorio, etc. The author is called a *librettist* (It., *libretti′sta*).

Licenza (It., lē-chen′tsäh). Freedom, license ... *Con alcuna licenza,* with a certain (degree of) freedom.

Lieblich (Ger., lēp′līyh). Lovely, sweet, charming.

Lied (Ger., leed). A song, particularly an art song; the plural is *lieder.*

Liedertafel. A general name for a German male choral society.

Ligature. 1. A tie; a syncopation.—2. A group or series of notes to be executed in one breath, to one syllable, or as a legato phrase.

Light opera. An operetta.

Limpido (It., lim'pē-dŏh). "Limpid"; clearly, distinctly.

Linear counterpoint. A modern term describing a type of contrapuntal writing in which individual lines are the main considerations in the ensemble.

Lip. 1. The upper and lower lips of a flue pipe are the flat surfaces above and below the mouth.—2. Lipping; that is, the art of so adjusting the lips to the mouthpiece of a wind instrument as to get a good tone.

Lirico. Italian word for *lyric*.

Liscio (It., lē'shŏh). Smooth, flowing.

L'istesso (It., lē-stes'sŏh). The same.

L'istesso tempo. The same tempo.

Litany. A song of supplication, priests and choir alternating.

Liturgy. The total service of the Christian church.

Liuto (It., lē-oo'tŏh). A lute.

Lo (It., loh). The.

Lobgesang (Ger., lŏhb'gĕ-săng^k). Song of praise.

Loco (It., lô'kŏh). "Place"; following 8*va* it means, "perform the notes as written."

Locrian mode. An ecclesiastical mode based on the seventh degree of the major scale.

Lointain (Fr., loo-an-tehn'). Distant; faint sounding.

Long. A Plainchant note equal to 2 (or 3) breves.

Lontananza, in (It., in lŏhn-tăh-năhn'tsăh). At a distance.

Lontanissimo (It., lŏhn-tăh-nis'sē-mŏh). Very far away.

Lontano (It., lŏhn-tah′nŏh). Far away . . . *Da lontano,* from a distance.

Loud pedal. The pianoforte pedal which lifts the dampers; the right pedal.

Lourd (Fr., loor). Heavy.

Lourdement (Fr., lŏŏr-deu-mǎn′). Heavily.

Loure (Fr., loor). A dance in 6/4 or 3/4 time and slow tempo, the downbeat strongly marked.

Louré (Fr., loorā). Slurred, legato, *non staccato.*

Luftig (Ger., lŏŏf′tĭyh). Airy, light.

Lugubre (It., lŏŏ-goo′brĕh). Mournful.

Lunga (It., lŏŏn′gah). Long; sustained, prolonged. Written over or under a hold (⌒) it means that the pause is to be decidedly prolonged; often written *Pausa lunga,* long pause.

Lunghe (It., lŏŏn′gĕh. Plural of *lunga*). Prolonged.

Lur. A primitive wooden trumpet in use by shepherds in Scandinavia.

Lusingando (It., loo-zin-gähn′dŏh).
Lusingante (It., —gähn′tĕh).
Lusinghevole (It., —gā′vŏh-lĕh).
Lusinghevolmente (It., —gĕh-vŏh-men′tĕh).
Lusinghiero (It., —gē-â′rŏh).
Coaxingly, caressingly, flatteringly, seductively.

Lustig (Ger., lŏŏs′tĭyh). Merry, merrily.

Lute. A general term for a variety of plucked, stringed instruments, popular from the 16th through 18th centuries.

Luthier (Fr., leu-tieh′). A maker of lutes, and generally speaking, of any string instruments.

Luttosamente (It., lŏŏt-tŏh-săh-men′tĕh).
Luttuosamente (It., lŏŏt-tŏŏ-ŏh-săh-men′tĕh).
Mournfully, plaintively.

Luttoso (It., lŏŏt-toh′sŏh). ⎫
Luttuoso (It., lŏŏt-tŏŏ-oh′sŏh). ⎭
    Mournful, doleful, plaintive.

Lydian mode. The church mode that begins on the fourth
    note of the major scale.

Lyre. 1. An ancient Greek stringed instrument, the body
    being a soundboard, from which rose 2 curving arms
    joined above by a crossbar; the strings, from 3 to 10 in
    number, were stretched from this crossbar to or over a
    bridge set on the soundboard, and were plucked with a
    plectrum.—2. The lyre of military bands consists of loosely
    suspended steel bars tuned to the scale and struck with a
    hammer.

Lyric, lyrical. Pertaining to or proper for the lyre, or for
    accompaniment on (by) the lyre; hence, adapted for sing-
    ing, or for expression in song; opposed to *epic* (narrative)
    and *dramatic* (scenic, accompanied by action) . . . *Lyric
    drama,* the opera . . . *Lyric opera,* one in which the lyric
    form predominates . . . *Lyric stage,* the operatic stage.

Lyrics. A colloquial term for the text of a popular song or of
    a musical.

M

M. Stands for It. *mano* or Fr. *main* (hand); for *Manual*
    (organ); and for *Metronome* (usually M. M.).

Ma (It., mäh). But . . . *Allegro ma non troppo,* rapidly, but not
    too fast.

Mächtig (Ger., mäyh′tĭyh). Powerful, mighty.

Madrigal. A short lyric poem; also, a vocal setting of such a
    poem, in from 3 to 8 parts, contrapuntal, and usually for
    unaccompanied chorus; there are also madrigals in simple
    harmony, in dance rhythms, etc., or accompanied by in-
    struments.

Maestà, con (It., kŏhn măh-ĕ-stah′).

Maestade, con (It., kŏhn măh-ĕ-stah′dĕh).

Maestevole (It., măh-ĕ-stā′vŏh-lĕh).

Maestevolmente (It., —stā-vŏhl-men′tĕh).

Maestosamente (It., —stŏh-săh-men′tĕh).
  With majesty, with dignity, majestically.

Maestoso (It., măh-ĕ-stoh′sōh). Majestic, dignified; in a style characterized by lofty breadth.

Maestro (It., măh-ĕh′strŏh). Master . . . *Maestro di cappella,* choirmaster; conductor.

Maggiore. In Italian, major.

Maggot. A madrigal in old English; the word meant "a whimsical notion," and was used in the sense of a song dedicated to a lady.

Magnificat (L., măhg-nē′fē-kăht). "Magnificat anima mea dominum" (my soul doth magnify the Lord), the canticle of the Virgin Mary (Luke I, 46-55) sung as part of the Office of Vespers in the Roman Catholic Church.

Main (Fr., măn). Hand . . . *Main droite* (*gauche*), right (left) hand; often written *m. d., m. g.*

Maître (Fr., mä′tr). Master . . . *Maître de chapelle,* choirmaster; conductor.

Majestätisch (Ger., măh-yes-tä′tish). Maestoso.

Majeur. French for major.

Major. "Greater"; opposed to minor, "lesser." See INTERVAL . . . *Major cadence,* one closing on a major triad . . . *M. chord* or *triad,* one having a major third and perfect fifth.

Major scale. A scale consisting of 2 major seconds, 1 minor second, 3 major seconds, and 1 minor second in this order.

Major second. An interval of 2 semitones.

Major seventh. An interval 1 semitone short of an octave.

Major third. An interval of 2 whole tones.

Malagueña (Sp., măh-lă-gay'nyăh). Type of Spanish folk music originating in the provinces of Malaga and Murcia.

Malinconia, con (It., kŏhn măh-lin-kŏh-nē'ăh).
Malinconicamente (It., măh-lin-kŏh-nē-kăh-men'tĕh).
With melancholy expression; dejectedly.

Malinconico (It., măh-lin-kô'nē-kŏh). Melancholy, dejected. (Also *Malinconioso, Malinconoso*.)

Mambo. A ballroom dance of West Indian origin similar to the cha-cha and rumba.

Mancando (It., măhn-kăhn'dŏh). Decreasing in loudness, dying away.

Mandola (It., măhn-dô'lăh). A large mandolin.

Mandolin(e). A small kind of lute, the body shaped like half a pear; with wire strings tuned pairwise, played with a plectrum and stopped on a fingerboard.

Mandolinata (It., măhn-dŏh-lē-nah'tăh). 1. A mandolin piece of quiet character, like a serenade.—2. A direction in piano playing to play with a mandolin effect.

Mandolino (It., măhn-dŏh-lē'nŏh). A mandolin.

Mandora, Mandore. Same as MANDOLA.

Maniera (It., măh-nē-â'răh). Manner, style, method . . . *Con dolce maniera,* in a suave, delicate style.

Mano (It., mah'nŏh). Hand . . . *Mano destra* (*sinistra*), right (left) hand.

Manual. An organ keyboard; opposed to *pedal.*

Manualiter (L., mă-nü-ăl'ĭ-tŭr). On the manual(s) alone.

Maracas. Latin American rattles, usually in pairs, shaken vigorously.

Marcando (It., mar-kăhn'dŏh, "marking").
Marcate (It., măr-kah'tĕh, "marked," "mark!").
Marcato,-a (It., mar-kăh'tŏh, -tăh, "marked").
With distinctness and emphasis.

Marcatissimo (It., mar-käh-tis′sē-mŏh). With very marked emphasis.

March. A composition of strongly marked rhythm, suitable for timing the steps of a body of persons proceeding at a walking pace.—*March form* is in duple (2/4), compound duple (6/8), or quadruple (4/4) time, with reprises of 4, 8, or 16 measures, followed by a Trio section, and ending with a repetition of the march.

Marche (Fr., marsh). }
Marcia (It., mar′chäh). }
 March . . . *Alla marcia,* in march style.

Marche funèbre. Funeral march.

Marimba. South American and African xylophone with tuned resonators placed underneath the wooden bars.

Markiert (Ger., mar-keert′). Accented, marked.

Marsch (Ger., marsh). March.

Martellato (It., mar-tel-lah′tŏh). "Hammered"; on the violin, play the notes with a sharp, decided stroke (♪); on the piano, strike the keys with a heavy, inelastic plunge of the finger, or (in octave playing) with the arm staccato.

Mattinata (It., mäh-tē-näh′tă). Morning song.

Marziale (It., mar-tsē-ah′lĕh). Martial, war-like.

Masque. A kind of musical drama, popular in the 16th and 17th centuries; a spectacular play with vocal and instrumental music.

Mass. In the Roman Catholic Church, the musical service taking place during the consecration of the elements, with 5 divisions; (1) Kyrie, (2) Gloria (including the Gratias agimus, Qui tollis, Quoniam, Cum Sancto Spiritu), (3) Credo (with the Et incarnatus, Crucifixus, Et resurrexit), (4) Sanctus and Benedictus (with the Hosanna), (5) Agnus Dei (with the Dona nobis) . . . *High Mass,* one celebrated at church festivals, with music and incense . . . *Low Mass,* one without music.

Mässig (Ger., mä'sĭyh). Measured; moderate ... *Mässig langsam,* moderately slow; *mässig geschwind,* moderately fast.

Matins. The music sung at morning prayer; the first of the Canonical Hours.

Mazurka (Polish, măh-zoor′kăh). A Polish national dance in triple time and moderate tempo with a variable accent on the third beat.

M.d. Abbreviation for "main droite," *right hand* in French, or "mano destra" in Italian.

Me stands for Mi, in Tonic Sol-fa.

Measurable music. Mensurable music.

Measure. 1. The notes and rests comprised between 2 bars; the metrical unit in composition, with regular accentuation, familiarly called a "bar" ... *Measure note,* a note shown by the time signature to be an even divisor of a measure; thus 3/4 shows that each measure has 3 quarter notes, and the measure note is then a quarter note ... *Measure rest,* see Rest.

Mechanism. A literal (and bad) translation of the French *mécanisme,* which means technical ability or skill, mechanical dexterity or training.

Medesimo (It., měh-dā′zē-mŏh). The same.

Mediant. The 3d degree of the scale.

Medley. See Potpourri.

Meistersinger (Ger., mī′ster-zing′er; *singular and plural*). Mastersinger(s); in Germany, the 15th–16th century artisan successors to the 12th–14th century aristocratic Minnesingers.

Melancolia (It., mä-lăhn-kŏh-lē′ăh). Melancholy.

Mélange (Fr., mä-lahn′zh). A medley, potpourri.

Melisma. A melodic ornament or grace; coloratura.— *Melismatic,* ornamented, embellished; *melismatic song,* that in which more than one tone is sung to a syllable; opposed to syllabic song.

Melodeon. The original American organs were called Melodeons, or Melodiums. See REED ORGAN.

Melodia. An organ stop resembling the Clarabella; a kind of stopped diapason.

Melodia (It., mĕh-lŏh-dē'äh). Melody . . . *Marcata la melodia,* the melody (should be) marked.

Melodic. 1. In the style of a melody; progressing by single tones.—2. Vocal, singable; as a melodic interval.

Melodico (It., mĕh-loh'dē-kŏh). }
Melodioso (It., mĕh-lŏh-dē-oh'sŏh). }
Melodious, singing.

Melodion. A piano in which steel bars pressed against a revolving cylinder took the place of strings; invented by J. C. Dietz, of Emmerich, Germany.

Melodium. A Melodeon.

Melodrama. Originally, a musical drama; now (1) stage-declamation with a musical accompaniment; (2) a romantic and sensational drama in which music plays a subordinate part.

Melody. 1. The rational progression of single tones; contrasted with Harmony, the rational combination of several tones.—2. The leading part (usually the soprano).—3. An air or tune.

Melograph. Name of various mechanical devices for recording the music played on a pianoforte.

Melos (Gk., mā'lŏhs, "song"). The name bestowed by Wagner on the style of recitative employed in his later musical dramas.

Même (Fr., mäm). Same . . . *À la même,* tempo primo.

Meno (It., mā'nŏh). Less; not so . . . *Meno allegro,* not so fast.—*Meno* alone stands for *meno mosso,* not so fast.

Mensurable notation. Various types of rhythmic notations in use from the 13th to the 17th centuries.

Menuet (Fr., mŭ-nü-ā′).

Menuett (Ger., mā-noo-et′). $\Big\}$

A minuet.

Messa (It., mes′säh).

Messe (Fr., mess). $\Big\}$

Messe (Ger., mes′sĕ).

Mass.

Messa di voce (It., mes′säh dē voh′chĕh). The attack of a sustained vocal tone *pianissimo,* with a swell to *fortissimo,* and slow decrease to *pianissimo* again:

Mestamente (It., mĕh-stäh-men′tĕh).

Mestizia, con (kŏhn mĕh-stē′tsē-äh). $\Big\}$

Plaintively, grievingly.

Mesto (It., mĕh′stŏh). Pensive, sad, melancholy.

Mesuré (Fr., mŭ-zü-rā′). 1. Measured, moderate.—2. In exact time.

Meter, Metre. 1. In music, the symmetrical grouping of musical rhythms.—2. In verse, the division into symmetrical lines. The metre of English hymns is classified according to the kind of feet used, as iambic, trochaic, or dactylic; the figures show the number of syllables in each line:

IAMBIC METRES: *Common metre* (C.M.), 8 6 8 6; *Long metre* (L.M.), 8 8 8 8; *Short metre* (S.M.), 6 6 8 6. These have regularly 4 lines to each stanza; when doubled to 8 lines they are called *Common metre double* (C.M.D.), *Long metre double* (L.M.D.), and *Short metre double* (S.M.D.). They may also have 6 lines in each stanza and are then named *Common particular metre* (C.P.M.), 8 8 6 8 8 6; *Long particular metre* (L.P.M.), or *Long metre 6 lines,* 8 8 8 8 8 8; and *Short particular metre* (S.P.M.), 6 6 8 6 6 8. Besides the above, there are *Sevens and Sixes,* 7 6 7 6; *Tens,* 10 10 10

10; *Hallelujah metre,* 6 6 6 6 8 8 (or 6 6 6 6 4 4 4 4), etc.

TROCHAIC METRES: *Sixes,* 6 6 6 6; *Sixes and Fives,* 6 5 6
5; *Sevens,* 7 7 7 7; *Eights and Sevens,* 8 7 8 7, etc.

DACTYLIC METRES: *Elevens,* 11 11 11 11; *Elevens and
Tens,* 11 10 11 10, etc. These are most of the metres in
general use.

Metronome. The familiar "time-keeper" of music students;
a double pendulum moved by clockwork, and provided
with a slider on a graduated scale marking the number of
beats the metronome makes per minute. M. M. stands for
"Maelzel's Metronome" after the reputed inventor, Maelzel of Vienna (1816). Modern metronomes are electric and
have no pendulum.

Mezzo,-a (It., med'zŏh, -zăh). 1. Half.—Written alone, as an
expression mark, it refers to either an *f* or a *p* just preceding, thus meaning "mezzo *forte*" or "mezzo *piano*" . . .
Mezzo forte, half-loud . . . *Mezzo legato,* in piano playing,
calls for a light touch with less pressure than in legato. . . .
Mezzo piano, half soft (less loud than *mezzo forte*) . . .
Mezzo voce, "with half the power of the voice"; calls for
mezzo forte, both in singing and playing.

Mezzo-soprano (It., med'zŏh-sŏh-prah'nŏh). The female
voice between soprano and alto, partaking of the quality of
both, and usually of small compass (a-f^2, or a-g^2), but very
full toned in the medium register.

M.g. Abbreviation for "main gauche," *left hand* in French.

Mi. The third Aretinian syllable; name of the note *E* in
France, Italy, etc.

Middle C. The *C* in the middle of the piano
keyboard:

Militarmente (It., mē-lē-tar-men'tĕh). In military (march)
style; *alla militare.*

Military band. An orchestra attached to a branch of the military service consisting of woodwinds, brass, and percussion.

Military music. Instruments of percussion and wind instruments only, admitting the cornet, bugle, saxophones, etc.

Mimodrama. A dramatic or musical spectacle in which the performers convey the dramatic action by gestures and choreography, without speaking; same as PANTOMIME.

Minaccevole (It., mē-năht-chā′vŏh-lĕh).

Minaccevolmente (It., —chā-vŏhl-men′tĕh).

Minacciando (It., —chāhn′dŏh).

Minacciosamente (It., —chŏh-săh-men′tĕh).

Minaccioso (It., —choh′sŏh).

In a menacing or threatening manner.

Miniature score. An orchestral score reproduced in a small size so that it can be used for study purposes.

Minim. A half note . . . *Minim rest,* a half rest.

Minnesänger (Ger., min′nĕ-zeng′er).

Minnesinger (Ger., min′nĕ-zing′er).

(*Either form is both singular and plural.*) The German aristocratic poet-musicians of the 12th–14th centuries.

Minor. Latin word for "smaller," used in music in 2 different senses: 1. To indicate a *smaller* interval of a kind, as in minor second, minor third, minor sixth, minor seventh, minor ninth, and minor tenth;—2. To define a key, as in *a* minor, or a scale as in *a* minor scale, or a minor triad; in minor keys the third of the scale forms an interval of a minor third from the root.

Minore (It., mē-noh′rĕh). Minor.

Minor harmonic scale. A minor scale with the raised seventh degree providing a leading tone.

Minor melodic scale. A minor scale which eliminates the interval of an augmented second between the sixth and seventh degrees of the harmonic minor scale, thereby providing a smoother melodic progression. When ascending, the sixth and seventh degrees are raised; when descending, these notes are unaltered.

Minor natural scale. A minor scale without chromatic alterations, and therefore lacking the leading tone.

Minstrels. In the Middle Ages, professional musicians who sang or declaimed poems, often of their own composition, to a simple instrumental accompaniment.

Minuet. An early French dance form. As an art product it is usually a double minuet, the first section repeated after the second (the Trio). It is in triple time.

Minuetto (It., mē-noo-et′tŏh). Minuet.

Miracle play. Sacred dramas, often with music, which were popular in England in the Middle Ages; the stories were usually on Biblical subjects or parables, which were also called *Moralities.*

Mirliton (Fr., meer′lĕ-tŏhn). Small tubular musical instrument, the sound of which is produced by a membrane set vibrating by the human voice. Same as KAZOO.

Mirror canon. A canon which sounds the same when sung or played backwards; a musical palindrome.

Missa (Latin). The Mass ... *Missa brevis,* short Mass ... *Missa solemnis,* high Mass.

Misteriosamente (It., mē-stĕh-rē-ŏh-săh-men′tĕh).
Misterioso (It., mē-stĕh-rē-oh′sŏh).
Mistero, con (It., kŏhn mē-stâ′rŏh).
In a style suggestive of mystery, or of hidden meaning.

Misura, alla (It., ăhl′lăh mē-zoo′răh).
Misurato (It., mē-zoo-rah′tŏh).
With the measure; in exact time.

Mit (Ger., mit). With ... *Mit Ausdruck,* with expression ... *Mit Begleitung,* accompanied ... *Mit Bewegung,* with animation, con moto ... *Mit halber Stimme,* mezza voce ... *Mit innigster Empfindung,* with deepest emotion ... *Mit Kraft,* powerfully, *con forza.*

Mixed cadence. See CADENCE ... *Mixed chorus, quartet, voices,* vocal music combining male and female voices.

Mixolydian mode. A mode corresponding to the progression from *G* to *G* on the white keys of the piano.

Mixture. A compound auxiliary flue stop with from 3 to 6 ranks of pipes sounding as many harmonics of any note played.

Mobile (It., mô′bē-lĕh). Readily responsive to emotion or impulse.

Modal harmony. The type of harmony which is derived from church, exotic, or invented modes, apart from the common major and minor keys.

Mode. 1. A generic term applied to ancient Greek melodic progressions and to church scales established in the Middle Ages and codified in the system of Gregorian chant. The intervals of the Greek modes were counted downwards, and those of the medieval modes were counted upwards, so the intervallic contents were different between the Greek and the church systems. However, the church modes retained the Greek names of the modes. If played on the white keys of the piano, the church modes are: from *C* to *C*, Ionian; from *D* to *D*, Dorian; from *E* to *E*, Phrygian; from *F* to *F*, Lydian; from *G* to *G*, Mixolydian; from *A* to *A*, Aeolian; and from *B* to *B*, Locrian. The modes continued to underlie all western music through the 17th century, then gradually gave way to the common major and minor keys.—2. The distinction between a major key (mode) and minor key (mode).—3. Any scalar pattern of intervals, either traditional to a culture (Indian, Japanese, etc.) or invented.—4. A system of rhythmic notation used in the 13th century.

Moderato (It., mŏh-dĕh-rah′tŏh). Moderate; that is, at a moderate tempo, or rate of speed . . . *Allegro moderato,* moderately fast.

Moderatamente (It., mŏh-dĕh-**r**ăh-tăh-men′tĕh). ⎫
Moderazione, con (kŏhn mŏh-dĕh-**r**ăh-tsē-oh′nĕh). ⎬
   With moderation (of either tempo or emotion).

Modern music. The term is now used in 2 different senses: 1. Musical composition as it developed at the turn of the 20th century, in which modulation from one key to another reached complete freedom of diatonic and chromatic progressions, and dissonances acquired equal rights with traditional concords; Several keys could be combined in a technique called POLYTONALITY, and the melody was allowed to veer away from its tonal foundations becoming sometimes completely atonal; main themes were organized into a system known as DODECAPHONY.—2. Loosely speaking, all popular music, particularly in America and England, including jazz and rock, as contrasted to traditional classical music.

Moderno,-a (It., mŏh-dâr′nŏh, -näh). Modern . . . *Alla moderna,* in modern style.

Modulate. To pass from one key or mode into another.

Modulation. Passage from one key or mode into another . . . *Chromatic modulation,* one effected by use of chromatic intervals . . . *Diatonic mod.,* one effected by use of diatonic intervals . . . *Enharmonic mod.,* one effected by using enharmonic changes to alter the significance of tones or intervals . . . *Final mod.,* one in which the new key is retained, or still another follows . . . *Passing, Transient, Transitory mod.,* one in which the original key is speedily regained.

Möglich (Ger., mö′glïyh). Possible . . . *So rasch wie möglich,* as fast as possible.

Moll (Ger., mōhl). Minor.

Molto,-a (It., mŏhl′tŏh, -täh). Very, much . . . *Molto adagio,* very slowly . . . *Molto allegro,* very fast . . . *Con molta passione,* with great passion, very passionately . . . *Di molto* or *Molto molto,* exceedingly, extremely; as *crescendo molto molto,* growing very much louder.

Monochord. A very ancient musical instrument. As the name indicates, it had a single string, which was stretched over a soundbox and a shifting bridge that allowed the string to be adjusted to different pitches.

Monodrama. A dramatic or musical presentation, with a single performer.

Monody. The recitative-like accompanied song style of early 17th-century Italy.

Monophonous. Capable of producing but one tone at a time.

Monophony. Unaccompanied melody.

Monothematic. A composition with a single subject.

Monotone. 1. A single unaccompanied and unvaried tone.—2. Recitation (intoning, chanting) on such a tone.

Moralities. A later form of the Miracle plays.

Morbidezza, con (It., kŏhn mor-bē-det′săh). With tenderness; softly.

Morbidissimo (It., mor-bē-dis′sē-mŏh). Very tenderly, softly.

Morbido (It., môr′bē-dŏh). Soft, tender.

Morceau (Fr., mor-sōh′). A piece, composition . . . *Morceau de genre* (zhahn′r), characteristic piece.

Mordant (Fr., mor-dähn′). ⎫
Mordent (Ger., mor′dent). ⎬

A grace consisting of the single rapid alternation of a principal note with an auxiliary a minor second below:

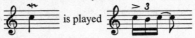

     is played

Inverted mordent, the alternation of the principal note with the higher auxiliary:

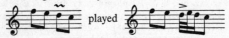

     played

Morendo (It., mŏh-ren′dŏh). Dying away.

Moresca (It., mŏh-rĕs′căh). A Moorish dance.

Morgenlied (Ger., mor′gĕn-lēt). Morning song.

Mormorando (It., mor-mŏh-rähn′dŏh).
Mormorevole (It., —ra′voh-leh).
Mormoroso (It., —roh′sŏh).
Murmuring, murmurous; in a very gentle, subdued tone.

Mormorio (It., mor-mŏh-rē′ŏh). Murmur. *Come un mormorio,* like a murmur.

Morris dance. An old English dance, often in the form of a symbolic character play.

Mosso (It., môhs′sŏh). "Moved." Standing alone, as a tempo mark, it is the same as *"con moto."* It means "rapid" in the phrases *meno mosso* (less rapid), *più mosso* (more rapid), and *poco mosso* (somewhat rapid) ... *Allegretto poco mosso,* a rather lively allegretto, almost allegro ... *Mosso agitato,* a fast and agitated movement; *assai mosso e agitato,* very rapid and agitated.

Motet. A sacred vocal composition in contrapuntal style, and without accompaniment. (Pieces in *anthem* style are, however, sometimes called *motets.*)

Motet (Fr., mŏh-tā′).
Motette (Ger., mŏh-tet′tĕ).
Motet.

Motif (Fr., mŏh-tēf′). Motive.

Motion. 1. The progression or conduct of a single part or melody; it is *conjunct* when progressing by steps, *disjunct* when progressing by skips.—2. The movement of one part in relation to that of another; in *contrary* or *opposite* motion one part ascends while the other descends; in *oblique* motion one part retains its tone while the other moves; in *parallel* motion, both parts move up or down by the same interval; in *similar* motion both move up or down together by dissimilar intervals; in mixed motion, two or more of the above varieties occur at once between several parts.

Motive. 1. A short phrase or figure used in development or imitation.—2. A Leading motive . . . *Measure motive,* one whose accent coincides with that of the measure.

Moto (It., mộ'tŏh). Motion; speed; movement, tempo.— *Con moto,* with an animated and energetic movement . . . *Moto precedente,* at the former tempo . . . *Più (meno) moto,* same as *più (meno) mosso.*

Moto perpetuo. "Perpetual motion" in Italian, applied to short pieces in very fast tempo in rondo form.

Motteggiando (It., mŏht-ted-jăhn'dŏh). In a bantering, facetious style.

Mottetto (It., mŏht-tet'tŏh). Motet.

Mouth organ. A harmonica.

Mouthpiece. That part of a wind instrument which a player places upon or between his lips.

Mouvement (Fr., moov-măhn'). Movement; tempo.

Movable Doh. A system of solffegio in which the tonic of every major scale is called Doh, the second degree called Re, the third Mi, etc., following the scale of Guido d'Arezzo.

Movement. 1. Tempo.—2. A principal division or section of a composition.

Movendo il tempo (It., mŏh-ven'dŏh ēl tem'pŏh). Growing faster.

Movimento (It., moh-vē-měn'toh). Movement.

M.s. Abbreviation for "mano sinistra," *left hand* in Italian.

Munter (Ger., mŏŏn'ter). Lively, gay, animated.

Musette (Fr., mü-zet'). 1. A small oboe.—2. A kind of bagpipe; also, a short piece imitating this bagpipe, with a drone bass.—3. A reed stop on the organ.

Musica (It., moo'zē-kăh). Music . . . *Dramma per musica,* an opera.

Musica ficta (L., moo′zē-că fĭk′tah). In music from the 10th through the 16th centuries, theoretically questionable chromatic alterations suposely made in performance.

Musica figurata (It., moo′zē-că fĭ-gyoor-a′tah). Music arranged in contrasting contrapuntal figurations.

Musica reservata (L., moo′zē-căh rĕ-zer-văh′tah). A 16th-century term applied to a particularly sophisticated type of contrapuntal music, related to musica ficta and "reserved" for masters of the craft.

Music drama. The original description of opera as it evolved in Florence early in the 17th century (*dramma per musica*); Wagner adopted this term in order to emphasize the dramatic element in his spectacles.

Musical. A colloquial description for an American or English musical revue.

Musical box, Music box. The Swiss music box has a metal cylinder or barrel, studded with pins, and turned by clockwork; in revolving, the pins catch and twang a comb-like row of steel teeth, each tooth producing a tone.

Musical saw. A special quasi-musical instrument producing a twanging sound when stroked.

Musicology. The science of music. The concept includes all branches of music—theory, history, esthetics, lexicography, bibliography, etc.

Musique (Fr., mü-zēk′). Music.

Musique concrète (Fr., —con-crĕt′). "Concrete music"; a practice developed by French electrical engineers and radio men in 1948, in which all kinds of incidental musical, nonmusical and unmusical sounds and noises are made use of, similar to the technique of collage in modern art.

Muta (It., moo′tăh). "Change!" (crook or instrument).

Mutation. 1. Change of voice.—2. Change of position, shifting (violin).

Mutation stop. In the organ, any stop (except a mixture) whose pipes produce tones neither in unison nor in octaves with the foundation stops (8′ stops); that is, all tierce and quint stops, and their octaves.

Mute. 1. A heavy piece of metal fitted to the bridge of a violin, etc., to deaden the sound. The direction for putting on the mutes is "con sordini"; for taking them off, "senza sordini."—2. A leather covered pad, paste-board cone, or wooden cylinder inserted in the bell of the horn or trumpet to modify the tone.

Mut(h)ig (Ger., moo′tĭyh). Spiritedly, boldly.

Mysteries. Medieval bible plays, often with vocal and instrumental music. In the form called *Moralities,* abstract ideas were personified on the stage.

N

Nach (Ger., năh). After; according to.

Nachahmung (Ger., năh-ăh′mŭng^k). Imitation.

Nach Belieben (Ger., năh bĕ-lē′ben). A piacere.

Nachdrücklich (Ger., năh′drük′lĭyh). ⎫
Nachdruck, mit (Ger., mit năh′drŏŏk). ⎭
With emphasis, strongly marked.

Nachgebend (Ger., năh′gā′bent). ⎫
Nachgiebig (Ger., năh′gē′bĭyh). ⎬
Nachlassend (Ger., năh′lăh′sent). ⎭
Yieldingly, slower and slower; *rallentando.*

Nachgiebiger (Ger., năh′gē′bĭyh-er). Still slower.

Nachlässig (Ger., năh′les′sĭyh). Carelessly.

Nachschlag (Ger., năh′shlăyh). The end notes of a trill.

Nachthorn (Ger., năh′t-horn). A covered stop in the organ, having covered pipes of 2′, 4′, or 8′ pitch.

Nachtmusik (Ger., năht′-moo-zĭk). Night music, a serenade.

Nachtschall (Ger., năht′shähl). See NACHTHORN.

Nachtstück (Ger., năht′shtük). "Night piece," a nocturne.

Nach und nach (Ger., năh ŏŏnt năh′). Little by little, gradually.

Nail fiddle. A primitive instrument in use for a time in the 18th century. It consisted of a wooden board with nails of different sizes affixed in a semicircle; it was played with an ordinary violin bow on the nails.

Naked Fifth. A harmonic Fifth without an added Third.

Napolitana. An old type of Italian madrigal, which was revived in modern times in the form of a popular song.

Narrante (It., năr-răhn′tĕh). Narrating; as if telling a story; calls for distinct declamation.

Nasard (Fr., năh-zar′). ⎫
Nasat (Ger., năh-zaht′). ⎭
The Twelfth (organ stop) of $2\frac{2}{3}$-foot pitch (large sizes $10\frac{2}{3}$ and $5\frac{1}{3}$, smaller size $1\frac{1}{3}$).

Nason flute. An organ stop having stopped pipes of mild, suave tone.

Natural. 1. The sign ♮.—2. A white key on the keyboard ... *Natural harmonics,* those produced on an open string ... *Natural horn,* the French horn without valves ... *Natural interval,* one found between any two tones of a diatonic major scale ... *Natural key,* C major ... *Natural pitch,* that of any wind instrument when not overblown ... *Natural scale,* C major, having neither sharps nor flats ... *Natural tone,* any tone obtained on a wind instrument with cupped mouthpiece, without using keys, valves, or the slide.

Naturale (It., năh-too-rah′lĕh). ⎫
Naturalmente (It., —răhl-men′tĕh). ⎭
In a natural, unaffected style.

Neapolitan sixth. The first inversion of a flat two chord (♭II); in C major, the notes F, A♭, D♭.

Negli (It., nāl′yē). In the.

Negligente (It., nĕh-glē-jen′tĕh). ⎫
Negligentemente (It., —jen-tĕh-men′tĕh). ⎬
Negligenza, con (It., kŏhn nĕh-glē-jen′tsäh). ⎭
     In a style expressive of negligence, carelessness.

Negro spirituals. Songs of a religious character sung by Negro slaves on the Southern plantations in America.

Nei (nă′ē), **nel, nell', nella, nelle, nello** (It.). In the.

Nervoso (It., nâr-voh′sŏh). In a forcible, agitated style.

Nettamente (It., net-tăh-men′tĕh). ⎫
Netto,-a (It., net′tŏh, -tăh). ⎬
     In a neat, clear, distinct style.

Neumes. Signs used, in the early Middle Ages, to represent tones.

Nicht (Ger., nĭyht). Not . . . *Nicht zu langsam,* not too slow.

Niente (It., nē-en′tĕh). Nothing . . . *Quasi niente,* barely audible.

Ninth. The interval of an octave, plus a major or minor Second.

Nobile (It., nô′bē-lĕh). ⎫
Nobilità, con (It., kŏhn nŏh-bē-lē-tah′). ⎬
Nobilmente (It., nŏh-bēl-men′tĕh). ⎭
     In a refined , chaste, lofty style.

Noch (Ger., nŏh). Still; yet . . . *Noch rascher,* still faster.

Nocturne (Fr., nŏhk-tūrn′). A piece of a dreamily romantic or sentimental character, without fixed form.

Nocturns. Services of the Church held during the night.

Nodal figures. The figures corresponding to the "nodal lines" of a vibrating plate of wood, glass, etc.; rendered visible by strewing fine dry sand on the plate, this sand being tossed by the vibrating portions of the plate to the "nodal lines," which are points of perfect or comparative rest . . . *Nodal point,* see NODE.

Node. A point or line in a vibrating body (such as a string, soundboard, trumpet, bell), which remains at rest during the vibration of the other parts of the body.

Noël (Fr., nōĕl). A Christmas carol or hymn.

Noire (Fr., nwăhr). Quarter note.

Non (It., nŏhn). Not.

Nonet. A composition for nine voices or instruments.

Nonnengeige (Ger., noh′nen-gī′gĕ). Literally, "nun violin"; a curious nickname for the tromba marina, which itself is a curious name for a monochord, a box with one string. German nuns were supposed to favor this instrument.

Nota cambiata. A "changed note" in Italian; an extra note inserted one diatonic degree above the principal note before descending to the next note (as the note *D* inserted between *C* and *B*).

Notation. The art of representing musical tones, and their modifications, by means of written characters.

Note. One of the signs used to express the relative time value of tones . . . *Note against note,* counterpoint in equal notes.

Notturno (It., nŏht-toor′nŏh). A Nocturne.

Novellette (Ger., nŏh-vel-let′tĕ). An instrumental piece free in form, bold in harmony, romantic in character, of considerable length, and with a variety of contrasting themes.

Nuance (Fr., nü-ahnss′). Shading; change in musical expression, either in the tone-color, tempo, or degree of force.

Number. 1. A subdivision of an opera or oratorio.—2. A smaller, and more or less complete, portion of a large work, such as a song, aria, interlude, etc.—3. Any single piece on a program.—4. An opus number.

Nun's fiddle. See TROMBA MARINA.

Nuovo, di (It., dē nŏŏ-ô′vŏh).   ⎫

Nuovamente (It., nŏŏ-ŏh-văh-men′tĕh). ⎬

    Again, anew.

Nut. 1. The ridge over which the strings pass at the end of the fingerboard next to the head of a violin, etc.—2. The sliding projection at the lower end of the violin bow, by means of which the hair is tightened or slackened.—3. The "lower nut" on the violin is the ridge between the tailpiece and tailpin (or button).

O

O. A small circle signifies (*a*) an open string; (*b*) the harmonic mark; (*c*) the diminished fifth.

O (It., ŏh). Or. (Written before either vowels or consonants; *od* is an unusual form.)

Obbligato (It., ŏhb-blē-gah′tŏh). Required, indispensable. An *obbligato* part is a concerted (and therefore essential) instrumental part; especially when accompanying and vying with a vocal solo.

Obligato (Ger. spelling, ŏh-blē-gah′tŏh). Obbligato.

Oblique motion. A type of 2-part counterpoint in which one voice moves and the other remains stationary.

Oboe. [Ger. *Oboe* (oh-boh′ĕ); It. *òboe* (oh′bŏh-ĕh).] 1. An orchestral instrument with conical wooden tube, 9 to 14 keys, and a double reed; compass 2 octaves and a Seventh, from $b\flat$ to a^3. Tone very reedy and penetrating, though mild. Only 2 kinds are in ordinary use, the treble oboe (just described), and the English horn (alto oboe) of lower pitch.—2. In the organ, an 8′ reed stop, with conical pipes surmounted by a bell and cap.

Oboe da caccia (It., oh′boh-eh dăh căh′tchăh). Literally, "oboe of the hunt." An instrument tuned a fifth below the oboe. It was in use during the Renaissance period but was eventually replaced by the English horn.

Oboe d'amore (It., —dăh-moh′reh). Literally, "oboe of love." An oboe that sounds a minor third below the written notation; used in many old scores, and also in some modern revivals.

Ocarina (It., ô-kăh-rē′năh). "Goose-pipe"; a bird-shaped wind instrument of terra cotta, with finger holes and a whistle mouthpiece.

Octave. 1. A series of 8 consecutive diatonic tones.—2. The interval between the 1st and 8th tones of such a series.—3. In the organ, a stop whose pipes sound tones an octave higher than the keys touched; like the Principal ... *Concealed, covered,* or *hidden octaves* (or *fifths*), parallel octaves (or fifths) suggested by the progression of 2 parts in similar motion to the interval of an octave (or fifth) ... *Rule of the octave,* a series of harmonies written over the diatonic scale as a bass ... *Short octave,* the lowest octave of some old organ manuals, in which some keys (and pipes) are omitted.

Octave coupler. One uniting the 8′ tones of one keyboard with those an octave higher on another.

Octave flute. 1. The piccolo.—2. An organ stop of 4′ pitch.

Octave stop. See OCTAVE 3.

Octet. A composition for 8 voices or instruments.

Octuor (Fr., ŏhk-tü-ohr′). An octet.

Ode. A chorus in ancient Greek plays; a musical work of praise.

Oder (Ger., oh′der). Or; or else.

Off. In organ music, a direction to push in a stop or couplet ... *Off the pitch,* false in pitch or intonation.

Offertoire (Fr., ŏh-făr-twah′r). ⎫
Offertorio (It., ŏhf-făr-tô′rē-ŏh). ⎬
Offertorium (L., ô-fŭhr-tō′rē-ŭm). ⎭

Offertory; in the Roman Catholic Mass, the verses or anthem following the Credo, and sung by the choir while the priest is placing the consecrated elements on the altar, during which the offerings of the congregation are collected.

Ohne (Ger., oh′nĕ). Without.

Oliphant. An ancient hunting horn, sometimes made of elephant's tusk (*oliphant* is an old English word for "elephant").

Omnitonic. Having or producing all tones; chromatic (instrument).

Ondeggiamento (It., ŏhn-ded-jäh-men′tŏh). Undulation; rocking (as by waves).

Ondeggiante (It., ŏhn-ded-jähn′tĕh). Undulating, billowy, rocking.

Ondes musicales. The name for the electronic musical instrument invented by Martenot; sometimes called *Ondes Martenot.*

Ondulé (Fr.). Undulated, wavy.

One step. American ballroom dance of the 1910's and 1920's in 2/4 time.

Ongarese (It.). Hungarian.

Open diapason, harmony, note, order, pipe, etc. See the nouns.

Open harmony. In 4-part harmony, an arrangement of voices such that the 3 upper voices have a total range of more than an octave (as in C, G, E, C).

Open pedal. The loud piano pedal.

Open string. A string on the violin, viola, or cello sounding its natural tone without being stopped by the finger.

Opera. A form of drama, of Italian origin, in which vocal and instrumental music are essential and predominant. The several acts, usually preceded by instrumental introductions, consist of vocal scenes, recitatives, songs, arias, duets, trios, choruses, etc., accompanied by the orchestra. This is the *Grand* or *Heroic opera*; a *Comedy opera* is a versified comedy set to music; a *Comic opera* has spoken interludes.

Opéra bouffe (Fr., ŏh-pā-räh boof'). ⎫
Opera buffa (It., ôh'pä-räh bŏŏf'fäh). ⎭
Light comic opera.

Opéra comique (Fr., ŏh-pā-räh kŏh-mēk'). French opera with spoken dialogue instead of recitative. It is not necessarily comic in nature.

Opera seria (It., ôh'pä-räh sä'rē-äh). Serious (grand, heroic, tragic) opera.

Operetta (It., ŏh-pĕh-ret'täh). ⎫
Opérette (Fr., ŏh-pā-ret'). ⎭
A "little opera"; the poem is in a comic, mock-pathetic, parodistic, or anything but serious vein; music light and lively, often interrupted by dialogue.

Ophicleide (ŏf'ĭ-klīd). The bass instrument of the key bugle family; now little used.

Opposite motion. Contrary motion.

Oppure (It., ŏhp-poo'rĕh). Or; else; often written *opp.*

Opus (Latin). Work; often written *Op.*, or *op* . . . *Opus-number,* one number in the series with which a composer marks his works.

Oratorio (It., ŏh-räh-tô'rē-ŏh). An extended, more or less dramatic, composition for vocal solos and chorus, with accompaniment by orchestra or organ (or both) sung without stage play or scenery.

Orchester (Ger., or-kĕs'ter). Orchestra.

Orchestra (or'kĕs-träh). A company of musicians performing on the instruments usually employed in opera, oratorio, or symphony; hence, the instruments, taken together.

Orchestral (or-kĕs'tral, or or'kĕs-tral). Pertaining to, or resembling, the orchestra . . . *Orchestral piano playing,* the style of Liszt and his disciples, who try to imitate orchestral effects on the piano.

Orchestration. The art of writing music for performance by an orchestra; the science of combining, in an effective manner, the instruments constituting the orchestra.

Orchestrion. A large stationary barrel organ, generally played by clockwork.

Order. The arrangement of the chord tones above a given bass, *open* and *close order* being the same as open and close harmony.

Organ. The church organ, or pipe organ, is a keyboard wind instrument consisting of few or many sets of pipes played from one or more keyboards; there may be 5 keyboards for the fingers (manuals), and there is generally 1 for the feet (pedal, or pedal keyboard). The pipes, of which there are two main divisions, flue pipes and reed pipes, are arranged in sets (registers, or stops), and made to speak by wind admitted from the bellows on pressing the keys.

Organo (It., or′gäh-nŏh). Organ . . . *Organo pleno,* full organ.

Organ point. A tone sustained in one part to harmonies executed in the other parts, usually a bass tone, tonic or dominant (or both).

Organ tone. The tone of the 8′ Open Diapason on the Great Organ manual is considered the distinctive "organ-tone." (Also called "Diapason tone.")

Organum (L., ôr′gän-ŭm). 1. An organ.—2. The earliest attempts at harmonic or polyphonic music, in which 2 parts progressed in parallel fifths and fourths.

Orgel (Ger., ohr′gel). ⎫
Orgue (Fr., ohrg). ⎬
    Organ.

Orgue de barbarie. A street organ, operated by a crank, and producing a "barbarous" crackling sound while playing a tune.

Ornament. A grace, embellishment.

Osservanza, con (It., kŏhn ŏhs-sâr-văhn'tsăh). With care, observing all signs.

Osservato (It., ŏhs-sâr-vah'tŏh). Carefully observed; *stile osservato,* strict style.

Ossia (It., ŏhs-sē'ăh). Or; or else; indicates an alternative (or facilitated) reading or fingering of a passage. (Also *Oppure, Ovvero.*)

Ostinato (It., ŏh-stē-nah'tŏh). Obstinate; *basso ostinato,* a ground bass; hence, an "ostinato" is the incessant repetition of a theme with a varying contrapuntal accompaniment.

Ottava (It., ŏht-tah'văh). Octave ... *All' ottava* (written *8va*------- or *8*-------, "at the octave," an octave higher... *Coll'ottava,* "with the octave," that is, in octaves ... *Ottava alta,* the higher octave ... *Ottava bassa* (*8va bassa*), the lower octave, an octave below.

Ottavino. A piccolo.

Ottoni. In Italian, brass instruments.

Ottetto (It., ŏht-tet'tŏh). An octet.

Ou (Fr., oo). Or; or else.

Ouverture (Fr., oo-vâr-tür'). ⎫
Ouvertüre (Ger., oo-var-tü'rĕ). ⎭
Overture.

Overblow. With wind instruments, to force the wind through the tube in such a way as to cause any harmonic to sound.

Overstring. To arrange the strings of a piano in 2 sets, one lying over and diagonally crossing the other; a piano so strung is called an *overstrung* piano, in contradistinction to *vertical.*

Overtone. Harmonic tone.

Overture. A musical introduction to an opera, oratorio, etc.—A concert overture is an independent composition in sonata form.

Ovvero (It., ŏhv-vâh'rŏh). Or; or else.

P

P. Stands for *Pedal* (*P.* or *Ped.*); *piano* (*p*), *pp* or *ppp*, *pianis-simo; P. F.,* pianoforte; *pf,* pianoforte (soft, increasing to loud); *fp,* forte piano (loud, diminishing to soft instantly); *mp,* mezzo piano (half soft); *Pointe* (Fr., "toe").

Padovana (It., păh-dŏh-vah'năh). A Pavane. (Also *Pado-vane, Paduana, Paduane,* etc.)

Paired notes. Two parallel series of notes played on the piano with one hand.

Pandiatonicism. A modern term for a system of diatonic harmony making use of all 7 degrees of the scale in disso-nant combinations, as for instance in the concluding chord *C, G, E, A, D, G.*

Pandora. A string instrument of great antiquity, plucked like a lute.

Panpipes. A set of reeds of different sizes; the name is ex-plained by the legend that the god Pan invented it.

Pantomime. A ballet-like performance without speech or singing, in which the action is suggested by gestures and choreography. The word *pantomime* means "all imitating" in Greek.

Parallel motion. Voice leading in harmony or counterpoint in which intervals move in the same direction. In tradi-tional harmony parallel thirds and sixths are recom-mended, but parallel fifths and octaves are forbidden.

Paraphrase. A transcription or rearrangement of a vocal or instrumental piece for some other instrument or instru-ments, with variations.

Parlando (It., par-lăhn'dŏh).⎫
Parlante (It., par-lăhn'tĕh). ⎭
"Speaking"; singing with clear and marked enuncia-tion.—In piano playing, *parlante* calls for a clear, crisp *non legato.*

Parlato (It., par-lah'tŏh). Spoken.

Parody. As used in old music theory, this term meant "like something else," and was quite devoid of the contemporary sense of travesty. A *parody Mass* is a work with thematic material taken from a work by another composer.

Part. 1. The series of tones written for and executed by a voice or instrument, either as a solo or together with other voices or instruments.—2. A division of a homophonic movement devoted to the exposition of one melody, or musical idea; like the 2-part and 3-part song forms.

Parte (It., par'tĕh). Part ... *Colla parte,* a direction to accompanists to follow yieldingly and discreetly the solo part or voice.

Partial stop. A half stop.

Partial tone. An harmonic tone.

Partita (It., par-tē'tăh). A suite.

Partition (Fr., păr-tē-sĭ-ohn'). ⎫
Partitur (Ger., păr-tē-toor). ⎬
A score. ⎭

Part music. Concerted or harmonized vocal music.

Part singing. The singing of part music, usually without instrumental accompaniment.

Part song. A composition for at least 3 voices in harmony, without accompaniment, and for equal or mixed voices. It is properly a melody with choral harmony, with any reasonable number of voices to each part.

Paspy. A passepied.

Passacaglia (It., păhs-săh-cahl'yăh). An old Italian dance in triple time and stately movement, written on a ground bass of 4 measures.

Passacaille (Fr., păh-săh-cah'ē). Passacaglia.

Passage. 1. A portion or section of a piece, usually short.—2. A rapid repeated figure, either ascending or descending. A scale passage is generally called a run.

Passamezzo (It., păhs-săh-mĕd'zŏh). An old Italian dance in duple time, like the Pavane, but faster.

Passepied (Fr., păhs-p'yā'). A Paspy; an old French dance in 3/8 or 6/8 time, with 3 or 4 reprises; like the minuet in movement, but quicker.

Passing notes or tones. Notes or tones foreign to the chords which they accompany, and passing by a step from one chord to another. They differ from suspensions in not being prepared, and in entering (usually) on an unaccented beat.

Passion, Passion music. A musical setting of a text descriptive of Christ's sufferings and death (passion).

Passionatamente (It., păhs-sē-ŏh-năh-tăh-men'tĕh). ⎫
Passionato, -a (It., păhs-sē-ŏh-năh'tŏh, -tăh). ⎬
Passione, con (It., kŏhn păhs-sē-oh'nĕh). ⎭
    Passionately, in an impassioned style, fervently.

Pasticcio (It., păhs-tit'chŏh). ⎫
Pastiche (Fr., păhs-tēsh'). ⎬
    A musical medley of extracts from different works, pieced together and provided with new words so as to form a "new" composition.

Pastoral. 1. A scenic cantata representing pastoral life; a pastoral opera.—2. An instrumental piece imitating in style and instrumentation rural and idyllic scenes.

Pastorale (It., păhs-tŏh-rah'lĕh). ⎫
Pastorale (Fr., păhs-tŏh-răhl'). ⎬
    A Pastoral.

Pateticamente (It., păh-tĕh-tē-kăh-men'tĕh). Pathetically.

Patetico,-ca (It., păh-tā'tē-kŏh, -kăh). Pathetic.

Patimento (It., păh-tē-men'tŏh). Suffering, grief; *con espressione di patimento,* with mournful or plaintive expression.

Patter song. A humorous song sung in parlando style, usually quite fast.

Pauken (Ger., pow'ken). Kettledrums.

Paura (It., păh-oo'răh). Fear, dismay.

Pauroso (It., păh-ŏŏ-roh'sŏh). Fearful, timid.

Pausa (It., pah'ŏŏ-zăh). A rest; a pause . . . *Pausa lunga,* long pause; *pausa generale,* pause for all performers.

Pause. 1. A full stop.—2. A rest.—3. A hold ⌒.

Pavana (It., păh-vah'năh). ⎫
Pavan(e). ⎭
A stately dance of Italian or Spanish origin, in slow tempo and alla breve time.

Paventato (It., păh-ven-tah'tŏh). ⎫
Paventoso (It., păh-ven-toh'sŏh). ⎭
Fearfully, timidly.

Pearly. A style of piano touch producing a clear, round, smooth effect of tone, especially in scale passages.

Ped. Stands for *Pedal;* signifies that the right (loud) piano pedal is to be pressed; or (in organ music) that notes so marked are to be played on the pedals.

Pedal. 1. A foot key on the organ or pedal piano.—2. A foot lever; as the piano pedals, or the organ swell-pedal.—3. A treadle, like those used for blowing the reed organ.—4. A stop knob or lever worked by the foot (organ).—5. A contraction for PEDAL POINT.

Pedale doppio (It., pĕh-dah'lĕh dô'pē-ŏh). Pedal-part in octaves.

Pedale ogni battuta (It., pĕh-dah'lĕh ŏhn'yē băht-too'tăh). "Take pedal with each measure."

Pedalier. A set of pedals, either (1) so adjusted as to play the low octaves of the piano, after the manner of organ pedals, or (2) provided with separate strings and action, to be placed underneath the piano.

Pedal note. See PEDAL TONE.

Pedal organ. The set of stops controlled by the organ pedals.

Pedal piano. A pianoforte provided with a pedalier.

Pedal point. An organ point.

Pedal tone. A sustained or continuously repeated tone.

Pedanteria, con (It., kŏhn pĕh-dăhn-tĕh-rē′ăh).⎫
Pedantisch (Ger., pĕh-dăhn′tish).   ⎬
   Pedantically; in an even, unemotional style.

Pensiero (It., pen-sē-â′roh). A thought... *Pensiero del(la)*—, Souvenir of—, Recollections of—.

Pensieroso (It., pen-sē-ĕh-roh′sŏh).⎫
Pensoso (It., pen-soh′sŏh).   ⎬
   Pensive, thoughtful.

Pentatonic scale. A 5-tone scale, usually that which avoids semitonic steps by skipping the 4th and 7th degrees in major, and the 2d and 6th in minor.

Per (It., pĕr). For, by, from, in, through... *Per l'organo,* for the organ; *Per il flauto solo,* for solo flute.

Percussion. 1. The striking or sounding of a dissonance.—2. The striking of one body against another... *Instruments of percussion* are the drums, the tambourine, cymbals, bells, triangle, etc., and the dulcimer and pianoforte.

Percussion stop. A reed organ stop, which strikes the reed a smart blow when sounding it, to render its vibration prompter and stronger.

Percussive. Sounded by striking.

Perdendosi (It., pâr-den′dŏh-sē). Dying away; *morendo* or *diminuendo,* together (in modern music) with a slight *rallentando.*

Perduna. Bourdon (organ stop).

Perfect cadence. A cadence consisting of the dominant triad followed by the tonic triad.

Perfect intervals. The standard octave, fifth, and fourth.

Perfect pitch. ABSOLUTE PITCH.

Perigordino (It., pĕh-rē-gor-dē'nŏh). ⎫
Périgourdine (Fr., pā-rē-goor-dēn'). ⎬
    An old Flemish dance. ⎭

Period. A complete musical thought of 8 (12) or 16 measures, ending with an authentic CADENCE.

Perlé (Fr., pâr-lā'). ⎫
Perlend (Ger., pâr'lent). ⎬
    Pearly. ⎭

Perpetual canon. A canon in which the final cadence leads back into the opening measures, like a round.

Perpetuum mobile. Latin for perpetual motion; a type of short and rapid composition, usually for a solo instrument.

Pesante (It., pĕh-sähn'tĕh). Heavy, ponderous; firm, vigorous.

Peu à peu (Fr., pö ăh pö'). Little by little ... *Un peu,* a little.

Pezzi (It., pet'sē). Pieces ... *Pezzi concertati,* concerted pieces... *Pezzi staccati,* any detached numbers taken from an opera, etc.

Pezzo (It., pet'sōh). A piece; a number (of an opera, etc.).

Phantasie (Ger., făhn-täh-zē'). Fancy, imagination.

Phantasiestück (Ger., făhn-täh-zē'shtük). A fantasia; in modern music, a short piece of a romantic and intensely subjective cast, with no set form.

Phrase. Half of an 8-measure period.—Also, any short figure or passage complete in itself and unbroken in continuity.

Phrase mark. A curved line connecting the notes of a phrase.

Phrasing. 1. The bringing out into proper relief of the phrases (whether motives, figures, subjects, or passages).—2. The signs of notation devised to further the above end.

Phrygian mode. A church MODE corresponding to the scale from *E* to *E* on the white keys of the piano.

Piacevole (It., p'yăh-chā'vŏh-lĕh). Pleasant, agreeable; calls for a smooth, suave delivery, free from strong accents.

Piacevolezza, con (It., kŏhn p'yăh-chā-vŏh-let'săh). PIACEVOLE.

Piacevolmente (It., p'yăh-chā-vŏhl-men'tĕh). PIACEVOLE.

Piacimento (It., p'yăh-chē-men'tōh). PIACERE.

Piangendo (It., p'yăhn-jen'dōh).

Piangente (It., p'yăhn-jen'tĕh).

Piangevole (It., —jā'vŏh-lĕh).

Piangevolmente (It., —jā-vŏh-men'tĕh).

"Weeping, tearfully"; in a mournful, plaintive style.

Pianino (It., pē-ăh-nē'nŏh). An upright pianoforte.

Pianissimo (It., pē-ăh-nēs'sē-moh). Very soft; abbreviated *pp*.

Pianississimo (It., pē-ăh-nēs-sēs'sē-moh). Very, very soft; abbreviated *ppp*.

Piano (It., pē-ah'nŏh). Soft, softly (sign *p*) . . . *Piano pedal,* the soft or left pedal of the pianoforte.

Piano. Familiar abbreviation of Pianoforte.

Piano à queue (Fr., pyăh'noh ah kü). Grand piano; literally, "piano with a tail."

Pianoforte (It., pē-ăh-nŏh-fôr'tĕh; Engl., pĭ-ăn'oh-fort). A keyboard stringed instrument of percussion, the tones being produced by hammers striking the strings. The principal parts are the *Frame,* the *Soundboard,* the *Strings,* the *Action,* and the *Pedals.* The hammer action was first practically developed by Bartolommeo Cristofori of Padua in 1711.

Pianola. Trade name for the player piano.

Piano quartet. Composition for piano, violin, viola, and cello.

Piano quintet. Composition with piano and string quartet.

Piano score. An arrangement of an orchestral work for piano.

Piano trio. A composition for piano, violin, and cello.

Piatti (It., p'yăht'tē). Cymbals.

Pibroch (pē'brŏh). Variations for the bagpipe.

Picardy third. The frequent practice in Baroque music of ending a piece in a minor key with a major chord; the Picardy third in this case is the major third from the tonic.

Piccanteria, con (It., kŏhn pik-kăhn-tĕh-rē'ăh). With piquant, sprightly expression.

Picchettato (It., pik-ket-tah'tŏh). ⎱
Picchiettato (It., pik-kē-et-tah'tŏh). ⎰
Detached, *staccato*. See Piqué.

Piccolo (It., pik'kŏh-lŏh, "little"). The octave flute, a small flute pitched an octave higher than the orchestral flute. (The Italians call it *Flauto piccolo*, or *Ottavino*.)

Pick. To pluck or twang the strings of a guitar, mandolin, etc.—Also (*noun*), a plectrum.

Piece. 1. A musical composition.—2. An instrument, taken as a member of an orchestra or band.

Pièce (Fr., p'yess). A piece . . . *Suite de pièces,* a set of pieces.

Pieno (It., p'yâ'nŏh). 1. Full.—2. A mixture stop.

Pietosamente (It., pē-ĕh-tŏh-săh-men'tĕh). ⎱
Pietoso (It., pē-ĕh-toh'sŏh). ⎰
"Pitiful(ly), moving(ly)"; demands a sympathetic and expressive delivery.

Piffero (It., pif'fĕh-rŏh). 1. A fife; also, a primitive kind of oboe or shawm.—2. Same as Bifara.

Pincé (Fr., păn-sā'). 1. Plucked; as the strings of the harp.— 2. Pizzicato (in violin playing).

Pipe. 1. A rude flageolet or oboe.—2. An organ pipe; in *Flue pipes* the tone is produced by the vibration of a column of air within a tube or body; they are *open* or *covered* (*stopped, plugged*), a stopped pipe yielding a tone an octave lower than an open pipe of like length.—In *Reed pipes* the tone is produced by a reed.

Piqué (Fr., pē-kā′). In violin playing, the mezzo-staccato called for by a slur with staccato dots; notes so marked to be played in one bow (*picchiettato*).

Piston. See VALVE.

Pitch. The position of a tone in the musical scale. Pitch is relative, or absolute. The *relative* pitch of a tone is its position (higher or lower) as compared with some other tone. (See INTERVAL.) Its *absolute* pitch is its fixed position in the entire range of musical tones.

To indicate absolute pitch, the musical scale is divided into a fixed series of octaves, named and lettered as on p. xi, "Table of Clefs."

The number of vibrations made by a tone establishes its absolute pitch; the standard *French pitch* (also called *International,* or *low,* pitch) gives the tone a^1 435 double vibrations per second. The standard of pitch in the United States is a^1 = 440 double vibrations per second.

Pitch pipe. A small wooden or metal reed pipe which sounds one or more tones of fixed pitch, to give the tone for tuning an instrument, or for a choir.

Più (It., pew). More.—When *più* stands alone, as a *tempo* mark, *mosso* is implied; as an *expression* mark, it refers to the next preceding *f* or *p* . . . *Più mosso, più moto,* faster . . . *Più mosso ancora,* still faster . . . *Con un poco più di moto,* with a little more movement (that is, somewhat faster).

Piuttosto. (It., pew-tos′toh). Somewhat, or rather.

Pivot chord. In modulation, a chord pivotal to both the old key and the new key; particularly in chromatic modulation, the diminished seventh chord functions as such a passe-partout device.

Pizzicato (It., pit-sē-kah′tŏh). "Pinched"; plucked with the finger; a direction, in music for bow instruments, to play the notes by plucking the strings. (Abbrev. *pizz.*)

Placidamente (It., plăh-chē-däh-men′tĕh). ⎫
Placidezza, con (It., kŏhn plăh-chē-det′săh). ⎬
Placidly, tranquilly. ⎭

Placido (It., plah′chē-dŏh). Placid, smooth.

Plagal cadence. A cadence in which the subdominant chord is followed by the tonic chord.

Plagal mode. A church mode in which the final keynote is a fourth above the lowest tone of the mode. See AUTHENTIC MODE.

Plainchant, Plainsong. The unison vocal music of the Christian church, probably dating from the first centuries of the Christian era, the style being still obligatory in the Roman Catholic ritual.

Player piano. Trade name of a mechanical piano in which the keyboard action is produced by a rotating perforated roll.

Plectrum. A pick; a small piece of ivory, tortoise shell, or metal, held between the forefinger and thumb, or fitted to the thumb by a ring, and used to pluck or twang the strings of the mandolin, zither, etc.

Plein (Fr., plăn). Full.

Plein-jeu (Fr., plăn-zhö′). 1. A stop or combination of stops bringing out the full power of the organ, harmonium, etc.—2. Same as FOURNITURE.

Plus (Fr., plü). More.

Po' (It., pô; contraction of *poco*). Little ... *Con un po' d'espansione,* with a certain display of emotion... *Alzando un po' la voce,* raising the voice a little ... *Ritenendo un po',* becoming a trifle slower.

Pochette (Fr., pŭ-shĕt′). "Little pocket"; a very small violin that could be carried in the pocket of a dancing master to accompany his pupils in rehearsals.

Pochissimo (It., poh-kee′cee-moh). Very little.

Poco (It., pô′kŏh). Little ... *A poco a poco,* little by little ... *Poco allegro,* rather fast ... *Poco largo,* rather slow ... *Poco meno;* when standing alone as a tempo mark, *mosso* is implied; i.e., *poco meno mosso,* a little less fast (a little slower) ... *Poco più,* standing alone, also implies *mosso* ("a little faster") ... *Poco più lento della prima volta,* somewhat slower than the first time.

Poi (It., pô′ē). Then, thereafter.

Point d'orgue (Fr., pwōhn dôrg). 1. Organ point.—2. Pause.—3. Cadenza.

Pointe (Fr., pwăn′t). 1. Point or head of a bow.—2. Toe (abbrev. *p.*).

Polacca (It., pŏh-lăhk′kăh). A Polonaise ... *Alla polacca,* in the style of a Polonaise.—(Better, *Pollacca.*)

Polca (It., pôl′kăh). Polka.

Polka (pōl′kăh; Bohemian, *pulka*). A lively round dance in 2/4 time, originating about 1830 as a peasant dance in Bohemia.

Polka mazurka. A form of mazurka accommodated to the steps of the polka.

Polo (Sp., poh′loh). A syncopated Spanish dance in triple time, from Andalusia.

Polonaise (Fr., pŏh-lôh-näz′). A dance of Polish origin, in 3/4 time and moderate tempo; formerly in animated processional style, but now merely a slow promenade opening a ball.

Rhythm:

Last measure:

Polonese (It., pŏh-lŏh-nä′zĕh). Same as POLACCA.

Polyphonic. 1. Consisting of 2 or more independently treated melodies; contrapuntal.—2. Capable of producing 2 or more tones simultaneously, like the piano, harp, or organ.

Polyphony. The combination in harmonious progression of 2 or more independent melodies; the independent treatment of the parts; counterpoint, in the widest sense.

Polytonality. Simultaneous use of two or more different tonalities or keys. In much modern music polytonality has become a standard technique.

Pompa, con (It., kŏhn pŏhm′päh).

Pomposamente (It., pŏhm-pŏh-säh-men′tĕh).

Pomposo (It., pŏhm-pŏh′sŏh).
Pompously, loftily; in a majestic, dignified style.

Ponderoso (It., pŏhn-dĕh-roh′sŏh). Ponderous; in a vigorous, impressive style.

Ponticello (It., pŏhn-tē-chel′lŏh). Bridge.—*Sul ponticello,* near the bridge.

Pop music. A kind of popular music of the second half of the 20th century which rejects all pretentions of artistry, but aims instead at the brash reflection of contemporary life, with its artless permissiveness, neurotic gaiety, and youthful vigor of tunes, rhythms, and raucous sound projection. The discotheque is the natural habitat of pop music, as is the nightclub.

Portamento (It., por-täh-men′tŏh). A smooth gliding from one tone to another, differing from the legato in its more deliberate execution, and in the actual (though very rapid and slurring) sounding of the intermediate tones.

Portando (It., por-tähn′dŏh). "Carrying"; i.e., the *portamento* effect . . . *Portando la voce,* vocal *portamento.*

Portate la voce (It., por-tah′tĕh läh voh′chĕh). "Carry the voice," that is, sing *portamento.*

Portative. A small portable organ which could be used in religious processions.

Portunal flute. A flute stop on the organ, with open (seldom stopped) wooden pipes, wider at top than at the mouth.

Posato (It., pŏh-sah′tŏh). Sedate, dignified.

Posaune (Ger., pŏh-zow′nĕ). Trombone. Also, a reed stop in the organ, of 8′ pitch (manuals) or 16′ pitch (pedal).

Positif (Fr., pah-zē-tēf). Choir organ.

Position. 1. The place of the left hand on the fingerboard of the violin, etc. In the 1st position, the forefinger stops the tone (or semitone) above the open string; by shifting up, so that the 1st finger takes the place previously occupied by the 2d, the 2d position is reached, and so on. In the half position the 2d, 3d, and 4th fingers occupy the places taken, in the 1st position, by the 1st, 2d and 3d fingers.—2. The arrangement of notes in a chord, with reference to the lowest part; in the 1st, or fundamental position, the lowest part takes the root; in the 2d, it takes the third; etc.—3. Close (open) position, see HARMONY, *close* and *open*.

Possibile (It., pŏhs-sē′bē-lĕh). Possible; *pianissimo possibile,* as soft as possible; *il più presto possibile,* as rapid as possible.

Post horn. A horn without valves or keys, used on post coaches.

Postlude. A closing voluntary on the organ.

Posto, di (It., dē pôs′toh). See SLANCIO.

Potpourri (Fr., pŏh-pŏŏ-rē′). A musical medley, all kinds of tunes, or parts of tunes, being connected in an arbitrary manner.

Poussé (Fr., pŏŏs-sā′). Up-bow.

pp. Pianissimo.

ppp. Pianississimo.

Prächtig (Ger., prĕyh′tĭyh). Grandly, majestically.

Præludium (L., prä-loo'dē-oom). Prelude.

Pralltriller (Ger., prähl'trĭl-er). Upper mordent.

Precedente (It., prĕh-chĕh-den'tĕh). Preceding ... *Moto precedente,* in the preceding tempo.

Precentor. A director and manager of the choir, and of the musical services in general.

Precipitando (It., prĕh-chē-pē-tähn'dŏh). ⎫
Precipitatamente (It., —täh-täh-men'tĕh). ⎪
Precipitato (It., —tah'tōh). ⎬
Precipitoso (It., —toh'sōh). ⎭
  With precipitation, impetuosity, dash.

Precisione, con (It., kŏhn prĕh-chē-zē-oh'nĕh). ⎫
Preciso (It., prĕh-chē'zōh). ⎭
  With precision.

Prelude. A musical introduction to a composition or drama.

Preludio (It., prĕh-loo'dē-ōh). Prelude.

Preparation. The preparation of a dissonance consists in the presence, in the preceding chord and same part, of the tone forming the dissonance.

Prepared piano. A modernistic practice initiated by the American composer John Cage, in which the timbre of the piano is altered by placing such objects as screws, bolts, and clips on the strings of the grand piano.

Pressando (It., pres-sähn'dŏh). ⎫
Pressante (It., pres-sähn'tĕh). ⎭
  Pressing on, accelerating.

Pressez (Fr., pres-sā'). Accelerate; go faster.

Prestamente (It., prĕh-stâh-men'tĕh). Rapidly.

Prestant (Fr., pres-tähn'). An open flue stop, usually of 4′ pitch; equivalent to English *Principal.*

Prestezza, con (It., kŏhn prĕh-stet'säh). With rapidity.

Prestissimo (It., prĕh-stis′sē-mŏh). Very rapidly.

Presto (It., prâ′stŏh). Fast, rapid; faster than *allegro* . . . *Presto assai,* very, extremely rapid . . . *Presto parlante,* "speaking rapidly (volubly)"; a direction in recitatives, etc.

Prima. See Primo.

Primary accent. The downbeat, or thesis; the accent beginning the measure, directly following the bar.

Primary triad. One of the 3 fundamental triads of a key (those on the 1st, 5th, and 4th degrees).

Prime. The first note of a scale.

Primo,-a (It., prē′mŏh, -măh). First . . . *Prima buffa,* leading lady in comic opera . . . *Prima donna,* leading lady in opera . . . *Prima vista,* at first sight . . . *Prima volta,* the first time (written *Ima volta,* or simply *I,* or 1); indicates that the measure or measures under its brackets are to be played the first time, before the repeat; whereas, on repeating, those marked *Seconda volta* (or *IIda volta,* or *II,* or 2) are to be performed instead.

Primo (It.). A first or leading part, as in a duet.

Principal. In the organ, a stop of open metal flue-pipes of 4′ pitch on the manuals and 8′ pitch on the pedal.

Principal chords. The basic chords of a key—the triads on the tonic, dominant, and subdominant, with the dominant seventh chord.

Principal work. See Stop 2.

Principio (It., prin-chē′pē-ŏh). Beginning, first time . . . *In principio,* at the beginning . . . *Più marcato del principio,* more marked than the first time.

Processional. A hymn sung in church during the entrance of choir and clergy.

Program music. A class of instrumental compositions intended to represent distinct moods or phases of emotion, or to depict actual scenes of events; sometimes called "descriptive music."

Progress. To advance or move on: in *melody,* from one tone to another; in *harmony,* from one chord to another.

Progression. The advance from one tone to another, or from one chord to another; the former is *melodic,* the latter *harmonic* progression.

Progressive composition. In song writing, the setting of each strophe to different music, following the changing mood more closely than in the ballad or folk song, where melody and harmony are generally the same for each verse.

Progressive stop. A compound organ stop in which the number of ranks increases as the pitch rises.

Prontamente (It., prŏhn-tăh-men′tĕh).

Pronto (It., prŏhn′tŏh).

Promptly, swiftly.

Pronunziato (It., prŏh-nŏŏn-tsē-ah′tŏh). Pronounced, marked; *ben pronunziato,* well, clearly enunciated.

Proportion. A term of medieval music theory, relating to the proportionate duration of the notes of the melody, and also the ratio of vibrations of these notes.

Psalm. A hymn; a sacred song.

Psaltery (sôl′ter-ĭ). An ancient instrument in use to the 17th century; known to the Hebrews as the *Kinnor,* to the Germans as the *Rotta;* a kind of harp-zither, with a varying number of strings plucked by the fingers or with a plectrum.

Psaume (Fr., sohm). Psalm.

Pulsatile (—tĭl) **instruments.** Instruments of percussion.

Pulse. A beat or accent.

Pult (Ger., poolt). Music stand.

Punta. (It., pŏŏn′tăh). Point (of the bow) ... *Colla punta dell'arco,* at the point of the bow.

Pupitre (Fr., pü′pētr). Music stand.

Pyramidon. An organ stop having short covered pipes more than 4 times as wide at top as at mouth, and of 16′ or 32′ tone.

Q

Quadrille (kwŏ-drĭl′). A square dance consisting of 5 (or 6) figures named *le Pantalon, l' Été, la Poule, la Pastourelle* (*la Trenise*), and *la Finale.* The time alternates between 3/8 (6/8) and 2/4.

Quadruple counterpoint. See COUNTERPOINT.

Quadruple meter or **time.** That characterized by 4 beats to the measure.

Quadruplet. A group of 4 equal notes, to be executed in the time of 3 or 6 of the same kind in the regular rhythm; written:

Quality of tone. That characteristic peculiarity of any vocal or instrumental tone which distinguishes it from the tone of any other class of voices or instruments. Also called *Tone color, Timbre.*

Quarter note. A crotchet (♩).

Quarter rest. A rest equal in time value to a quarter note (¼, or ♩).

Quarter tone. Half a semitone; an interval which is sometimes used in modern compositions. Also used in some non-Western music.

Quartet(te). 1. A concerted instrumental composition for 4 performers.—2. A composition, movement, or number, either vocal or instrumental, in 4 parts.—3. Also, the performers as a group.

Quasi (It., kwah′zē). As if; as it were; nearly; approaching ... *Andante quasi allegretto,* andante approaching allegretto.

Quatre (Fr., kăh′tr). ⎫
Quattro (It., kwăht′trŏh). ⎬ Four.

Quatuor (Fr., kwăh-tü-or′). A quartet, vocal or instrumental.

Quaver. British term for an eighth note.

Quickstep. A march, usually in 6/8 time.

Quindecima (It., kwin-dā′chē-măh). A fifteenth (either the interval or the organ stop) ... *Alla quindecima* (written simply *15ma*), 2 octaves higher (or lower).

Quint. 1. The interval of a Fifth.—2. A $5\frac{1}{3}′$ organ stop, sounding a fifth higher than the normal 8′ pitch.—3. The *E* string of the violin.

Quintadena. An organ stop of small stopped metal pipes, in whose tone the twelfth (2d harmonic) is prominent.

Quintatön (Ger., kvin-tăh-tön′). In the organ, a covered flue stop of 8′, 16′, or 32′ pitch.

Quintet(te). 1. A concerted instrumental composition for 5 performers.—2. A composition, movement, or number, vocal or instrumental, in 5 parts.—3. Also, the performers as a group.

Quintole. A quintuplet.

Quintuor (Fr., kăn-tü-or′). A quintet.

Quintuple rhythm, time. Has 5 beats to the measure.

Quintuplet. A group of 5 equal notes to be executed in the time of 4 of the same kind in the regular rhythm; written:

Quitter (Fr., kē-tā′). To quit, leave ... *Sans quitter la corde,* without quitting the string.

Quodlibet. A musical medley; potpourri; Dutch concert. Originally, a piece employing several well-known tunes from various sources, performed either simultaneously or in succession.

R

R. Stands for right (Ger., *rechte*); *r. h.* right hand (*rechte Hand*). In French organ music, R stands for *clavier de récit* (swell manual).

Rabbia, con (It., kŏhn răhb′bē-äh). With passion, frenzy; furiously.

Raccoglimento, con (It., kŏhn răhk-kŏhl-yē-men′tŏh). Collectedly, coolly; meditatively.

Raccontando (It., răhk-kŏhn-tăhn′dŏh). Narrating, as if telling a story.

Raddolcendo (It., răhd-dŏhl-chen′dŏh). ⎫
Raddolcente (It., răhd-dŏhl-chen′těh). ⎬
Growing calmer and gentler. ⎭

Raddolcito (It., răhd-dŏhl-chē′tŏh). Gentler, calmer.

Raga. A generic term for a Hindu scale, consisting of 5, 6, or 7 different notes and calculated to create a certain mood. Each raga is suited to a particular time of the day. The word itself comes from the Sanskrit meaning "color," so that an infinite variety of nuances is possible in the playing of ragas by musicians of India.

Ragtime. A syncopated American music of black origins, popular from about 1896 to 1918. During this period, the term included vocal and instrumental music, and dance styles associated with the music. As an instrumental genre, it existed as both a popular ballroom style and as the earliest form of Jazz. In today's usage, the term usually refers to ragtime for piano.

Rallentamento (It., răhl-len-tăh-men′tŏh). A slackening in tempo.

Rallentando (It., răhl-len-tăhn′dŏh). Growing slower and slower.

Rallentare (It., răhl-len-tah′rĕh). To grow slower; *senza rallentare,* without slackening the pace.

Rallentate (It., răhl-len-tah′tĕh). Go slower.

Rallentato (It., răhl-len-tah′tŏh). At a slower pace.

Rank. A row of organ pipes. A mixture stop is said to have 2, 3, or more ranks, according to the number of pipes sounded by each digital (key).

Rant. An old country dance, or a reel.

Ranz des vaches (Fr., răhns dā văh′sh). One of the airs sung, or played on the alpine horn, in the Swiss Alps as a call to the cattle.

Rapidamente (It., răh-pē-dăh-men′tĕh). ⎫
Rapidità, con (It., kŏhn răh-pē-dē-tah′). ⎬
Rapido (It., răh′pē-dŏh). ⎭
  With rapidity, rapidly.

Rasch (Ger., răhsh). Fast, rapid, swift . . . *Noch rascher,* still faster . . . *So rasch wie möglich,* as fast as possible.

Rauschquinte (Ger., rowsh′kvin′tĕ). A mixture stop of 2 ranks. (Also *Rauschflöte, -pfeife, -quarte, -werk.*)

Ravvivando il tempo (It., răhv-vē-văhn′dŏh). Accelerating the tempo.

Ray. Stands for RE, in Tonic Sol-fa.

Re (It., ră). ⎫
Ré (Fr., ră). ⎬
  Second of the Aretinian syllables, and the name of the note *D* in France, Italy, etc.

Rebec. A medieval violin, shaped like a half pear, with 3 gut strings.

Recapitulation. A return of the initial section of a movement in sonata form.

Recessional. A hymn sung in church during the departure of choir and clergy after a service.

Recht (Ger., rĕyht). Right; *rechte Hand,* right hand.

Recital. A concert at which either (*a*) all the pieces are executed by one performer, or (*b*) all pieces performed are by one composer.

Recitando (It., rĕh-chē-tähn′dŏh). ⎫
Recitante (It., rĕh-chē-tähn′tĕh). ⎬
In declamatory style.

Récitatif (Fr., rā-sē-tăh-tēf′). ⎫
Recitativ (Ger., rā-tsē-tăh-tēf′). ⎪
Recitative (rĕs′ĭ-ta-tēv′). ⎬
Recitativo (It., rĕh-chē-tăh-tē′vŏh). ⎭

1. Declamatory singing, free in tempo and rhythm.—2. In piano playing, calls for a crisp delivery of the melody, free in tempo and rhythm.

Reciting note. The tone on which most of each verse in a chant (psalm or canticle) is continuously recited; the dominant.

Recorder. Type of flute of the end-blown variety with a whistle mouthpiece.

Redoubled interval. A compound interval.

Redowa. A Bohemian dance, like the Mazurka, though less strongly accented, in 3/4 time and lively tempo.

Reduce. In organ music, a direction to decrease the volume of tone by retiring the louder stops.

Reduction. Rearrangement of a composition for a smaller number of instruments, while preserving its form as far as possible.

Redundant. Augmented.

Reed. A thin strip of cane, wood, or metal, so adjusted before an aperture as nearly to close it, fixed at one end, and set by an air current in vibration, which it communicates either to an enclosed column of air (organ pipe, oboe), or directly to the free atmosphere, thus producing a musical tone. A *Free reed* vibrates within the aperture without striking the edges; a *Beating reed* strikes on the edges. A *Double reed* is two beating reeds which strike against each other.

Reed fifth. A stopped quint register in an organ.

Reed instrument. One whose tone is produced by the vibration of a reed in its mouthpiece.

Reed nasat. See Reed fifth.

Reed organ. A keyboard instrument whose tones are produced by free reeds; (*a*) the *Harmonium* (invented 1843 by A. Debain of Paris), the bellows forcing compressed air *outward* through the reeds; (*b*) the *American organ,* in which a suction bellows draws the air *in* through them. Either style has a variety of stops of different quality.

Reed pipe. See Pipe.

Reed work. See Stop (noun) 2.

Reel. A lively dance of Scotland and Ireland, usually in 4/4 (sometimes 6/4) time, with reprises of 8 measures; danced by 2 couples.

Refrain. A recurring melody of a song, usually at the end of a stanza; in popular music, a chorus.

Regal. A portable organ with reed pipes used during the 16th and 17th centuries.

Reggae. Jamaican popular music, marked by insistent square rhythms, in the manner of rock 'n' roll.

Register. 1. A set of pipes or reeds controlled by one drawstop; a stop (organ stop).—2. A portion of the vocal compass: as *high* or *low* register; *chest-* or *head*-register.—3. A portion, in the range of certain instruments, differing in quality from the other portions.

Registration. 1. The art of effectively employing and combining the various stops of the organ.—2. The combinations of stops employed for any given composition.

Relation(ship). The degree of affinity between keys, chords, and tones.

Relative key. A minor key is relative to that major key, the tonic of which lies a minor Third above its own; a major key is relative to that minor key, the tonic of which lies a minor Third below its own.

Relative pitch. Ability to name an interval, or the exact note after hearing a given note.

Religiosamente (It., rĕh-lē-jŏh-săh-men'tĕh).⎫
Religioso (It., rĕh-lē-joh'sŏh).   ⎬
In a devotional style.   ⎭

Remote key. An unrelated key.

Renaissance. In music history, the period from 1400 to 1600.

Repeat. 1. The sign: or or , *a* signifying that the music between the double-dotted bars is to be repeated; *b* and *c,* that the preceding and also the following division is to be repeated.—2. A section or division of music which is repeated.

Repercussion. 1. Repetition of a tone or chord.—2. In a fugue, the regular reentrance of subject and answer after the episodes immediately following the exposition.

Répétiteur (Fr., rĕh-pĕh-tē-tŭhr'). A choral assistant; anyone who conducts rehearsal.

Répétition (Fr., rĕh-pĕh-tē-sē-on'). A rehearsal.

Répétition générale (Fr., —zhĕh-nĕh-rahl'). A dress rehearsal.

Repetizione (It., rĕh-pĕh-tē-tsē-oh'nĕh). See Ripetizione.

Replica (It., râ'plē-kăh). A repeat or reprise . . . *Da capo senza replica,* play from beginning without observing the repeats.

Reprise (Fr., rŭ-prēz'). 1. A Repeat 2.—2. The revival of a work.—3. Break 3.—4. Repercussion 2.—5. Reentrance of a part or theme after a rest or pause.

Requiem. The first word in the Mass for the dead; hence, the title of the musical setting of that Mass. Its divisions are (1) Requiem, Kyrie, (2) Dies iræ, Requiem, (3) Domine Jesu

Christe, (4) Sanctus, Benedictus, (5) Agnus Dei, Lux æterna.

Resolution. The progression of a dissonance, whether a simple interval or a chord, to a consonance. *Direct resolution* is immediate progression from the dissonance to the consonance; *Indirect* (or *delayed, deferred, retarded*) *resolution* passes through some intermediate dissonance or dissonances before reaching the final restful consonance.

Resonance-box. A hollow resonant body like that of the violin or zither.

Response. 1. Responsory.—2. Answer.—3. The musical reply, by the choir or congregation, to what is said or sung by the priest or officiant.

Responsory. 1. That psalm, or part of one, sung between the missal lessons.—2. The Gradual.—3. A Respond; that is, a part of a psalm (formerly an entire psalm) sung between the lessons at the canonical hours.

Rest. A pause or interval of silence between two tones; hence, the sign indicating such a pause. See "Notes and Rests," p. viii.

Restez (Fr., res-tā′). "Stay there!" In music for bow instruments this direction means (*a*) "Play on the same string," or (*b*) "Remain in the same position (shift)."

Retardation. 1. A holding back, decreasing in speed.—2. A suspension resolving upward.

Retarded progression. A suspension resolving upward.

Retarded resolution. See Resolution.

Retenu. French for Ritenuto, holding back.

Retrograde. Performing a melody backwards; a crab movement.

Réveil (Fr., rā-vä′ēu). ⎫
Reveille. ⎭
The military signal for rising.

Reverse motion. Contrary motion.

Reversion. Retrograde imitation.

Rapsodie (Fr., răhp-sŏh-dē′). A Rhapsody; generally an instrumental fantasia on folk songs or on motives taken from primitive national music.

Rhythm. The measured movement of similar tone-groups; that is, the effect produced by the systematic grouping of tones with reference to regularity both in their accentuation and in their succession as equal or unequal in time value. *A Rhythm* is, therefore, a tone-group serving as a pattern for succeeding identical groups.

Rhythm and blues. A type of black, urban, popular music combining the elements of strong repetitive rhythms, simple melodies and harmonies and blues. Precursor of early rock 'n' roll.

Rhythm section. Percussion section in a jazz band consisting of piano, bass, and drums, supplying the main beat.

Ribattuta (It., rē-băht-too′tăh). 1. A Beat 3.—2. A device for beginning a trill by dwelling longer on the principal tone than on the auxiliary.

Ribs. The curved sides of the violin, connecting belly and back.

Ricercare (It., rē-châr-kăh′rĕh). Instrumental composition of the 16th and 17th centuries generally characterized by imitative treatment of the theme or themes.

Riddle canon. A canon which is not written out so that the performer must find out when the imitating voices must come in.

Rigadoon. A lively French dance, generally in 4/4 time (sometimes 2/2, rarely 6/4) with an *Auftakt* of a quarter note; it consists of 3 or 4 reprises.

Rigaudon (Fr., rē-goh-dŏhn′).
Rigodino (It., rē-gŏh-dē′nŏh).
Rigodone (It., rē-gŏh-doh′nĕh).
 A rigadoon.

Rigor (It., rē-gohr′). ⎫
Rigore (It., rē-goh′rĕh). ⎭
  Rigor, strictness . . . *Al* (or *con*) *rigore di tempo* (or *a rigor di tempo*), in strict time.

Rigoroso (It., rē-gŏh-roh′sŏh). In strict time.

Rilasciando (It., rē-lăh-shăhn′dŏh). ⎫
Rilasciante (It., rē-lăh-shăhn′tĕh). ⎭
  RALLENTANDO.

Rimettendo (It., rē-met-ten′dŏh). ⎫
Rimettendosi (It., —ten′dŏh-sē). ⎭
  "Resuming" a preceding tempo, whether after accelerating or retarding.

Rinforzando (It., rin-for-tsăhn′dŏh). ⎫
Rinforzato (It., rin-for-tsah′tŏh). ⎭
  With special emphasis; indicates a sudden increase in loudness, either for a tone or chord, or throughout a phrase or short passage.

Rinforzare, senza (It., sen′tsăh rin-for-tsah′rĕh). Without growing louder.

Ripetizione (It., rē-pĕh-tē-tsē-oh′nĕh). Repetition.

Ripieno (It., rē-p'yâ′nŏh). "Filling up"; "supplementary." 1. A *ripieno* part is one reinforcing the leading orchestral parts by doubling them or by filling in the harmony.—2. In scores, *ripieno* is a direction calling for the entrance of the full string band (or, in military music, the clarinets, oboes, etc.).—3. A combination stop drawing all registers of any given manual.

Ripigliando (It., rē-pēl-yăhn′dŏh). Resuming.

Ripigliare (It., rē-pēl-yah′rĕh). To resume.

Riposatamente (It., rē-pŏh-săh-tăh-men′tĕh). ⎫
Riposato (It., rē-pōh-sah′tŏh). ⎬
Riposo, con (It., kŏhn rē-pô′sŏh). ⎭
  In a calm, tranquil manner; reposefully.

Riprendendo (It., rē-pren-den′dŏh). Resuming; *riprendendo poco a poco il tempo,* gradually regaining the preceding rate of speed.

Riprendere (It., rē-pren′dĕh-rĕh). To resume; *stringendo per riprendere il* 1^0 *tempo,* hastening, in order to regain the former tempo.

Risentito (It., rē-sen-tē′tŏh). Energetic, vigorous; expressive.

Risolutamente (It., rē-sŏh-lŏŏ-tăh-men′tĕh).

Risolutezza, con (It., kŏhn rē-sŏh-lŏŏ-tet′săh).

Risoluto (It., rē-sŏh-loo′tŏh).

Risoluzione, con (It., kŏhn rē-sŏh-lŏŏ-tsē′oh′nĕh).
In a resolute, vigorous, decided style.

Risvegliato (It., rē-svăl-yah′tŏh). Lively, animated.

Ritardando (It., rē-tar-dăhn′dŏh). Growing slower and slower.

Ritardare, senza (It., sen′tsăh rē-tar-dah′rĕh). Without slackening the pace.

Ritardato (It., rē-tar-dah′tŏh). At a slower pace.

Ritenendo (It., rē-tĕh-nen′dŏh).
Ritenente (It., rē-tĕh-nen′tĕh).
RALLENTANDO.

Ritenuto (It., rē-tĕh-noo′tŏh). Held back; at a slower rate of speed.

Ritmico (It., rit′mē-kŏh). Rhythmical; MISURATO.

Ritmo (It., rit′mŏh). Rhythm.

Ritornello (It., rē-tor-nel′lŏh).
Ritournelle (Fr., rē-toor-nel′).
1. The burden of a song.—2. A repeat.—3. In accompanied vocal works, an instrumental prelude, interlude, or post-lude (refrain).—4. In a concerto, the orchestral refrain.

Robustamente (It., rŏh-bŏŏ-stăh-men′tĕh).
Robusto (It., rŏh-bŏŏ′stŏh).
Firmly and boldly.

Rock. A term that covers a variety of popular American styles of the 1960's and 1970's: *acid rock, folk rock, hard rock, jazz rock, mellow rock, punk rock, soft rock,* etc. It is an outgrowth of the ROCK 'N' ROLL of the 1950's, but features amplified guitars and keyboards.

Rock 'n' roll. A popular American style of the 1950's that emerged from the black ethnic style of RHYTHM AND BLUES. As opposed to the prevailing popular style of the time, which featured singers with smooth orchestral background, rock 'n' roll featured a percussively heavy reinforcement of the meter (beat) played by JAZZ-like combos consisting of tenor saxophone, piano, bass, drums, and sometimes guitar. BLUES harmonic structures were common, but without the characteristic BLUE NOTES or blues mood.

Rococo. An architectural term applied to music, descriptive of the ornamental type of composition current from about 1725 to 1775. As a musical period, it overlaps and joins late Baroque and early Classicism.

Rohr-flöte (Ger., rōhr′-flö′te). ("Reed flute"), a diapason organ stop.

Rohr-quint (Ger., rōhr′-quĭnt). ("Reed fifth"), an organ stop which sounds a fifth above the diapasons.

Roll. 1. A tremolo or trill on the drum. The sign in notation is

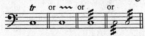

Long roll, the prolonged and reiterated drum signal to troops, for attack or rally.—2. In organ playing, a rapid arpeggio.—3. On the tambourine, the rapid and reiterated hither- and thither-stroke with the knuckles.

Romance. Originally, a ballad, or popular tale in verse, in the Romance dialect; now, a title for epico-lyrical songs, or of short instrumental pieces of sentimental or romantic cast, and without special form.—The French romance is a simple love ditty; *Romances sans paroles* [rŏh-mähns′ sähn päh-rŏhl′], "Songs without Words."

Romanesca. A type of court dance which originated in the Roman countryside in Italy in the 17th century.

Romantic. In music history, the period from about 1815 to c. 1910, overlapping with late Classicism on one end, and Impressionism and Expressionism on the other end.

Romanza. Italian term for a short romantic song or a solo instrumental piece.

Rondeau. A medieval French song with instrumental accompaniment, consisting of an aria and a choral refrain.

Rondel. A type of rondeau.

Rondo (It., Rondò [rŏhn-doh′]). An instrumental piece in which the leading theme (I) is repeated, alternating with the others. A typical pattern, with letters representing thematic sections, would be: A-B-A-C-A-B-A.

Root. The lowest note of a chord in the fundamental position.

Rosalia. A type of a sequence modulating a whole tone higher, popular in semiclassical pieces of the 19th century; named after an Italian song *Rosalia mia cara.*

Rota. A round; also a Latin name for a *hurdy-gurdy.*

Rotondo (It., rŏh-tŏhn′dŏh). Round, full.

Roulade (Fr., roo-lähd′). A grace consisting of a run or *arpeggio* from one principal melody tone to another; a vocal or instrumental flourish.

Roulante. French for rolling; *caisse roulante* is a tenor drum.

Round. A kind of vocal canon at the unison, without coda; sometimes with an harmonic support or accompaniment, the *pes.*

Roundelay. A lay or song containing some continued reiteration or refrain.

Rovescio (It., roh-vĕs′shoh). An inverse motion; *al rovescio* usually means a retrograde or a crab movement, but it may also indicate the inversion of intervals in a melody, so that upward progressions become downward progressions, and vice versa.

Rubando (It., roo-băhn′dŏh). Performing in a *rubato* style . . . *Affrettando e rubando il tempo,* perform with increasing speed, and dwell on accented tones.

Rubato (It., roo-băh′tŏh). "Robbed"; meaning "dwell on, and (often almost insensibly) prolong prominent melody tones or chords." This requires an equivalent acceleration of less prominent tones, which are thus "robbed" of a portion of their time value.

Ruhig (Ger., roo′īyh). Quiet, calm, tranquil.

Rührung (Ger., rü′rŏŏng^k). Emotion.

Rumba. A syncopated Cuban dance music that was popular in the United States in the 1930's–1950's.

Run. 1. A rapid scale passage; in vocal music, usually such a passage sung to one syllable.—2. The wind in the wind-chest (organ) *runs* when it leaks into a groove.

Rustico (It., rŏŏ′stē-kŏh). Rural, pastoral.

Ruvidamente (It., roo-vē-dăh-men′tĕh). ⎫
Ruvido (It., rŏŏ′vē-dŏh). ⎬
In a rough, harsh style. ⎭

Rythmé (Fr., rit-mā′). Measured . . . *Bien rythmé,* well-balanced and elegant in rhythmical effect.

S

S. Stands for *Segno* in the phrases *al Segno, dal Segno;* for *Senza, Sinistra, Solo, Soprano, Sordini;* and for *Subito* in thr phrase *Volti subito* (V.S.).

Sackbut. 1. Early form of trombone.—2. In the Bible, the translation of *sabbek,* supposed to have been a harp-like instrument.

Saite (Ger., zī′tĕ). A string.

Salicet.
Salicional.

An organ stop having open metal flue pipes, usually of 8′ pitch, also of 4′, 2′, and (on the pedal) 16′ pitch, with mellow, reedy tone.

Salmo. Italian for psalm.

Salsa. Modern Latin American dance in a raucous rhythmic manner; *salsa* means "sauce" in Spanish.

Saltarella, Saltarello (It., săhl-tăh-rel′lăh, -lŏh). A second division in many 16th-century dance tunes, in triple time,

the skipping step marked in the rhythm $\underline{}$.

—Also, an Italian dance in 3/4 or 6/8 time.

Saltato (It., săhl-tah′tŏh). See SPRINGING BOW.

Salto (It., săhl′tŏh). Leap; *di salto,* by a leap or leaps.—Also, skip or "cut."

Samba. Popular dance from Brazil.

Sanctus. See MASS.

Sanft (Ger., zăhnft). Soft, low.

Sans (Fr., săhn). Without.

Saraband.
Sarabanda (It., săh-răh-băhn′dăh).
Sarabande (Fr., săh-răh-bahn′d).
Sarabande (Ger., săh-răh-băhn′dĕ).

A stately dance of Spanish or Oriental origin. The instrumental *S.* has usually two 8-measure reprises, in slow tempo and triple time; its place in the Suite, as the slowest movement, is before the Gigue.

Sardana. A rapid, rustic dance of Catalonia.

Sarrusophone. A brass wind instrument with a double reed, invented (1863) by and named after the bandmaster Sarrus of Paris.

Satz (Ger., săhtz). Movement, as of a sonata or symphony.

Saudade (Port., săh-oo-dăh′dē). A Brazilian dance characterized by nostalgia or longing.

Sautillé (Fr., soh-tē-yā′). Technique of string playing with a bouncing bow.

Saxhorn. A brass wind instrument invented c. 1840 by Adolphe Sax, a Belgian. It is essentially an improved key bugle or ophicleide, having from 3 to 5 valves instead of keys.

Saxophone. A metal wind instrument invented about 1840 by Adolphe Sax of Dinant-sur-Meuse, Belgium, having a clarinet mouthpiece with single reed, the key mechanism and fingering also resembling those of the clarinet. It has a mellow, penetrating tone of veiled quality.

Saxotromba. A valve trumpet invented by Sax.

Sbalzato (It., zbăhl-tsah′tŏh). Dashingly, impetuously.

Scale. 1. The series of tones which form, (*a*) any major or minor key (*diatonic* scale), or (*b*) the *chromatic* scale of successive semitonic steps.—2. The compass of a voice or instrument; also, the series of tones producible on a wind instrument.—3. In the tubes of wind instruments (especially organ pipes), the ratio between width of bore and length.

Scat singing. A type of jazz performance in which a singer improvises nonsense words, sometimes imitating the sounds produced by musical instruments.

Scemando (It., shĕh-măhn′dŏh). Same as DIMINUENDO.

Scena (It., shâ′năh). An accompanied dramatic solo, consisting of arioso and recitative passages, and often ending with an aria.

Schalkhaft (Ger., shăhlk′hăft). Roguish, sportive, wanton.

Schallplatte (Ger., shăhl′-plăht-tĕ). Phonograph record.

Schaurig (Ger., show′rĭyh). In a style expressive of (or calculated to inspire) mortal dread; weirdly.

Schelmisch (Ger., shĕl'mish). Joking, roguish.

Scherzhaft (Ger., shârts'hähft). Sportive; jocose, burlesque.

Scherzando (It., skâr-tsähn'dŏh). ⎫
Scherzante (It., skâr-tsähn'tĕh). ⎪
Scherzevole (It., skâr-tsa'vŏh-lĕh). ⎬
Scherzoso (It., skâr-tsoh'sŏh). ⎭
In a playful, sportive, toying manner; lightly, jestingly.

Scherzo (It., skâr'tsŏh). A joke, jest.—1. An instrumental piece of a ligh , piquant, humorous character.—2. A vivacious movement in the symphony, with strongly marked rhythm and sharp and unexpected contrasts in rhythm and harmony; usually the third movement.

Schiettamente (It., skē-et-täh-men'tĕh). ⎫
Schiettezza, con (It., kŏhn—tet'säh). ⎬
Schietto (It., skē-et'tŏh). ⎭
Simply, quietly; neatly, deftly.

Schlag (Ger., shläyh). A beat or stroke; *Schlaginstrumente,* percussion instruments.

Schleppen (Ger., shlep'pen). To drag, retard ... *Nicht schleppen,* do not drag.

Schleppend (Ger., shlep'pent). Dragging.

Schluss (Ger., shlŏŏss). Close, cadence; end.

Schlüssel (Ger. shlüsel). Clef.

Schmachtend (Ger., shmah'tent). Languishing(ly), longing(ly).

Schmeichelnd (Ger., shmī'yhelnt). Flatteringly; in a coaxing, caressful style.

Schmelzend (Ger., shmel'tsĕnt). "Melting," lyrical.

Schmerzhaft (Ger., shmârts'häft). ⎫
Schmerzlich (Ger., shmârts'līyh). ⎬
Painful(ly), sorrowful(ly), plaintive(ly).

Schmetternd (Ger., shmet′ternt). A term calling for brass instruments to be played with a blared or "brassy" tone.

Schnell (Ger., shnel). Fast, quick, rapid . . . *Schneller,* faster; *nach und nach schneller,* gradually faster.

Schottische (shot′ish). A round dance in 2/4 time, a variety of the Polka.

Schwach (Ger., shväh). Weak; soft, faint, low.

Schwächer (Ger., shvĕyh′er). Softer, fainter.

Schwebend (Ger., shvä′bent). Floating, soaring; buoyant(ly); in a lofty, elevated style.

Schwegelpfeife (Ger., shvä′gel-pfī′fĕ). An open flue pipe in the organ, of 8′ or 4′ pitch, the pipes slightly tapering at the top.

Schweizerflöte (Ger., shvī′tser-flötĕ). An 8′ metal flue stop in the organ, of penetrating tone; the same of 4′ pitch is called *Schweizerpfeife;* of 16′ pitch, on the pedal, *Schweizerflötenbass.*

Schwellen (Ger., shvel′len). To swell, as in an organ.

Schwellwerk (Ger., shvel′verk). Swell organ.

Schwer (Ger., shvār). Heavy, ponderous; difficult.

Schwermüt(h)ig (Ger., shvār′mü′tīyh). Sad, melancholy.

Schwindend (Ger., shvin′dent). Dying away, *morendo.*

Schwung, mit (Ger., mit schvŏŏng[k]). ⎫
Schwungvoll (Ger., shvŏŏng[k]′fōhl). ⎬
    Swingingly; buoyantly; with sweep and passion.

Scintillante (It., shin-til-lähn′tĕh). Sparkling, brilliant.

Scioltamente (It., shŏl-täh-men′tĕh). ⎫
Scioltezza, con (kŏhn shŏhl-tet′säh). ⎬
Sciolto,-a (It., shôl-tŏh, -täh). ⎭
    Freely, fluently, nimbly.

Scivolando (It., shē-vŏh-lähn′dŏh). Same as *Glissando,* in piano playing.

Scoop. Vocal tones are "scooped" when taken, instead of by a firm and just attack, by a rough *portamento* from a lower tone.

Scordatura (It., skŏhr-dăh-too′răh). A change in the ordinary tuning of a stringed instrument, to obtain special effects or easier execution.

Score. A systematic arrangement of the vocal or instrumental parts of a composition on separate staves one above the other ... *Close* or *compressed score,* a Short score ... *Full* or *orchestral score,* one in which each vocal and instrumental part has a separate staff ... *Pianoforte score,* a piano arrangement of an orchestral score, the words of any leading vocal parts being inserted *above* the music without their notes... *Open score,* a Full score ... *Organ score,* like Pianoforte score, sometimes with a third staff for pedal bass... *Short score,* any abridged arrangement or skeleton transcript; also, a 4-part vocal score on 2 staves ... *Supplementary score,* one appended to the body of the score when all parts cannot be written on one page ... *Vocal score,* that of an *a cappella* composition; also, the vocal parts written out in full, usually on separate staves, the piano accompaniment being arranged or compressed (from the full instrumental score) on 2 staves below the rest.

Scoring. Instrumentation, orchestration.

Scorrendo (It., skŏhr-ren′dŏh). ⎫
Scorrevole (It., skŏhr-rā′vŏh-lĕh). ⎬
    Fluent, flowing, gliding.

Scotch snap or **catch.** The rhythmic motive 𝄞♪. found in many Scotch airs.

Scozzese, alla (It., ăhl′lăh skŏht-tsā′zĕh). In Scotch style.

Sdegno, con (It., kŏhn zdăn′yŏh). ⎫
Sdegnosamente (It., zdăn-yŏh-săh-men′tĕh). ⎬
Sdegnoso (It., zdăn-yoh′sŏh). ⎭
    In a style expressing scorn, disdain, wrath, or indignation.

Sdrucciolando (It., zdrŏŏt-chŏh-lähn′dŏh). Sliding, *glissando*.

Se (It., sā). If . . . *Se bisogna,* if necessary . . . *Se piace,* if you please.

Sea chanty. A seafaring song.

Sec (Fr., sek). Dry, simple.

Secche (It., sek′kĕh). Plural of SECCO.

Secco (It., sek′kŏh). Dry, simple; not dwelt on . . . *Recitativo secco,* one with a simple figured-bass accompaniment.

Sécheresse, avec (Fr., ăh-vēk sā-shŭ-ress′). Dryly; without dwelling on or embellishing.

Second. 1. The interval between 2 conjunct degrees.—2. The alto part or voice.—3. Performing a part lower in pitch than first, as second bass, second violins.—4. Lower in pitch, as second string.—5. Higher; as second line of staff.

Secondary chords. Subordinate chords.

Secondo,-a (It., sĕh-kŏhn′dŏh, -dăh). Second; also a second part or performer in a duet.

Section. A short division (one or more periods) of a composition, having distinct rhythmic and harmonic boundaries; specifically, half a phrase.

Secular music. Music other than that intended for worship and devotional purposes.

Seelenvoll (Ger., zeh′len-fol). Soulfully.

Segno (It., sān′yŏh). A sign . . . *Al segno,* to the sign; *Dal segno,* from the sign;—directions to the performer to turn back and repeat from the place marked by the sign (𝄋) to the word *Fine,* or to a double-bar with hold (⌢).

Segue (It., sā′gwĕh). 1. Follows; *segue l'aria,* the aria follows.—2. Simile.

Seguendo (It., sĕh-gwen′dŏh). }
Seguente (It., sĕh-gwen′tĕh). }

Following ... *Seguendo il canto,* same as *col canto, colla voce.*

Seguidilla (Sp., sā-gwē-dil′yäh). A Spanish dance in triple time, some varieties being slow, others lively; usually in minor, accompanied by guitar and voice, and at times by the castanets.

Sehnsucht, mit (Ger., mit zān′zŏŏht).⎱
Sehnsüchtig (Ger., zān′züyh′tīyh). ⎰
　Longingly; in a style expressive of yearning.

Sehr (Ger., zār). Very.

Semibiscroma. Sixty-fourth note in Italian.

Semibreve. A whole note.

Semicroma. Sixteenth note in Italian.

Semiminima. Quarter note in Italian.

Semiquaver. Sixteenth note.

Semitone. A half tone.

Semplice (It., sem′plē-chĕh).⎱
Semplicemente (It., sem-plē-chĕh-men′tĕh).⎰
　In a simple, natural, unaffected style.

Sempre (It., sem′prĕh). Always, continually; throughout.

Sensibile (It., sen-sē′bĕ-lĕh). Audible; sensitive ... *Nota sensibile,* leading-note.

Sensibilità, con (It., kŏhn sen-sē-bē-lē-tah′). With feeling.

Sentence. A passage of symmetrical rhythmic form, generally not over 16 measures long, and usually ending with a full tonic cadence.

Sentimentale (It., sen-tē-men-tah′lĕh).⎱
Sentimento, con (It., kŏhn sen-tē-men′tŏh).⎰
　Feelingly.

Sentito (It., sen-tē′tŏh). With feeling, expression, special emphasis.

Senza (It., sen′tsäh). Without. (Abbreviated S.)—*Senza di* *slentare,* without retarding . . . *S. misura,* "without measure," that is, not in strict time . . . *S. passione,* without passion, quietly . . . *S. piatti,* "drum alone" (where one performer plays the cymbals and bass drum) . . . *S. rallentare,* without retarding . . . *S. sordini,* see SORDINO . . . *S. suono,* "without tone," that is, spoken . . . *S. tempo,* same as *senza misura.*

Sept. The interval of a Seventh.

Sept chord. Seventh chord.

Septet(te). A concerted composition for seven voices or instruments.

Septimole (Ger., sep-tē-moh′lĕ).⎫
Septole (Ger., sep-toh′lĕ). ⎭
 A septuplet.

Septuor (Fr., sep-tü-ohr′). A septet.

Septuplet. A group of 7 equal notes to be performed in the time of 4 or 6 of the same kind in the regular rhythm.

Sequence. 1. The repetition, at different pitch levels, oftener than twice in succession, of a melodic motive.—2. In the Roman Catholic Church, a kind of hymn.

Serenade. 1. An "evening song"; especially such a song sung by a lover before his lady's window.—2. An instrumental composition imitating the above in style.

Serenata (It., sĕh-rĕh-nah′täh). 1. A species of dramatic cantata in vogue during the 18th century.—2. An instrumental composition midway between Suite and Symphony, but freer in form than either, having 5, 6, or more movements, and in chamber music style.—3. See SERENADE.

Serenità, con (It., kŏhn sĕh-rĕh-nē-tah′).⎫
Sereno (It., sĕh-rā′nŏh). ⎭
 In a serene, tranquil style.

Serial music. Modern technique of composition in which all thematic materials are derived from a series of 12 different notes of the chromatic scale, graduated dynamics, a set of different rhythms and different instrumental timbres. Serial music represents an expansion of the 12-tone method of composition into the domain of note values, dynamics and instrumental timbres.

Serietà, con (It., kŏhn sĕh-rē-ĕh-tah′). Seriously.

Serio,-a (It., sâ′rē-ŏh, -ăh). Serious ... *Opera seria,* grand or tragic opera ... *Tenore serio,* dramatic tenor.

Serioso (It., sĕh-rē-oh′sŏh). In a serious, grave, impressive style.

Serpent. 1. A bass wind instrument invented by Canon Guillaume of Auxerre in 1590. Nearly obsolete.—2. In the organ, a reed stop.

Serré (Fr., sĕh-rā′, *pressed*). Playing faster and with more excitement.

Sesquialtera (L., sĕs-kwē-ahl′tĕ-rah). In the organ, either a mutation stop a fifth above the fundamental tone, or (usually) a compound stop of from 2 to 5 ranks.

Sestet. A Sextet.

Sestetto (It., ses-tet′tŏh). A sextet.

Sestole, Sestolet. A sextuplet.

Settimino (It., set-tē-mē′nŏh). A septet.

Seventeenth. 1. Interval of 2 octaves plus a third.—2. Same as Tierce (organ stop).

Seventh chord. A chord of the 7th, composed of a root with its third, fifth, and seventh.

Severamente (It., sĕh-vĕh-răh-men′tĕh). ⎫
Severità, con (It., kŏhn sĕh-vĕh-rē-tah′). ⎬
Severo (It., sĕh-vâ′rŏh). ⎭
  Strictly, with rigid observance of tempo and expression marks.

Sext. 1. The interval of a sixth.—2. The office of the fourth

Canonical Hour.—3. A compound organ stop of 2 ranks (a 12th and a 17th) a sixth apart.

Sextet. A concerted composition for 6 voices or instruments, or for 6 *obbligato* voices with instrumental accompaniment.

Sextole, Sextolet. A sextuplet.

Sextuplet. A group of 6 equal notes to be performed in the time of 4 of the same kind in the regular rhythm. In the *true* sextuplet the 1st, 3d, and 5th notes are accented; the *false* sextuplet is simply a double triplet.

Sfogato (It., sfŏh-gah′tŏh). "Exhaled"; a direction, in vocal music, to sing lightly and airily.—*Soprano sfogato,* a high soprano voice.

Sforzando (It., sfŏhr-tsăhn′dŏh). ⎫
Sforzato (It., sfŏhr-tsah′tŏh). ⎬
   (Written, *sfz, sf,* > ∧ ⸙). A direction to perform the tone

or chord with special stress, or marked and sudden emphasis.

Sfumate (It., sfŏŏ-mah′tĕh). ⎫
Sfumato (It., sfŏŏ-mah′tŏh). ⎬
   Very lightly, like a vanishing smoke-wreath.

Shading. 1. In the interpretation of a composition, the combination and alternation of any or all the varying degrees of tone power between *fortissimo* and *pianissimo,* for obtaining artistic effect.—2. The placing of anything so near the top of an organ pipe as to affect the vibrating column of air within.

Shake. A trill . . . *Shaked graces,* the shaked Beat, Backfall, Cadent, and Elevation, and the Double Relish (all obsolete).

Shanty. A characteristic song of the English working class in olden times; the word comes from the French *chanter,* "to sing."

Sharp. The character ♯, which raises the pitch of the note before which it is set by a semitone; the Double sharp, symbolized by a cross or the letter X, raises the note by 2 semitones.

Sharp (*adjective*). 1. (Of tones or instruments.) Too high in pitch.—2. (Of intervals.) Major or augmented.—3. (Of keys.) Having a sharp or sharps in the signature.—4. (Of organ stops.) Shrill.—5. (Of digitals; *plural.*) The black keys; or any white key a semitone above another.

Shawm. A medieval high-pitched wind instrument.

Shift. In playing the violin, etc., a change by the left hand from the first position; the 2d position is called the *half-shift,* the 3d the *whole shift,* and the 4th the *double shift.* When out of the 1st position the player is "on the shift," and *shifting up* or *down,* as the case may be.

Shimmy. An American dance in quick ragtime rhythm.

Shofar. An ancient Jewish ritual trumpet, made from a ram's horn.

Si (It., sē). 1. The 7th solmisation syllable.—2. One; it . . . *Si leva il sordino,* take off the mute . . . *Si levano i sordini,* take off the mutes . . . *Si piace, si libet,* at pleasure . . . *Si replica,* repeat . . . *Si segue,* proceed . . . *Si tace,* be silent . . . *Si volta,* turn over . . . *Si ha s'immaginar la battuta di* 6/8, imagine the time to be 6/8.

Siciliana (It., sē-chē-lē-ah′năh).⎫
Sicilienne (Fr., sē-sē-l'yen′).   ⎭
  Dance of the Sicilian peasants; a kind of pastorale in moderately slow tempo and 6/8 or 12/8 time, frequently in minor . . . *Alla siciliana,* in the style of the above.

Side drum. The most commonly used drum in symphonic bands and in symphonic scores; it is also called SNARE DRUM.

Sight reading. An ability to read unfamiliar music with ease. In singing, it is synonymous with solfeggio. All professional instrumentalists must be able to read at sight as a matter of routine, but there are some extraordinary pianists who can play complicated works with great precision and fluency at sight.

Signal horn. A bugle.

Signature. The signs set at the head of the staff at the beginning of a piece or movement; the *Key signature* is the chromatic sign or signs (sharps or flats); the *Time signature* is the figures or signs indicating the measure.

Silenzio (It., sē-len′tsē-ŏh). Silence . . . *Lurgo silenzio,* a long pause.

Similar motion. Motion of voices in the same direction, as distinguished from contrary motion.

Simile (It., sē′mē-lĕh). Similarly; a direction to perform the following measures or passages in the same style as the preceding . . . *Simile mark,* ⨊ or ⨋ ; means that a measure or group must be repeated.

Simple. (Of tones or intervals.) Not compound.—(Of counterpoint, imitation, rhythm, etc.) Not compound or complex, undeveloped, not varied.

Simplement (Fr., săn-plᵘ-mähn′). Simply, *semplice.*

Sinfonia (It., sin-fŏh-nē′äh). 1. A symphony.—2. An opera overture.

Sinfonie (Ger., sin-fŏh-nē′). Symphony.

Sinfonietta (It., sin-fŏh-nē-ĕt′ah). A small symphony, sometimes for a chamber orchestra.

Singbar (Ger., zingᵏ′bar). Singable; *cantabile . . . Sehr singbar vorzutragen,* perform in a very singing style.

Singend (Ger., zing′ent). Singing, melodious, *cantabile.*

Singhiozzando (It., sin-g′yŏht-tsähn′dŏh). Sobbing; catching the breath.

Singspiel (Ger., zingᵏ′shpēl). A type of German opera established during the 18th century; usually light, and characterized by spoken interludes.

Singstimme (Ger., zing^k′shtim′mĕ). The singing voice; the voice.

Sinistra (It., sē-nĭ′străh). Left ... *Mano sinistra* (m. s.), left hand ... *Colla sinistra,* with the left hand.

Sino (It., sē′nŏh). To, up to, as far as, till ... *Sino* (or *sin'*) *al fine,* to the end.

Sistrum. An ancient instrument which was used in Egyptian religious ritual; it had a semicircular metal frame with crossbars overhung with tinkling rings.

Sitar. A popular instrument of India, in the shape of a lute, plucked with a plectrum.

Sixth. Interval containing 6 diatonic degrees.

Sixteenth note. Half the value of an eighth note.

Sixth chord. First inversion of a triad.

Six-four chord. Second inversion of a triad.

Skip. Melodic progression by an interval wider than a Second; *disjunct* progression.

Slanciante (It., zlăhn-chăhn′tĕh).
Slanciato (It., zlăhn-chah′tŏh).
    "Thrown off" lightly and deftly, or forcibly and vehemently.

Slancio, con (It., kŏhn zlăhn′chŏh). With dash, vehemence; impetuously. (Often *con islancio.*)

Slancio, di (It.). The direct and "hammer-like" attack of a higher or lower tone, contrasted with the "carry" of the Portamento. (Also *di posto.*)

Slargando (It., zlar-găhn′dŏh).
Slargandosi (It., zlar-găhn′dŏh-sē).
    Growing slower.

Slargato (It., zlar-gah′tŏh). Slower; *più sostenuto.*

Slentando (It., zlen-tăn′dŏh). Growing slower.

Slide. 1. The movable U-shaped tube in the trombone, etc.—2. In the organ, a slider.—3. Three or four swiftly ascending or descending scale tones.—4. On a violin bow, that part of the nut which slides along the stick.

Slide horn.
Slide trombone.
Slide trumpet. }
One played by the use of a slide instead of keys or valves.

Slur. A curved line under or over 2 or more notes, signifying that they are to be played *legato*. In vocal music the slur unites notes to be sung in one breath; the notes so sung are called a *slur*.

Slurred melody. One in which two or more tones are sung to one syllable: opposed to *syllabic* melody.

Small octave. See "Table of Clefs," p. xi.

Small orchestra. The usual orchestra minus the trombones, 2 horns, and perhaps the clarinets and kettledrums.

Smaniante (It., zmăh-nē-ăhn′těh). }
Smanioso (It., zmăh-nē-oh′sŏh). }
In an impetuous, passionate style.

Sminuendo (It., zmē-nŏŏ-en′dŏh). Same as DIMINUENDO.

Sminuito (It., zmē-nŏŏ-ē′tŏh). More softly.

Smorendo (It., zmŏh-ren′dŏh). Dying away.

Smorfioso (It., zmŏhr-fē-oh′sŏh). With affected expression.

Smorzando (It., zmŏhr-tsăhn′dŏh). }
Smorzato (It., zmŏhr-tsăh′tŏh). }
Dying away.

Snare drum. A side drum, across the lower head of which are stretched several gut strings, the "snares," whose jarring against the head reinforces the tone.

Soave (It., sŏh-ah′vĕh).

Soavemente (It., sŏh-ăh-vĕh-men′tĕh).

Soavità, con (It., kŏhn sŏh-ăh-vē-tah′).
    Suavely, sweetly, softly, flowingly.

Soffocato (It., sŏhf-fŏh-kah′tŏh). Muffled, damped; choked.

Soft pedal. The left pedal on the piano reducing the sound by
    shifting the keyboard, so that only 2 of the 3 strings in the
    middle register of the piano are struck by the hammers.

Soggetto (It., sŏhd-jet′tŏh). Subject, theme.

Sognando (It., sŏhn-yăhn′dŏh). Dreaming, dreamily.

Soh. Stands for *Sol,* in Tonic Sol-fa.

Sol (It., sôl). The fifth of the Aretinian syllables, and name of
    the note *G* in France, Italy, etc.

Solenne (It., sŏh-len′nĕh).

Solennemente (It., sŏh-len-nĕh-men′tĕh).

Solennità, con (It., kŏhn sŏh-len-nē-tah′).
    Solemn, solemnly, with solemnity, in a lofty style.

Sol-fa. 1. To sing *solfeggi,* especially to the solmisation sylla-
    bles.—2. Solmisation, and the syllables sung in it.

Solfeggio (It., sŏhl-fed′jŏh; plural *solfeggi* [-jē]). A vocal
    exercise either on one vowel, or on the solmisation-sylla-
    bles, or to words.

Soli (It., soh′lī). The plural of solo in Italian.

Solid chord. Flat chord.

Solito (It., sô′lē-tŏh). Accustomed, habitual . . . *Al solito,* as
    usual.

Solmisation. A method of teaching the scales and intervals
    by syllables, the invention of which is ascribed to Guido
    d'Arezzo (born 990?). It was based on the hexachord, or
    6-tone scale; the first 6 tones of the major scale, *c d e f g a,*
    were named *ut, re, mi, fa, sol, la.* The 7th syllable *si,* for the
    leading tone, was added during the 17th century; about the

same time, the name *ut* for *C* was changed to *do,* except in France.

Solo (It., soh′lŏh). Alone.—*Solo* is a piece or passage for a single voice or instrument, or in which one voice or instrument predominates. In orchestral scores, "Solo" marks a passage where one instrument takes a leading part. In a 2-hand arrangement of a piano concerto, *Solo* marks the entrances of the solo pianoforte.—*Violino solo* means either "violin alone" or "first violin" (accompanied).

Solo organ. A 4th manual controlling solo stops.

Solo pitch. Same as SCORDATURA.

Solo quartet. 1. A quartet consisting of 4 singers (4 "solo voices").—2. A piece or passage in 4 parts for 4 singers.—3. A nonconcerted piece for 4 instruments, one of which has a leading part.

Solo stop. See STOP.

Sombre (Fr., sŏhn′br). Dark, veiled, obscure.

Sommesso,-a (It., sŏhm-mes′sŏh, -säh). Subdued.

Sommo,-a (It., sŏhm′mŏh, -mäh). Utmost, highest, greatest, extreme.—*Con somma espressione,* with intensest feeling.

Son (Fr., sŏhn). Sound; tone.

Sonabile (It., sŏh-nah′bē-lĕh). ⎱
Sonante (It., sŏh-nähn′tĕh). ⎰
Sounding, resounding, sonorous, resonant.

Sonata (It., sŏh-nah′täh). An instrumental composition in 3 or 4 extended movements contrasted in theme, tempo, and mood; usually for a solo instrument or chamber ensemble.

Sonata-concerto form. A combination of the SONATA FORM with the RITORNELLO procedure.

Sonata form. (Also known as *sonata allegro form* and *first movement form.*) This is usually the procedure used for first movements of Classical symphonies, sonatas, and chamber works; it may be used for other movements as well.

Sonate (Fr., soh-naht′). Sonata.

Sonatina (It., sŏh-näh-tē′näh).
Sonatine (Fr., sŏh-näh-tēn′).
Sonatine (Ger., sŏh-näh-tē′nĕ).

A short sonata in 2 or 3 (rarely 4) movements, the first in the characteristic first-movement form, abbreviated.

Sonevole (It., sŏh-nä′vŏh-lĕh). Sonorous, resounding.

Song. A short poem with a musical setting characterized by a structure in simple periods. There are *Folk songs* and *Art songs*; the latter may be either *strophic* (each strophe sung to the same tune, with a change at most in the final one), or *progressively composed* [composed-through].

Song form. A form of composition, either vocal or instrumental, which has 3 sections and 2 themes, the second (contrasting) theme occupying the 2d section.

Sono (It., sô′nŏh). Sound; tone.

Sonoramente (It., sŏh-nŏh-räh-men′tĕh).
Sonore (It., [*plural*] sŏh-nô′rĕh).
Sonorità, con (It., kŏhn sŏh-nŏh-rē-tah′).
Sonoro,-a (It., sŏh-nô′rŏh, -răh).

Sonorously, resoundingly, resonantly, ringingly.

Sopra (It., soh′prah). On, upon; above, over; higher ... In piano music, *sopra* written in the part for either hand means that that hand is to play (reach) *over* the other ... *Sopra una corda,* on one string ... *Come sopra,* as above ... *Nella parte di sopra,* in the higher (or highest) part.

Sopran (Ger., sŏh-prahn′). Soprano.

Sopranino (It., soh-prah-nee′nŏh). "Little soprano"; the highest pitch of the soprano register, as in sopranino saxophones, and sopranino recorders.

Soprano (It., sŏh-prah′nŏh). The highest class of the human voice; the female soprano, or *treble,* has a normal compass from c^1 to a^2; solo voices often reach above c^3, some as high as c^4 ... *Soprano clef,* the *C* clef on the first line ... *S. drammatico, S. giusto,* a female soprano of dramatic power ... *S. leggiero,* a light soprano ... *S. sfogato,* see SFOGATO ... *Soprano string,* the *E* string on the violin.

Sordamente (It., sŏhr-däh-men'tĕh). With a veiled, muffled tone.

Sordino (It., sŏhr-dē'nŏh). 1. A mute; *con sordini,* with the mutes; *senza sordini,* without the mutes; *si levano i sordini,* take off the mutes.—2. Damper (of the piano); *senza sordini,* with damper pedal; so used by Beethoven, who wrote *con sordini* to express the release (raising) of the damper pedal, instead of ✳.

Sortita (It., sŏhr-tē'täh). 1. A closing voluntary.—2. The first number sung by any leading character in an opera. An *Aria di sortita* is, however, also an air at the conclusion of which the singer makes his exit.

Sospirando (It., sŏh-spē-rähn'dŏh). Sighing, sobbing; catching the breath.

Sospirevole (It., sŏh-spē-rä'vŏh-lĕh). ⎫
Sospiroso (It., sŏh-spē-roh'sŏh). ⎬
Sighing deeply; plaintive, mournful. ⎭

Sostenuto (It., sŏh-stĕh-noo'tŏh). Sustained, prolonged.— Standing alone, as a tempo-mark, it is much the same as *Andante cantabile*; it may also imply a *tenuto,* or a uniform rate of decreased speed ... *Più sostenuto* is much the same as *Meno mosso.*—*Sostenuto pedal,* sustaining pedal.

Sotto (It., sŏht'tŏh). Below, under ... In piano music, *sotto* written in the part for either hand means that that hand is to play (reach) *under* the other ... *Sottovoce* (or *sotto voce*), in an undertone, aside, under the breath.

Soubrette (Fr., soo-bret'). In comedy and comedy opera, a maidservant or lady's maid of an intriguing and coquettish character; also applied to various light roles of similar type.

Soul. A style of black rhythm and blues singing.

Sound. A noise of any kind. The word is often inexactly used instead of "tone" (musical tone).

Soundboard. The thin plate of wood placed below or behind the strings of various instruments to reinforce and prolong their tones.—In the organ it is the cover of the windchest.

Sound bow. The thick rim of a bell, against which the clapper strikes.

Sound hole. A hole cut in the belly of a stringed instrument.

Soundpost. In the violin, etc., the small cylindrical wooden prop set inside the body, between belly and back, just behind (nearly beneath) the treble foot of the bridge.

Sourdine (Fr., soor-dēn′). An harmonium stop which partially cuts off the wind supply, so that full chords can be played softly. Also, see SORDINO.

Sousaphone. A spiral type of bass tuba, which is coiled around the player, with a large bellow turned forwards. The sousaphone is named after Sousa, the "March King," who used it often in his bands.

Soutenu (Fr., soo-tĕh-nü′). Held or sustained.

Space. In the staff, the interval between two lines or ledger lines.

Space music. A modern development of performance, in which the placement of musicians and singers is considered as essential to the composition itself; in some modern works, the players are positioned at far distances from one another.

Spasshaft (Ger., shpahs′hähft). *Scherzando.*

Spianato,-a (It., sp′yäh-nah′tŏh, -täh). Smooth, even, tranquil.

Spiccato (It., spik-kah′toh). Sharp staccato. See SPRINGING BOW.

Spigliatezza (It., spēl-yäh-tet′säh). Agility, dexterity.

Spinet (spin′et *or* spī-net′). An obsolete keyboard stringed instrument like a harpsichord, but smaller.

Spinto (It., spin′toh). Compelled, intense; applied to a high voice in expressive emotional opera parts.

Spirito, con (It., kŏhn spē′rē-tōh).

Spiritosamente (It., spē-rē-tōh-säh-men′tĕh).

Spiritoso (It., spē-rē-toh′sŏh).

Spiritedly; with spirit, animation, energy.

Spiritual. A religious song, cultivated by Negro slaves in the South.

Spitze (Ger., shpit-sĕ). 1. Point (of the bow).—2. Toe (in organ playing).

Spitzflöte (Ger., shpits′flö′tĕ). In the organ, an open flue stop of organ metal, tin, or wood, of 8′, 4′, 2′, or 1′ pitch; tone rather thin, but pure and reedy.

Spitzig (Ger., shpit′ziyh). Sharp, pointed.

Sprechstimme (Ger., shpreh′shtim-meh). Literally, "speech song"; inflected spoken singing, with pitches indicated approximately on the music staff. This is a modern technique often used in contemporary opera.

Springing bow. In violin playing, a style of bowing in which the bow is allowed to drop on the string, making it rebound and quit the string between each two notes. There are two varieties: (1) The *Spiccato,* indicated by dots over the notes, and played near the middle of the bow with a loose wrist, for rapid passages in equal notes, employing the wrist stroke throughout for each detached note; (2) the *Saltato,* with a longer fall and higher rebound, generally employed when several equal *staccato* notes are to be taken in one bow.

Square dance. A parlor or country dance, such as a quadrille, performed by several couples in a square formation.

Square time. A popular term for 4/4 time; march time.

Squillante (It., skwil-lähn′tĕh). Ringing, tinkling; piercing.

Stabat Mater (L., stäh′bäht mäh′tĕr). A Latin sequence on the Crucifixion sung in the Roman Catholic liturgy.

Stabile (It., stah′bē-lĕh). Steady, firm.

Staccato (It., stăhk-kah′tŏh). Detached, separated; a style in which the notes played or sung are more or less abruptly disconnected. See SPRINGING BOW.

Staccato mark. A dot ($\dot{\rho}$) or wedge-shaped stroke ($\dot{\rho}$) over a note, the former indicating a less abrupt *staccato* than the latter; the *Mezzo-staccato* is indicated by dotted notes under a slur.

Staff. The 5 parallel lines used in modern notation; Plain-chant uses only 4 . . . *Staff notation,* the staff and all musical signs connected with it . . . *Grand* or *Great staff,* one of 11 lines, Middle *C* occupying the sixth.

Stanchezza, con (It., kŏhn stähn-ket′säh). Wearily, draggingly.

Stanco,-a (It., stähn′kŏh, -käh). Weary, dragging.

Ständchen (Ger., shtän′yhĕn). Serenade.

Stanza. A symmetric unit of a song.

Stark (Ger., shtark). Loud, forcible; *forte.*

Stärker (Ger., shtâr′ker). Louder, stronger; *più forte.*

Steam organ. The Calliope.

Steg (Ger., shteg). The bridge on string instruments; *am Steg,* bowing near the bridge.

Stem. The vertical line attached to a note head.

Stentando (It., sten-tähn′dŏh). Delaying, retarding, dragging.

Stentato (It., sten-tah′tŏh). Retarded, dragged.

Step. A melodic progression of a second.—Also, a degree . . . *Chromatic step,* progression of a chromatic Second . . . *Diatonic step,* progression between neighboring tones of any diatonic scale . . . *Half step,* step of a semitone . . . *Whole step,* step of a whole tone.

Sterbend (Ger., shtär′bent). Dying; *morendo.*

Stesso (It., stes'sŏh). The same ... *Lo stesso* (or *l'istesso*) *movimento,* the same movement.

Stil (Ger., shtēl). ⎫
Stile (It., stē'lĕh). ⎬
Stilo (It., stē'lŏh). ⎭
Style ... *Stile osservato,* strict style, especially of pure vocal music ... *Stile rappresentativo,* dramatic monodic song with instrumental accompaniment in chords; the kind of operatic recitative originating towards the close of the 16th century.

Stillgedackt (Ger., shtil'gĕ-dăhkt'). A soft-toned stopped organ register.

Stimme (Ger., shtim'mĕ). 1. Voice.—2. Part; *mit der Stimme,* COLLA PARTE.—3. Organ stop.—4. Soundpost.

Stimmung (Ger., shtim'mŏŏng^k). Tuning, *accordatura;* pitch; a mood, frame of mind ... *Stimmung halten,* to keep in tune ... *Stimmungsbild,* a "mood-picture," short, characteristic piece.

Stinguendo (It., stin-gwen'dŏh). Dying away.

Stiracchiato (It., stē-răhk-k'yah'tŏh.) ⎫
Stirato (It., stē-rah'tŏh). ⎬
Dragging, delaying.

Stiriana (It., stē-rē-ah'năh). STYRIENNE.

Stop. 1. That part of the organ mechanism which admits and "stops" the flow of wind to the grooves beneath the pipes.—2. A set or row of organ pipes of like character, arranged in graduated succession. These are called *speaking* or *sounding* stops; they are classed as *Flue work* (having flue pipes), and *Reed work* (having reed pipes); the Flue work has 3 subclasses, (a) *Principal work,* having cylindrical flue pipes of diapason quality, (b) *Gedackt work,* having stopped pipes, and (c) *Flute work,* including all flue stops of a scale too broad or too narrow to produce diapason-tone, together with such stopped pipes as have chimneys, and all 3- or 4-sided wooden pipes . . . *Auxiliary stop,* one to be drawn with some other stop or stops, to reinforce the tone of the latter . . . *Complete stop,* one having at least one pipe for each key of the manual to which it belongs . . . *Compound stop,* see MIXTURE STOP . . . *Divided stop,* one the lower half of whose register is controlled by a different stop-knob from the upper, and bears a different name . . . *Flue stop,* one composed of flue pipes . . . *Foundation stop,* one of normal 8′ pitch . . . *Half stop, incomplete* or *imperfect stop,* one producing (about) half the tones of the full scale of its manual . . . *Mechanical stop,* one not having a set of pipes, but governing some mechanical device; such are the couplers, tremulant, bell signal, etc. . . . *Mixture stop,* one with 2 or more ranks of pipes, thus producing 2 or more tones for each key (as the Mixture, Carillon, Cornet, Cymbal) . . . *Mutation stop,* one producing tones a major third or perfect fifth (or a higher octave of either) above the 8′ stops (as the Tierce, Twelfth, Quint) . . . *Partial stop,* a HALF STOP . . . *Pedal stop,* a stop on the pedal . . . *Reed stop,* one composed of reed pipes . . . *Solo stop,* one adapted for the production of characteristic melodic effects, whether on the solo organ or not . . . *Sounding* or *speaking stop,* one having pipes and producing musical tones.—3. (*a*) On the violin, etc., the pressure of a finger on a string, to vary the latter's pitch; a *double stop* is when 2 or more strings are so pressed and sounded simultaneously; (*b*) on wind instruments with finger-holes, the closing of a hole by finger or key to alter the pitch; (*c*) on wind instruments of the trumpet family, the partial closing of the bell by inserting the hand.

Stop knob. The projecting handle of a STOP 1.

Stopped notes. Tones obtained by stopping; opposed to *open.*

Stopped pipes. Organ pipes closed (plugged or covered) at the top; opposed to *open.*

Straccicalando (It., sträht-chē-cäh-lähn′dŏh). Babbling, prattling.

Strain. In general, a song, tune, air, melody; also, some well-defined passage in, or part of, a piece.—Technically, a period, sentence, or short division of a composition; a motive or theme.

Strappare (It., strähp-pah′rĕh). To pluck off; in piano playing, to throw off a note or chord by a rapid, light turn of the wrist.

Strascicando (It., sträh-shē-căhn′dŏh). ⎫
Strascinando (It., sträh-shē-năhn′dŏh). ⎭
Dragging, drawling ... *Strascinando l'arco,* drawing the bow so as to bind the tones.

Strascinare la voce (It., sträh-shē-nah′rĕh läh voh′chĕh). To sing a *portamento* with exaggerated dragging or drawling.

Strathspey (strath-spay′). A lively Scotch dance, somewhat slower than the reel, and also in 4/4 time, but progressing in dotted eighth notes alternating with 16ths, the latter often preceding the former (SCOTCH SNAP).

Stravagante (It., sträh-väh-gähn′tĕh). Extravagant, fantastic, whimsical.

Streichinstrumente (Ger., shtriyh′in-stroo-men′tĕ). Bow instruments.

Streng (Ger., Shtreng^k). Severe(ly), strict(ly).

Strepito, con (It., kŏhn strâ′pē-tŏh). ⎫
Strepitosamente (It., strĕh-pē-tŏh-säh-men′tĕh). ⎬
Strepitoso (It., strĕh-pē-toh′sŏh). ⎭
In a noisy, boisterous, impetuous style.

Stretch. On a keyboard instrument, a wide interval or spread chord whose tones are to be taken simultaneously by the fingers of one hand.

Stretta (It., stret′täh). A closing passage (coda) in swifter tempo than the one preceding . . . *Alla stretta,* in the style of a stretta.

Strette (Fr., stret). A STRETTO.

Strettissimo (It., stret-tis'sē-mŏh). Very hurriedly.

Stretto (It., stret'tŏh). A division of a fugue (usually a final development, for the sake of effect) in which subject and answer follow in such close succession as to overlap.

Stretto,-a (It., stret'tŏh, -tāh). Pressed together, narrowed; hurried . . . *Andante stretto,* same as *Andante agitato* . . . *Stretto pedale,* the quick, deft shifting of the loud piano pedal, in a strongly marked chord passage, so that the harmonies may be at once forcible and distinct.

Strict style. A style of composition in which (most) dissonances are regularly prepared and resolved.

Stridente (It., strē-den'tĕh). Strident; rough, harsh; *martellato.*

String. A tone producing cord . . . *First string,* the highest of a set . . . *Open string,* one not stopped or shortened . . . *Silver string,* one covered with silver wire . . . *Soprano string,* the *E* string of the violin . . . *The Strings,* the string group in the orchestra.

Stringed instruments. All instruments whose tones are produced by strings, whether struck, plucked, or bowed.

Stringendo (It., strin-jen'dŏh). Hastening, accelerating the movement, usually suddenly and rapidly, with a *crescendo.*

Stringere (It., strin'jĕh-rĕh). To hasten; *senza stringere,* without hastening.

String quartet. A quartet for 1st and 2d violin, viola, and 'cello.—Also, the string group in the orchestra.

String quintet. A quintet for 2 violins, 2 violas, and 'cello; or for 2 violins, 1 viola, and 2 'celli; or for 2 violins, viola, 'cello, and double bass.—Also, the string group in the orchestra.

Stringy. Having the quality of tone, string tone, peculiar to bow instruments.

Strisciando (It., strē-shähn′dŏh). Gliding, smooth, *legato*.

Strophe. Literally, a "turn" in Greek; a break in the continuity of a song, leading to a new section, but preserving the unity of rhythm and musical setting.

Strophic composition. See SONG.

Strumento (It., stru-men′toh). Italian word for instruments.

Stück (Ger., shtük). A piece; a number.

Study. An étude, a teaching piece.

Stürmisch (Ger., shtür′mish). Stormy, passionate, impetuous.

Sturm und Drang (Ger., stoorm ŏŏnt drahng). "Storm and stress"; a literary term borrowed to describe a highly emotional, minor key style that emerged during the early Classical period, in the 1770's.

Style galant (Fr., stēl ga-lähn′). "Elegant" style of composition, emphasizing entertainment valué, popular in the second half of the 18th century in France and elsewhere.

Styrienne (Fr., stē-rē-enn′). An air in slow movement and 2/4 time, often in minor, with a Jodler (yodel) after each verse; for vocal or instrumental solo.

Su (It., soo). On, upon, by, near ... *Arco in su,* up-bow.

Suave (It., sŏŏ-ah′vĕh). ⎫
Suavemente (sŏŏ-äh-vĕh-men′tĕh). ⎬
Suavità, con (kŏhn sŏŏ-äh-vē-tah′). ⎭
See SOAVE, etc.

Subbass, Subbourdon. An organ stop of 16′ or 32′ pitch, generally on the pedal, and stopped.

Subdominant. The tone below the dominant in a diatonic scale; the 4th degree.

Subitamente (It., sŏŏ-bē-täh-men′tĕh). ⎫
Subito (It., soo′bē-tŏh). ⎬

Suddenly, without pause . . . *Volti subito,* turn over (the page) quickly . . . *p subito* (after *f*), an abrupt change to *piano,* without gradation.

Subject. A melodic motive or phrase on which a composition or movement is founded; a theme.

Submediant. The 3d scale-tone below the tonic; the 6th degree.

Suboctave. 1. The octave below a given tone.—2. The double contra-octave.

Subordinate chords. Chords not fundamental or principal; the triads on the 2d, 3d, 6th, and 7th degrees, and all seventh chords but the dominant 7th.

Subprincipal. A subbass pedal stop of 32′ pitch.

Substitution. In contrapuntal progression, the resolution or preparation of a dissonance by substituting, for the regular tone of resolution or preparation, its higher or lower octave in some other part.

Subtonic. The leading note.

Suffocato (It., sŏŏf-fŏh-kah′tŏh). See SOFFOCATO.

Sugli (It., sool′yē).
Sui (It., soo′ē).
On the; near the.

Suite (Fr., süē′t′). A set or series of pieces in various (idealized) dance forms. The earlier suites have 4 chief divisions: The Allemande, Courante, Saraband, and Gigue; other forms introduced at will (*intermezzi*) are the Bourrée, Branle, Gavotte, Minuet, Musette, Passepied, Loure, Pavane, etc.—The modern orchestral Suite is more like a DIVERTIMENTO.

Suivez (Fr., süē-vä′). 1. Same as COLLA PARTE.—2. "Continue," "go on."

Sul, sull', sulla, sulle (It.). On the, near the . . . *Sulla corda La,* on the *A* string . . . *Sulla tastiera,* near or by the fingerboard . . . *Sul ponticello,* near the bridge.

Suonare (It., sŏŏ-ô-năh′rēh). Old form of the verb *sonare,* "to sound," "to play."

Suonata (It., sŏŏ-ô-năh′tăh). Alternate spelling of *sonata.*

Superbamente (It., sŏŏ-pâr-băh-men′tĕh).⎫
Superbo,-a (It., sŏŏ-pâr′bŏh,-băh).   ⎬
Proudly, loftily.   ⎭

Superdominant. The 6th degree of a diatonic scale.

Superfluous. Augmented.

Superoctave. 1. An organ stop of 2′ pitch.—2. A coupler bringing into action keys an octave above those struck, either on the same manual or another.—3. The octave above a given tone.

Supertonic. The 2d degree of a diatonic scale.

Supplicando (It., sŏŏp-plē-kăhn′dŏh). ⎫
Supplichevole (It.,—kā′vŏh′lĕh).   ⎬
Supplichevolmente (It., —kĕh-vŏhl-men′tĕh). ⎭
In a style expressive of supplication, entreaty, pleading.

Surprise cadence. See CADENCE.

Suspended cadence. See CADENCE.

Suspension. A dissonance caused by suspending (holding back) a tone or some tones of a chord while the other tones progress.

Süss (Ger., züss). Sweet(ly).

Sustain. To hold during the full time value (of notes); also, to perform in *sostenuto* or *legato* style.

Sustaining pedal. A piano pedal which holds up dampers already raised by depressed keys, thus prolonging the tones of strings affected.

Susurrando (It., sŏŏ-sŏŏr-răhn′dŏh).⎫
Susurrante (It., sŏŏ-sŏŏr-răhn′tĕh). ⎬
In a whispering, murmurous tone.   ⎭

Svanirando (It., zvăh-nē-răhn′dŏh). Vanishing; fainter and fainter.

Svegliato (It., zvĕhl-yah′tŏh). Lively, animated, brisk.

Svelto (It., zvel′tŏh). Light, nimble.

Swell. 1. In the organ, a set of pipes enclosed in a box with movable shutters which may be opened and closed by a pedal.—2. The swell organ (the pipes enclosed, and their keyboard).—3. A *crescendo* ($\prec$), or *crescendo* and *diminuendo* ($\prec\succ$).

Swing. A smooth, sophisticated style of jazz playing, popular in the 1930's. Its distinctive characteristic was a trend away from primitive jazz groups who improvised by instinct, towards a well-organized ensemble of professional instrumentalists. The main outline of melody and harmony was established during rehearsals, but jam sessions were freely interpolated, with extended solos. The new style of performance required a larger band, so that the "Swing Era" became synonymous with the "Big Band Era" forming a natural transition to rock'n'roll.

Syllabic melody. One each tone of which is sung to a separate syllable.

Syllable name. A syllable taken as the name of a note or tone; as *Do* for *C.*

Sympathetic strings. Strings stretched below or above the principal strings of lutes and other instruments to provide sympathetic resonance and thus enhance the sounds.

Symphonic. Resembling, or relating or pertaining to, a symphony . . . *Symphonic ode,* a symphonic composition combining chorus and orchestra . . . *Symphonic poem,* an extended orchestral composition which follows in its development the thread of a story or the ideas of a poem, repeating and interweaving its themes appropriately; it has no fixed form, nor has it set divisions like those of the symphony.

Symphonie (Fr., sahn-fŏh′nē). *Symphony.*

Symphony. An orchestral composition in from 3 to 5 distinct "movements," or divisions, each with its own theme or themes and its own development. Usual plan: I. *Allegro* (sonata form, often with a slow introduction); II. *Adagio*; III. *Minuet* or *Scherzo*; IV. *Allegro* or *Presto*.

Syncopate. To efface or shift the accent of a tone or chord falling on a naturally strong beat, by tying it over from the preceding weak beat; the latter then (generally) takes the accent.

Syncopated pedal. The release of the damper pedal on striking a chord, followed by immediate depression of the pedal.

Syncopation. The shifting of accents from strong beat to weak beat, or to between beats.

Syrinx. Pan pipes.

T

T. Stands for *Tasto, Tempo, Tenor, Toe* (in organ music), *Tre* (T. C. = *tre corde*), and *Tutti*.

Tablature. 1. The rules and regulations for the poetry and song of the *Meistersinger.*—2. Early musical notation for the lute, viol, and organ.

Tabor. A small drum accompanying a folk singer, and tapped with only one hand.

Tacet. Latin for "it is silent"; a common usage in orchestral parts to mark a movement in which an instrument in question is not playing.

Tafelmusik (Ger., täh'fel-moo-zik). "Table music"; that is, music performed informally at a dinner gathering.

Tail. Same as STEM.

Takt (Ger., tähkt). A beat; a measure; time . . . *Ein Takt wie vorher zwei,* one measure like two before (same as DOPPIO MOVIMENTO) . . . *Streng im Takt,* strictly in time.

Talea (L., täh'lā-ŭ). See ISORHYTHM.

Talon (Fr., tah-lohn′). The end of the bow of the violin; literally, "heel."

Tambour (Fr., tahn-bŏŏr). Drum.

Tambour de basque (Fr., —duh băhsk). A tambourine.

Tambourine. A small, shallow drum with one head of parchment; played by striking it with the right hand. Around the hoop are several pairs of loose metallic plates called *jingles.*

Tambour militaire (Fr., —mē-lē-tarh′). A military drum; a side drum.

Tam-tam. 1. A gong.—2. The Hindoo drum. (Also *Tom-tom.*)

Tändelnd (Ger., ten′delnt). In a toying, bantering style.

Tango. Argentinian dance, characterized by strongly marked syncopation; became popular in ballrooms in the U.S. and Europe around 1912.

Tanto (It., tăhn′tōh). As much, so much; too (much) . . . *Allegro non tanto,* not too fast . . . *A tanto possibile,* as much as possible.

Tanz (Ger., tăhnts). A dance.

Tarantella (It., tăh-răhn-tel′lăh). ⎫
Tarantelle (Ger., tăh-răhn-tel′lĕ). ⎬
A dance of southern Italy, in 6/8 time, the rate of speed gradually increasing, and the mode alternating between major and minor.—Also, an instrumental piece in 3/8 or 6/8 time, very rapid tempo, and bold and brilliant style.

Tardamente (It., tăr-dăh-men′tĕh). Slowly, lingeringly.

Tardando (It., tăr-dăhn′dōh). Delaying, retarding.

Tardato (It., tăr-dăh′tōh). Delayed, slower; retarded.

Tardo (It., tăr′dōh). Slow, lingering.

Tarentelle (Fr., tăh-răhn-tel′). TARANTELLA.

Tastiera (It., tăh-stē-â′răh). Keyboard; fingerboard . . . *Sulla tastiera,* on (near) the fingerboard.

Tasto (It., tăh′stōh). Key; fret; touch; fingerboard; *sul tasto,* on (near) the fingerboard . . . *Tasto solo* means that the bass part is to be played, either as written or in octaves, without chords.

Te. Stands for *Si,* in Tonic Sol-fa.

Technic (tek′nik), **Technique** (Fr., tek-nēk′). All that relates to the purely mechanical part of instrumental or vocal performance; mechanical training, skill, dexterity.

Tedesco,-a (It., těh-děh′skŏh, -skäh). German . . . *Alla tedesca,* in the German style (in waltz rhythms, with changing tempo).

Teil (Ger., tile). A part or section; a movement.

Tema (It., tâ′mäh). Theme.

Tema con variazioni (It., târ′mäh kŏhn vâr-ē-äh-tsē′ŏh-nē). THEME AND VARIATIONS.

Temperament. A system of tuning in which tones of very nearly the same pitch, like *C* sharp and *D* flat, are made to sound alike by slightly "tempering" them (that is, slightly raising or lowering them). When applied to all the tones of an instrument (as the piano), this system is called "equal temperament"; when only the keys most used are tuned (as was done formerly), the temperament is "unequal."

Tempestosamente (It., tem-pěh-stŏh-säh-men′těh). ⎱
Tempestoso (It., tem-pěh-stŏh′sŏh). ⎰
Stormily, passionately, impetuously.

Temple block. A hollow block of resonant wood, usually ornamented in an oriental manner, and struck with a drumstick; it is also called Chinese block, or Korean temple block.

Tempo (It., tem′pŏh). 1. Rate of speed, movement.—2. Time, measure . . . A TEMPO, return to the preceding pace . . . *In tempo,* same as A TEMPO; *sempre in tempo,* always at the same pace; *in tempo misurato,* in strict time (after *"a piacere"*). . . . *Tempo com(m)odo,* at a convenient pace . . . *Tempo di Ballo, Bolero, Minuetto,* etc., in the movement of a Ballo, Bolero, etc. . . . *Tempo giusto,* at a proper, appropriate pace . . . *Tempo rubato,* see RUBATO. . . *L'istesso tempo,* or *Lo stesso tempo,* the same tempo; indicates, at a change of rhythm, that the pace remains the same . . . *Senza tempo,* same as A PIACERE . . . *Tempo primo,* at the original pace.

Tempo mark. A word or phrase indicating the rate of speed at which a piece should be performed. Thus, "Adagio, M.M. = 56," signifies a tranquil movement in which a quarter note has the time value of one beat of the metronome set at 56.

Tenendo (It., tĕh-nen′dŏh). Sustaining

Teneramente (It., tĕh-nĕh-răh-men′tĕh). ⎫
Tenerezza, con (It., kŏhn tĕh-nĕh-ret′săh). ⎬
Tenero (It., tâ′nĕh-rŏh). ⎭
Tenderly, with tender emotion; delicately, softly.

Tenor. The high natural male voice; the *dramatic tenor,* of full and powerful quality, has a range from *c* to *b*[1]♭ the *lyric tenor,* sweeter and less powerful, from *d* to c^2 (or c^2♯).— 2. The viola.—3. A prefix to the names of instruments of similar compass; as *tenor trombone.*

Tenor C. Small *c:*

Tenor clef. The *C* clef on the 4th line.

Tenore (It., tĕh-noh′rĕh). Tenor.

Tenth. 1. The diatonic interval of an octave plus 2 degrees.—2. Same as DECIMA 2.

Tenuto (It., tĕh-noo′tŏh). "Held"; means (*a*) generally, that a tone so marked is to be sustained for its full time value; (*b*) occasionally, *legato* . . . *Forte tenuto* (*f ten.*), *forte* throughout . . . *Tenuto mark,* a short stroke over a note.

Tepidamente (It., tĕh-pē-dăh-men′tĕh). Lukewarmly; in an even, unimpassioned style.

Ternary. Composed of, or progressing by, threes . . . *Ternary form*, Rondo form . . . *Ternary measure*, simple triple time.

Tertian. An organ stop consisting of a tierce and a larigot combined.

Terz (Ger., târts). ⎫
Terza (It., târ′tsăh). ⎭
    The interval of a third.

Terzett (Ger., târ-tset′). ⎫
Terzetto (It., târ-tset′tŏh). ⎭
    Properly, a vocal trio (seldom an instrumental one).

Tessitura (It., tes-sē-too′răh). The range covered by the main body of the tones of a given part, not including infrequent high or low tones. In English we say that the part "lies" high or low.

Tetrachord. The interval of a perfect fourth; the four scale-tones contained in a perfect fourth.

Tetralogy. A connected series of 4-stage works or oratorios.

Text. Words to which music is set.

Thematic composition. A style based on the contrapuntal treatment or development of one or more themes. (Invention, Fugue, Canon.)

Theme. A Subject.—Specifically, a theme is an extended and rounded off subject with accompaniment, in period form, proposed as a ground-work for elaborate variations.

Theme and variations. A form of composition in which the principal theme is clearly and explicitly stated at the beginning, and is then followed by a number of variations.

Theme song. The most prominent song in a musical, or a movie, calculated to express the abiding sentiment of the entire production.

Theorbo. A kind of large, double-necked bass lute.

Thesis. Downbeat, strong beat. See Arsis.

Third. An interval embracing 3 degrees. Also, the third degree of the scale, the Mediant.

Third stream jazz. The effort by some JAZZ musicians and art composers, in the 1950's and 1960's to fuse elements of jazz and contemporary art music.

Thirteenth. An interval embracing an octave and a sixth; a compound sixth.

Thirty-second note. Half of the value of a sixteenth note.

Thorough bass. See BASSO CONTINUO.

Three step. The ordinary (Vienna) waltz.

Thumb position. The high positions in cello playing, where the thumb quits the neck of the instrument.

Tie. A curved line joining 2 notes of like pitch which are to be sounded as one note equal to their united time value.

Tied notes. 1. Notes joined by a tie.—2. Notes whose hooks are run together in one or more thick strokes.

Tierce (tĕrs). 1. Third.—2. In the organ, a mutation stop pitched $2\frac{1}{3}$ octaves above the Diapason.—3. One of the Canonical Hours.

Tierce de Picardie (Fr., t'yĕrs duh pē-kar′dē). Picardy third; major ending of a piece in a minor key.

Timbale (Fr., tăn-băhl′). ⎫
Timballo (It., tim-băhl′lŏh). ⎭
Kettledrum.

Timbre (Fr., tăn′br). Quality of tone.

Timbrel (Hebrew). A tambourine or tabor.

Time. 1. The division of the measure into equal fractional parts of a whole note (𝅝), thus regulating the accents and rhythmic flow of music. The sign for time is the *Time signature* (see below). There are 2 classes of time, *Duple* and *Triple.* In *Duple* time the *number of beats* to the measure is divisible by 2; in *Triple* time, by 3. There are also 2 subclasses, *Compound Duple time* and *Compound Triple time;*

in the former *each beat* contains a dotted note (or its equivalent in other notes or rests) divisible by 3; in the latter, not only the number of beats in each measure is divisible by 3, but also each beat, as above.

Timoroso (It., tē-mŏh-roh'sŏh). In a style expressive of timidity, hesitation, or fear.

Timpani (It., tim'păh-nē). KETTLEDRUMS ... *Timpani coperti,* muffled drums.

Tinto, con (It., kŏhn tin'tŏh). With shading; expressively.

Toccata (It., tŏhk-kah'tăh). A composition for organ or harpsichord (piano), free and bold in style, consisting of runs and passages alternating with fugued or contrapuntal work, generally in equal notes, with a flowing, animated, and rapid movement.

Todesgesang (Ger., tŏh'des-gĕsangᵏ).⎫
Todeslied (Ger., tŏh'des-lēt). ⎭
   A dirge; a musical composition commemorating the dead.

Tom-tom. Indian drum producing a dull but incisive tone.

Ton (Ger., tohn). A tone; key; mode; pitch; octave-scale.

Tonada (Sp., tŏh-nah'tăh). A generic name for a Spanish song or dance, also adopted in Latin America.

Tonadilla (Sp., tŏh-nah-dē'ya). A Spanish theater piece of a light genre.

Tonal. Pertaining to tones, or to a tone, mode, or key ... *Tonal imitation,* imitation within the key of a composition; nonmodulating imitation.

Tonal answer. An answer to the subject in a fugue, in which the tonic is answered by the dominant and the dominant is answered by the tonic, thus altering the intervallic content of the theme.

Tonality. See KEY.

Tonante (It., tŏh-nähn'tĕh). Thundering, thunderous.

Tonart (Ger., tohn'art). Key (tonality).

Tondichtung (Ger., tohn′diyh-tōōng^k). Tone poem.

Tone. See ACOUSTICS ... Half tone, a minor, or chromatic, second ... Whole tone, a major second.

Tone cluster. Several consecutive notes, of the diatonic, pentatonic, or chromatic scale played simultaneously in a "cluster." Diatonic piano tone clusters were introduced by the American composer Henry Cowell.

Tone color. Quality of tone.

Tone poem. See SYMPHONIC POEM.

Tone row. The fundamental subject in a 12-tone composition.

Tongue (*noun*). A reed; (*verb*) to employ the tongue in producing, modifying, or interrupting the tones of certain wind instruments.

Tonguing. The production of tone effects on wind instruments by the aid of the tongue ... *Single tonguing,* the effect obtained by the repeated tongue thrust to the nearly inaudible consonant *t* or *d*; *Double tonguing,* that obtained by the repetition of *t k*; *Triple tonguing,* by *t k t*; etc.

Tonic. 1. The keynote of a scale.—2. The triad on the keynote (tonic chord) ... *Tonic pedal,* organ-point on the keynote ... *Tonic section,* a section or sentence in the key in which the composition began, with a cadence to the tonic of that key.

Tonic Sol-fa. A method of teaching vocal music, invented by Sarah Ann Glover of Norwich, England, about 1812. Pupils are taught to recognize the tones of the scale by observing the mental impressions peculiar to each tone. It is based on the Movable Do system, and uses the syllables *doh, ray, me, fah, soh, lah, te.*

Tonkunst (Ger., tohn′künst). The art of music; *Tonkünstler* —composer.

Tonleiter (Ger., tohn′līter). Scale.

Tonsatz (Ger., tohn′sähtz). A composition.

Tonus peregrinus. Latin for "wandering mode"; an excerpt of plainchant used in a choral work.

Torch song. A highly emotional American ballad sung by a female who "carries the torch" for an unresponsive male.

Tornando (It., tohr-nähn′dŏh). Returning; *tornando al primo tempo,* or *tornando come prima,* returning to (resuming) the original tempo.

Tostamente (It., tŏh-stäh-men′tĕh). Rapidly and boldly.

Tostissimamente (It., tŏh-stis-sē-mäh-men′tĕh).⎫
Tostissimo (It., tŏh-stis′sē-mŏh).⎭
 Extremely fast.

Tosto (It., tŏ′stŏh). Swift, bold; soon ... *Allegro molto, più tosto presto,* very fast, nearly *presto.*

Totenlied (Ger., tō′ten-lēt). See TODESGESANG.

Touch. 1. The method and manner of applying the fingers to the keys of keyboard instruments.—2. The amount and kind of resistance overcome by the fingers in depressing the keys of an organ or piano; as a *heavy* or *light touch, an elastic* touch.

Touche (Fr., toosh). Fingerboard; *sur la touche* is an instruction for string players to bow on the fingerboard.

Toye. Short piece for the virginal composed during the 16th and 17th centuries.

Tragicamente (It., trăh-jē-kăh-men′tĕh). Tragically.

Tranquillamente (It., trähn-kwil-läh-men′tĕh).⎫
Tranquillezza, con (It., kŏhn trähn-kwil-let′säh).⎪
Tranquillità, con (It., kŏhn trähn-kwil-lē-tah′).⎬
Tranquillo (It., trähn-kwil′lŏh).⎭
 Tranquilly, quietly, calmly.

Transcendental. The piano style of Liszt and his followers; so called because it surpasses the playing of former pianists, and exceeds the limits of the piano by imitating the orchestra.

Transcription. The arrangement or adaptation of a piece for some voice or instrument other than that for which it was originally intended.

Transient. Passing; not principal; intermediate . . . *Transient chord,* an intermediate chord foreign both to the key left and that reached . . . *Transient modulation,* a temporary modulation, soon followed by a return to the key left.

Transition. 1. Modulation, especially a transient one.—2. In Tonic Sol-fa, a modulation without change of mode.

Transpose. To perform or write out a composition in a different key.

Transposing instruments. 1. Instruments whose natural scale is always written in *C* major, regardless of the actual pitch.—2. Instruments having some device by which the action or strings can be shifted so that higher or lower tones are produced than when they are in the normal position.

Transposition. Performance of a composition in a different key from the one in which it was originally written.

Transverse flute. Cross flute. See FLUTE.

Traps. Colloquial term for the drum set in a jazz band.

Trascinando (It., trăh-shē-năhn′dŏh). Dragging, delaying.

Trasporto, con (It., kŏhn trăh-spôr′tŏh). With transport, ecstatically.

Trattenuto (It., trăht-tĕh-noo′tŏh). Held back, retarded.

Trauermusik (Ger., trow′er-moo-zĭk). Funeral music.

Träumerisch (Ger., troy′mĕrish). Dreamy.

Traurig (Ger., trow′rĭyh). Sad, melancholy.

Trautonium. An electronic musical instrument introduced by the German electrical engineer Trautwein.

Traversflöte (Ger., trăh-vârs′flö′tĕ). The cross flute; or, a 4′ organ stop resembling it in timbre.

Tre (It., trā). Three . . . *A tre,* for 3 voices or instruments; *a tre voci,* for (in) 3 parts . . . *Tre corde,* see UNO, *Una corda.*

Treble. Soprano ... *Treble clef,* the *G* clef:

Treibend (Ger., trī′bent). Urging, hastening.

Tremando (It., trĕh-mähn′dŏh). ⎫
Tremante (It., trĕh-mähn′tĕh). ⎬
Tremolando (It., trĕh-mŏh-lähn′dŏh). ⎭
  With a tremolo effect.

Tremolo (It., trâ′mŏh-lŏh). A quivering, fluttering. 1. In singing, a tremulous, unsteady tone.—2. On bow instruments, an effect produced by the very rapid alternation of down-bow and up-bow, written: —3. On the piano, the rapid alternation of the tones of a chord.—4. The effect produced by the *tremolo stop,* or *tremulant* (organ).—5. The TREMULANT.

Tremoloso (It., trĕh-mŏh-loh′sŏh). With a tremulous, fluttering effect.

Tremulant. The tremolo stop in an organ.

Trepak (trĕh-pahk′). Russian dance in fast duple time.

Très (Fr., trä). Very; *molto.*

Triad. A "3-tone" chord composed of a given tone (the Root) with its third and fifth in ascending order in the scale.

Triangle. A steel rod bent into triangular shape, with one corner left slightly open; it is struck with a metal wand.

Trichord piano. One having 3 strings (unisons) to each tone throughout the greater part of its compass.

Trill. The even and rapid alternation of 2 tones a major or minor second apart; the lower tone is the *principal note,* the higher tone the *auxiliary.* Sign *tr* or *tr* 〰〰〰

Triller (Ger., tril′ler). ⎫
Trillo (It., tril′lŏh). ⎬
  A trill.

Trio (It., trē′ŏh). 1. A piece for 3 voices or in 3 parts.—2. In minuets, marches, etc., the *trio* or *alternativo* is a second dance or march, after which the first is repeated.

Trio sonata. A type of Baroque chamber music written in 3 parts, the 2 upper parts supported by a figured bass.

Triole (Ger., trē-oh′lě).
Triolet (Fr., trē-ŏh-lā).
Triplet.

Trionfale (It., trē-ŏhn-fah′lĕh). Triumphal.

Trionfante (It., trē-ŏhn-fähn′tĕh). Triumphant.

Triple concerto. Concerto for 3 solo instruments and orchestra.

Triple counterpoint. See Counterpoint.

Triple-croche (Fr., trēp′l krōsh). Thirty-second note.

Triplet. A group of 3 equal notes to be performed in the time of 2 of like value in the regular rhythm; written:

Triple time. Meter containing 3 units, as in 3/4 or 3/8.

Tristezza, con (It., kŏhn trī-stet′säh).
Tristo,-a (It., trī′stŏh,-stäh).
In a style expressive of sadness or melancholy.

Tritone. The interval of 3 whole tones, or the augmented fourth:

Trochee (tro′kē). A metrical foot of 2 syllables, long and short, accent on the first: ‿ ⌣

Tromba (It., trŏm-bäh′). Trumpet.

Tromba marina (It., —mah-rī′näh). A monochord, with a single string stretched over a very long wooden box, which was used in the Middle Ages for acoustical experiments, and which could easily produce a long series of harmonics.

There is no reasonable explanation for the origin of the name "marine trumpet" of this instrument.

Trombone. The middle instrument of the brass group, pitched below the trumpet and the horn and above the tuba. The name itself is the augmentative form of the Italian word *tromba,* trumpet, and therefore means "big trumpet."

Trommel (Ger., trôm′mel). Drum.

Trompette (Fr., trŏhm-pĕt′). Trumpet.

Trompette à pistons (Fr., —pēs-ton′). A regular trumpet with pistons.

Tronco,-a (It., trŏhn′kŏh, -kăh). Cut off short; stopped abruptly.

Trope. In medieval Roman liturgy, a trope was an insertion of a musical section, usually a hymn.

Troppo (It., trŏp′pŏh). Too, too much . . . *Allegro, ma non troppo,* rapid, but not too fast.

Troubadours. A class of poet-musicians originating in Provence, and flourishing in France, Spain, and Italy from the 11th century till toward the close of the 13th. Members of this class were called *Trouvères* in Northern France.

Trüb(e) (Ger., trüp, trü′bĕ). Gloomy, dismal; sad, melancholy.

Trumpet. A metal wind instrument with cupped mouthpiece and small bell; the tone is brilliant, penetrating, and of great carrying power. It is a transposing instrument; the ordinary compass is about 2 octaves.—In the organ the Trumpet is an 8′ reed stop of powerful tone.

Tuba. 1. The straight trumpet of the Romans.—2. A name applied to the 3 lowest members of the saxhorn family; they are metal wind instruments of ponderous tone, with a compass of some 4 octaves.—3. In the organ, a reed stop (*tuba mirabilis*) on a heavy pressure of wind, of very powerful and thrilling tone.

Tubular chimes. Metal bells made of long, hollow cylindrical tubes, suspended from a bar.

Tumultuoso (It., too-mŏŏl-too-oh′sŏh). Vehement, impetuous; agitated.

Tune. An air, melody; a term chiefly applied to short, simple pieces or familiar melodies.

Tuning. 1. The process of bringing an instrument into tune.—2. The *accordatura* of a stringed instrument ... *Tuning cone,* a hollow cone of metal, for tuning metal flue pipes in the organ ... *Tuning crook,* a CROOK 3 ... *Tuning fork,* a two-pronged instrument of metal, yielding one fixed tone (usually a^1 or c^2) ... *Tuning hammer,* a hand wrench for tuning pianos ... *Tuning horn,* a Tuning cone ... *Tuning key,* a Tuning hammer ... *Tuning slide,* a sliding U-shaped section of the tube in certain brass instruments, used to adjust their pitch to that of other instruments.

Turco,-a (It., toor′kŏh, -käh). Turkish ... *Alla turca,* in Turkish style, with a noisy and somewhat monotonous harmonic accompaniment.

Turn. A melodic grace consisting (usually) of 4 notes, a principal note (twice struck) with its higher and lower auxiliary. Sign ∾.

Tusch (Ger., toosh). In German usage, a complimentary fanfare played by orchestral musicians for an honored conductor or soloist.

Tutti (It., too′tē). The indication in an orchestral or choral score that the entire orchestra, or chorus, is to enter; usually placed after an extended solo passage.

Twelfth. 1. The interval of an octave plus a fifth; a compound fifth.—2. A mutation stop in the organ, pitched a Twelfth higher than the Diapason.

Twelve-tone technique. A method of composition, developed mainly by Schoenberg, in which the music is based on a pattern of 12 different tones. A synonymous term is DODECAPHONY.

Two step. Quick American ballroom dance popular in the 1900's and 1910's.

Tympani. An incorrect, but frequently encountered spelling of Timpani.

Tyrolienne (Fr., tē-rŏh-l'yen′). A Tyrolese dance or dance song, a peculiar feature of the latter being the yodel, especially as a refrain.—Hence, a modern round dance in 3/4 time and easy movement.

U

Üben (Ger., *ü′*ben). To practice.

Über (Ger., *ü′*ber). Over, above.

Übermässig (Ger., *ü′*ber-mä′sīyh). Augmented.

Übung (Ger., *ü′*bŏŏng^k). Exercise; practice.

Uguale (It., oo-gwăh′lĕh). Equal, like, similar.

Ugualità, con (It., kŏhn oo-gwăh-lē-tah′). ⎫
Ugualmente (It., oo-gwăhl-mĕn′tĕh). ⎭
    Equally, similarly; evenly, smoothly, tranquilly.

Ukulele. Popular guitar-type instrument.

Umano,-a (It., oo-mah′nŏh, -năh). Human . . . *Voce umana,* Vox humana, an organ stop.

Umore, con (It., kŏhn oo-moh′rēh). With humor.

Un (Fr., ön). ⎫
Une (Fr., ün). ⎭
    One; a or an . . . *Un peu plus lent,* a little slower.

Un (It., oon). ⎫
Uno,-a (It., oo′nŏh, -năh). ⎭
    One; a or an . . . *Una corda,* with the soft pedal; *Tre corde* then means release the soft pedal.

Und (Ger., oont). And.

Unda maris (Latin, "Wave of the sea"). In the organ, an 8′ flue stop pitched a trifle lower than the surrounding foundation stops, the interference of its tone with theirs producing beats and a wavy, undulatory effect of tone.

Undecuplet. A group of 11 equal notes to be performed in the time of 8 (or 6) notes of like value in the regular rhythm.

Undulazione (It., ŏŏn-doo-läh-tsē-oh′nĕh). On bow instruments, the *vibrato* effect.

Unequal voices. Voices different in compass and quality; mixed voices.

Ungebunden (Ger., ŏŏn′gĕ-bŏŏn′den). Unconstrained; *mit ungebundenem Humor,* with unconstrained humor, *burlando.*

Ungeduldig (Ger., ŏŏn′gĕ-dŏŏl′dĭyh). Impatient(ly).

Ungestüm (Ger., ŏŏn′gĕ-shtüm′). Impetuous(ly).

Ungherese (It., ŏŏn-gä-rā′sĕh). Hungarian.

Unison. A tone of the same pitch as a given tone; also, a higher or lower octave of the given tone.—In the piano, a group of 2 or 3 strings tuned to the same pitch and struck by one hammer, is called a *unison;* a string in such a group is called a *unison string.*

Unisono (It., oo-nē′sŏh-nŏh). Unison . . . *All′ unisono,* progressing in unison with or in octaves with.

Unitamente (It., oo-nē-täh-mĕn′tĕh). Unitedly, together.

Uniti (It., oo-nē′tē). This signifies, after *"divisi,"* that the instruments or voices again perform their parts in unison.

Unito,-a (It., oo-nē′tŏh, -täh). United, joined.

Uno (It.). See Un.

Un poco (It., oon pô′kŏh). "A little," as in *un poco più lento,* a little more slowly.

Unruhig (Ger., ŏŏn′roo′ĭyh). Restless(ly), unquiet(ly).

Unter (Ger., ŏŏn′ter). Under, below, sub-.

Unvocal. 1. Not suitable for singing.—2. Not vibrating with tone; *unvocal air* is breath escaping with a more or less audible sigh or hiss, due to unskilful management of the voice.

Upbeat. 1. The raising of the hand in beating time.—2. An unaccented part of a measure (see AUFTAKT).

Up-bow. The stroke of the bow in the direction from point to nut; the *Up-bow mark* is ∨ or ∧.

Upright piano. A piano standing up, with its strings arranged cross-wise (diagonally) along the vertical soundboard, as distinguished from a grand piano in which the strings and the soundboard are horizontal.

Ut. 1. The first of the solmisation syllables.—2. Name of the note *C* in France (pronounced üt).

V

V. Stands for *Vide, Violino, Volti,* and *Voce, Vv.,* for *Violini.*

Va (It., vah). Go on, continue . . . *Va crescendo,* go on increasing (in loudness).

Vacillando (It., văh-chē-lăhn′dŏh).⎫
Vacillante (It., văh-chē-lăhn′tĕh).⎭
Vacillating; means that the passage is to be performed in a wavering, hesitating style.

Vaghezza, con (It., kŏhn văh-gĕt′tsăh). With charm.

Vago (It., văh′gŏh). Vague, dreamy.

Valse (Fr., văhls). Waltz . . . *Valse chantée,* waltz-song . . . *Valse de salon,* a salon piece in waltz time for the piano.

Value. The value (better *time value*) of a note or rest is its length or duration as compared (*a*) with other notes in the same movement, or (*b*) with the standard whole note ○ or any fractional note.

Valve. In brass wind instruments, a device for diverting the air current from the main tube into an additional side tube, thus lengthening the air column and lowering the pitch of the instrument's entire scale. There are *Piston* valves and *Rotary* valves.

Valzer (It., văhl′tser). Waltz.

Vamp. Expression in popular music meaning to improvise an accompaniment.

Variamente (It., văh-rē-äh-men′tĕh). Variously, differently.

Variante (It., văh-rē-ähn′tĕh). ⎫
Variante (Fr., văh-rē-ähn′t′). ⎬
A variant; a different (optional) reading. See OSSIA.

Variation. One of a set or series of transformations of a theme (see THEME) by means of harmonic, rhythmic, and melodic changes and embellishments.

Variazioni (It., văh-rē-äh-tsē-oh′nē). Variations.

Varié (Fr., văh-rē-ā′). Varied . . . *Air* or *thème varié,* same as *Tema con variazioni.*

Varsoviana (It., var-sŏh-vē-ah′năh). ⎫
Varsovienne (Fr., var-sŏh-v'yen′). ⎬
A dance in moderate tempo and 3/4 time, with an *Auftakt* of a quarter note, the downbeat of every second measure being strongly marked.

Vaudeville (Fr., voh-d'-vēl′). A light comedy, often a parody, in which dialogue and pantomime alternate with witty and satirical couplets generally set to well-known popular airs.

Veemente (It., vĕh-ĕh-men′tĕh). ⎫
Veemenza, con (It., kŏhn vĕh-ĕh-men′tsäh). ⎬
Vehemently, passionately.

Veil. A voice the tone of which is not quite clear and bell-like, but somewhat obscured, is said to have a "veil," or to be "veiled."

Velato,-a (It., vĕh-lah′tŏh, -täh). Veiled.

Vellutato (It., vel-loo-tah′tŏh). Velvety.

Veloce (It., vĕh-loh′chĕh). Rapid, swift; often means that a passage is to be performed faster than those before and after, then being the opposite of *ritenuto*.

Velocemente (It., vĕh-lŏh-chĕh-men′tĕh).⎫
Velocità, con (kŏhn vĕh-lŏh-chē-tah′). ⎭
Rapidly, swiftly.

Velocissimamente (It., vĕh-lŏh-chis-sē-măh-men′tĕh).⎫
Velocissimo (It., vĕh-lŏh-chis′sē-mŏh). ⎭
Very fast, with extreme rapidity.

Vent. (Fr., vahn). "Wind," as in *instruments à vent*, wind instruments.

Ventil. A valve.

Venusto (It., vĕh-nŏŏ′stŏh). Graceful, elegant.

Vergnügt (Ger., fâr-gnüyht′). Cheerful(ly), cheery (cheerily).

Vergrösserung (Ger., fâr-grös′serŏŏng[k]). AUGMENTATION.

Verhallend (Ger., fâr-hähl′lent). Dying away.

Verismo (It., vĕr-ēz′mŏh). A realistic type of opera that emerged in Italy in the 1890's; its stories are based on contemporary fiction or actual "veristic" dramatic events.

Verkleinerung (Ger., fâr-klīn′erŏŏng[k]). See DIMINUTION.

Verlöschend (Ger., fâr-lö′shent). Dying away.

Vermindert (Ger., fâr-min′dert). Diminished (interval).

Verschiebung, mit (Ger., mit fâr-shē′bŏŏng[k]). With shifting (soft) pedal; *ohne Verschiebung*, release soft pedal. See UNO, *Una corda, Tre corde.*

Verschwindend (Ger., fâr-shvin′dent). Vanishing, dying away.

Verse. 1. In sacred vocal music, a portion of an anthem or service for a solo voice or solo voices.—2. A stanza.

Verse-anthem. One in which the verses (soli, duets, trios, quartets) predominate over the choruses . . . *Verse-service,* a choral service for solo voices.

Verset. 1. A short verse, usually forming but one sentence with its response; for example:

    Vers. O Lord, save Thy people,

    Resp. And bless Thine inheritance.

—2. A short prelude or interlude for organ.

Versetzung (Ger., fâr-set'zŏŏng^k). Transposition.

Versicle. A Verset 1.

Verstimmt (Ger., fâr-shtimt'). Out of tune; out of humor, depressed.

Verweilend (Ger., fâr-vī'lent). Delaying.

Vespers. Evensong; the 6th of the Canonical Hours.

Vezzosamente (It., vet-tsŏh-săh-men'tĕh).⎫

Vezzoso (It., vet-tsŏh'sŏh).   ⎭

    In a graceful, elegant style.

Vibraharp. A common name for the vibraphone.

Vibrante (It., vē-brähn'tĕh). With a vibrating, agitated effect of tone.

Vibraphone. A percussion instrument consisting of suspended metal bars in keyboard arrangement, which, when struck with mallets, produce tones that are amplified by resonator tubes below the bars. A motor-driven mechanism causes the vibrato that gives the instrument its name.

Vibration. Rapid oscillations of a sounding body, such as a string, or a column of air in wind instruments, which result in the production of definite tones. The human ear is capable of perceiving vibrations from about 16 per second to several thousand per second. The lowest *A* on the piano keyboard has $27\frac{1}{2}$ vibrations per second, and the high *C* on the keyboard vibrates at 4224 per second.

Vibrato (It., vē-brăh'tŏh). 1. On bow instruments, the wavering effect of tone obtained by rapidly shaking the finger on the string which it is stopping.—2. In singing, (*a*) a tremulous effect caused by very rapid partial interruptions of the tone; (*b*) strongly accented, and diminishing in intensity: ♩ (also instrumental effect).

Vicendevole (It., vē-chen-dā'vōh-lĕh). Changeably, inconstantly.

Vicino (It., vē-chē'nŏh). Near; *più vicino,* nearer (as of sounds coming nearer and growing louder).

Victrola. Trademark for phonograph.

Vide (L., vī'deh).⎱
Vedi (It., vē'dē).⎰
See . . . Vi - - de, written in scores, means that a "cut" is to be made, and directs the performers to skip from *Vi-* over to *de.*

Viel (Ger., fēl). Much, great . . . *Mit vielem Nachdruck,* with strong emphasis.

Vielle à roue (Fr., vē-ĕh'lĕh ăh roo). A medieval viol with a mechanical wheel attachment: a hurdy gurdy.

Vielstimmig (Ger., fēl'shtim-miyh). Polyphonic, manyvoiced.

Viennese school. Refers to various styles of composition centered around Austria. The *Classical Viennese School* includes Haydn, Mozart, Beethoven, Schubert, and others. Some observers perceive a continuity leading to the Strauss family in the later 19th century. The *20th Century Viennese School* refers to the group of modern composers, mainly Schoenberg and his disciples, who write in the DODECAPHONIC style.

Viertelnote (Ger., fēr'tĕhl-noh-tĕh). A quarter note.

Vif (Fr., vēf). Lively.

Vigore, con (It., kŏhn vē-goh'rĕh).⎱
Vigorosamente (It., vē-gŏh-rŏh-säh-men'tĕh).⎰
Vigoroso (It., vē-gŏh-roh'sŏh).
With vigor, energy.

Vihuela (Sp., bē-wĕh'lah). An old Spanish lute.

Villancico (Sp., bēl-yăhn-sē′cŏh). A Spanish choral song of the Renaissance period.

Villanella (It., vēl-läh-nel′läh). Type of 16th-century vocal music originating in Naples and of a rather lighthearted nature, less refined than the madrigal; used by some modern composers as a kind of instrumental rustic dance.

Viol. A very ancient type of bow instrument, differing from the violin family by having a *fretted* fingerboard, a variable number of strings (usually 6), and in the shape of the body. It was made in 4 sizes, like the violin, by which it was superseded in the orchestra, etc.

Viola (It., vē-ô′lah). The tenor violin. A bowed string instrument with its 4 strings tuned a fifth lower than the violin: *C, G, D, A.*

Viola da braccio (It., —brah′chŏh). Literally, "viol for the arm"; an old, bowed string instrument held in the arm like the violin or viola.

Viola da gamba (It., —gahm′bäh). Literally, "viol for the leg"; an old, bowed string instrument of the size approximating the cello, and held between the knees.

Viola d'amore (It., —dăh-moh′rĕh). Literally, "a viola of love"; an ancient stringed instrument in the middle range, supplied with sympathetic strings.

Viole (Fr., v'yohl′). A viol; a viola.

Violentamente (It., vē-ŏh-len-täh-men′tĕh).⎫
Violento (It., vē-ŏh-len′tŏh).   ⎬
In a violent, impetuous style.   ⎭

Violin family. The familiar 4-stringed bow instruments, constructed in 4 sizes, tuned as follows:

Double bass (Written)

Violina. A metal flue stop in the organ, of stringy *timbre,* usually of 4′ pitch.

Violinata (It., vē-ŏh-lē-nah′tăh). 1. A piece for violin.—2. A piece for another instrument, imitating the violin style.

Violin clef. The *G* clef ♪ .—*French violin clef,* the *G* clef set on the lowest line of the staff.

Violin diapason. A diapason stop of stringy tone.

Violino (It., vē-ŏh-lē′nŏh). Violin.

Violon (Fr., v'yŏh-lŏhn′). 1. Violin.—2. Violin diapason.

Violoncello (It., vē-ŏh-lŏhn-chel′lŏh). A 4-stringed bow instrument of violin type (see VIOLIN), held, while playing, between the knees; familiarly called the 'cello.

Violone (It., vē-ŏh-loh′nĕh). 1. The bass viol.—2. An organ stop on the pedal, of 16′ pitch and violoncello-like *timbre.*

Virelai (Fr., vēr-eh-lā′). A medieval French song or ballad; the name comes from *Vire,* in Normandy.

Virginal. A small kind of harpsichord.

Virtuoso,-a (It., vēr-too-oh′sŏh, -săh). A highly proficient instrumentalist or vocalist.

Vista (It., vĭ′stăh). Slight . . . *A* (*prima*) *vista,* at (first) sight.

Vistamente (It., vĭ′stăh-men′tĕh).

Visto,-a (It., vĭ′stŏh, -stăh).
Briskly, animatedly.

Vite (Fr., veet). Fast.

Vivace (It., vē-vah′chĕh). Lively, animated, brisk. As a tempo-mark standing by itself, *Vivace* calls for a movement equalling or exceeding *Allegro* in rapidity.

Vivacetto (It., vē-văh-chet′tŏh). Less lively than *Vivace,* about *Allegretto.*

Vivacemente (It., vē-văh-chĕh-men′tĕh). ⎫
Vivacezza, con (It., kŏhn vē-văh-chet′săh). ⎬
Vivacità, con (It., kŏhn vē-văh-chē-tah′). ⎭
     Lively, spirited, animated, brisk; *vivace.*

Vivacissimo (It., vē-văh-chis′sē-mŏh). Very lively, *presto.*

Vivente (It., vē-ven′tĕh). ⎫
Vivido (It., vē′vē-dŏh). ⎬
Vivo (It., vē′vŏh). ⎭
     Lively, spiritedly, briskly.

Vocal. Pertaining to the voice; suitable for the singing voice ... *Vocal cords,* the 2 opposed ligaments set in the larynx, whose vibration, caused by expelling air from the lungs, produces vocal tones ... *Vocal glottis,* the aperture between the vocal cords while singing.

Vocal score. An opera score arranged for voices and piano.

Vocalise (Fr., vŏh-căh-lēz′). A vocal exercise or étude, sung to the vowels or solmisation syllables.

Voce (It., voh′chĕh; *plural* **Voci** [voh′chē]). Voice; part ... *A due* (*tre*) *voci,* for 2 (3) parts or voices; in 2 (3) parts ... *Mezza voce, Sotto voce,* see MEZZA; SOTTO.

Voce di petto (It., —dē pet′tŏh). Chest voice.

Voce di testa (It., —dē tĕs′tăh). Head voice.

Voice. 1. The singing voice, divided into 6 principal classes: Soprano, Mezzo-soprano, Contralto (Alto), Tenor, Baritone, and Bass.—2. The word *voice* is often used instead of "part," in imitation of foreign usage; the practice cannot be recommended.

Voice leading. The art of arranging the voices in a polyphonic composition, so that each part would have a logical continuation.

Voice part. 1. A vocal part.—2. A Part [improper usage].

Voicing. Tuning (said of organ pipes).

Voix (Fr., v'wăh). Voice; part . . . *À deux (trois) voix,* for 2 (3) voices; in 2 (3) parts.

Volante (It., vŏh-lähn'tĕh). Flying; light, swift.

Volata (It., vŏh-lah'tăh).
Volate (Ger., vŏh-lah'tĕ).
Volatine (Fr., vŏh-lăh-tēn').
A short vocal run or trill; a run or division; a light, rapid series of notes.

Volatina (It., vŏh-lăh-tē'năh). A short *Volata.*

Volkslied (Ger., fŏhlks'lēt). Folk song.

Volkstümlich (Ger., fŏhlks'tüm'lĭyh). Like a German folk song, or popular music.

Volkston, im (Ger., im fŏhlks'tohn). In the style of a folk song, or popular music.

Voll (Ger., fŏhl). Full . . . *Volles Orchester,* full orchestra . . . *Volles Werk,* full organ . . . *Mit vollem Chore,* with full chorus.

Volltönend (Ger., fŏlh-tön'ent). Sonorous, resonant.

Volta (It., vŏhl'tăh). A turn or time . . . *Prima volta* (or *Ima volta, Ima, Ia, I., 1.*), first time; *Secunda volta* (or *IIda volta,* etc.), second time; *una volta,* once; *due volte,* twice.

Volteggiando (It., vŏhl-ted-jähn'dŏh). Crossing hands on a keyboard.

Volti subito (It., vŏhl'tĕ soo'bē-tŏh). Turn over instantly.

Volubilmente (It., vŏh-loo-bēl-men'tĕh). Fluently, flowingly.

Voluntary. An organ solo before, during, or after divine service; or, a choral piece opening the service.

Voluttuoso (It., vŏhl-lŏŏt-too-oh'sŏh). Voluptuous.

Vom (Ger., fŏhm). From the . . . *Vom Anfang,* DA CAPO.

Vorausnahme (Ger., fohr-ows′nähme). See ANTICIPATION.

Vorhalt (Ger., fohr′hält). A suspension.

Vorher (Ger., fohr-här′). Before, previous(ly).

Vorig (Ger., fohr′īyh). Preceding, previous; as *voriges Zeit-mass* (*tempo precedente*).

Vorschlag (Ger., fohr′shläyh). See APPOGGIATURA.

Vorspiel (Ger., fohr′shpēl). Prelude, introduction; overture.

Vortrag (Ger., fohr′trah). Rendering, interpretation, performance, style, delivery, execution.

Vortragszeichen (Ger., fohr′trah-tsihen). Expression mark.

Vorwärts (Ger., fohr′vârts). Forwards; *etwas vorwärts gehend,* somewhat faster, *poco più mosso.*

Vox (L., vōx). Voice . . . *Vox angelica* (angelic voice), a 4′ stop corresponding to the 8′ Vox humana . . . *Vox humana* (human voice), an 8′ reed stop in the organ, the tone of which has a (fancied) resemblance to the human voice.

Vuoto (It., voo-oh′toh). "Empty"; used in the indication *corda vuota,* "open string."

W

Wachsend (Ger., văh′sent). Crescendo, "growing."

Wagner tuba. A brass instrument introduced by Wagner in his music dramas, in two sizes, tenor and bass.

Waits (also *Waytes, Wayghtes,* etc.). Originally, English street watchmen, who gave notice of their coming by sounding horns, etc.; later, town musicians; and, still later, various irregular bands of indifferent music makers.

Waldflöte (Ger., vählt′flö′tĕ). An open metal flue stop in the organ, of 2′ or 4′ pitch and suave, full tone.

Waldhorn (Ger., vählt′horn). The French horn without valves.

Waltz. A round dance in 3/4 time, varying in tempo from slow to moderately fast ... *Waltzsong,* a song in waltz rhythm.

Walzer (Ger. vähl′tser). Waltz.

Warble. See YODEL.

Wärme, mit (Ger., mit vârmĕ). With warmth, warmly; *mit grosser Wärme,* with great warmth.

Wehmut(h),mit (Ger., mit vä′moot).⎫
Wehmüt(h)ig (Ger., vä′mü′tïyh).⎭
In a style expressive of sadness or melancholy.

Weich (Ger., vïyh). Soft, tender; mellow, suave.

Weihnachtsmusik (Ger., vï′nahts-moo-zïk). Christmas music.

Well tempered. In equal temperament, as in Bach's *Well Tempered Clavier.*

Wenig (Ger., vä′nïyh). Little; *ein klein wenig langsamer,* a very little slower.

Whipping bow. A form of violin technique in which the bow is made to fall with a certain vehemence on the strings. Chiefly employed when one wishes to mark sharply single tones in rapid tempo, as:

White note. One with an open head: (o 𝅗𝅥).

Whole note. The note o.

Whole shift. See SHIFT.

Whole step. The step of a whole tone.—2. A whole tone.

Whole tone. A major Second.

Whole-tone scale. A scale consisting only of whole tones, and therefore lacking the dominant and either major or minor triads. It was popularized by Debussy and his followers, and is still often used to suggest an eerie and phantom-like mood.

Wie (Ger., vē). As.—*Wie oben,* as above; *wie vorher,* as before, as at first; *wie aus der Ferne,* as from a distance.

Wiegend (Ger., vē′ghent). Swaying, rocking.

Wiegenlied (Ger., vee′ghen-leed). A lullaby.

Wind band. 1. A company of performers on wind instruments.—2. The wind instruments in the orchestra; also, the players on, or parts written for, the same.

Wind instruments. Instruments whose tones are produced by wind (that is, compressed air).

Wolf. 1. The discord produced when playing, in certain keys, on an organ tuned in unequal temperament.—2. In bow instruments, an imperfect or jarring vibration caused by sounding some particular tone or tones.

Wood block. Another name for temple block.

Woodwind. Wind instruments that use reeds (clarinet, oboe, saxophone, etc.) and the flute (which formerly was made of wood and, in the recorder, still is).

Working-out. Development section in sonata form.

Wuchtig (Ger., vŏŏh′tĭyh). Weighty, weightily, ponderous(ly), with strong emphasis.

Würde, mit (Ger., mit vür′dĕ). ⎫
Würdevoll (Ger., vür′dĕ-fŏhl′). ⎬
   With dignity; loftily.

Wüt(h)end (Ger., vü′tent). Furious(ly), frantic(ally).

X

Xylophone. A very ancient instrument, consisting of a row of flat wooden bars fastened horizontally to two stretched cords, tuned to the tones of the scale, and struck (played on) with two mallets: a wooden dulcimer.

Y

Yodel. A type of singing in Switzerland and generally in the Alps, characterized by the frequent alternation of falsetto tones with chest tones; a kind of a warble. The original German spelling is *Jodel.*

Z

Zamacueca (Sp., thăh-măh-kwĕh′kăh). The national dance of Chile, in rapid triple time.

Zapateado (Sp., thăh-păh-tā-ăh′dō). Spanish dance in triple time, characterized by heel stamping to emphasize the strong syncopation.

Zart (Ger., tsăhrt). Tender, soft, delicate, *dolce;* slender ... *Mit zarten Stimmen,* with soft-toned stops.

Zartflöte (Ger., tsăhrt′flö′tĕ). In the organ, a 4′ flute stop of very delicate tone.

Zärtlich (Ger., tsâhrt′lĭyh). Tender(ly), caressing(ly).

Zarzuela (Sp., thăhr-thoo-āl′ăh). Type of Spanish opera with spoken dialogue.

Zeffiroso (It., dzef-fĕ-roh′sŏh). Zephyr-like.

Zeitmass (Ger., tzīt′-măhs). Tempo.

Zelo, con (It., kŏhn dzâ′lŏh).

Zelosamente (It., dzĕh-lŏh-săh-men′tĕh).

Zeloso (It., dzĕh-loh′sŏh).

   Zealously, enthusiastically, with energy and fire.

Ziemlich (Ger., tsēm′lĭyh). Somewhat, rather ... *Ziemlich bewegt und frei in Vortrag,* quite animated and free in delivery (style).

Zierlich (Ger., tsēr′lĭyh). Neat(ly), delicate(ly); graceful(ly).

Zigeunermusik (Ger., tsĭ-goy′ner-moo-zĭk). Gypsy music.

Zimbalon. An improved dulcimer much employed in Hungarian music, provided with dampers, and having a chromatic scale of 4 octaves: E to e^3.

Zingara, alla (It., ăhl'lăh tsin'găh-răh). ⎱
Zingarese, alla (It., ăhl'lăh tsin-găh-rā'zĕh). ⎰
In Gypsy style.

Zither (Ger., tsit'ter). The modern zither has 32 or more strings stretched over a shallow wooden resonance box, which has a fretted fingerboard on the side next the player; above the fingerboard are 5 melody strings, plucked with a metal "ring" worn on the right thumb.

Zitternd (Ger., tsit'ternt). Trembling, tremulous.

Zögernd (Ger., tsö'gernt). Hesitating, retarding.

Zu (Ger., tsoo). Too; to.

Zunehmend (Ger., tsoo'nā'ment). Increasing, *crescendo*.

Zurückgehend (Ger., tsoo-rük'gā'ent). Returning (to a preceding slower tempo).

Zurückhaltend (Ger., tsoo-rük'hähl'tent). Holding back, *ritardando*.

Zwei (Ger., tsvī). Two.

Zweihändig (Ger., tsvī'hen'dīyh). For 2 hands.

Zweistimmig (Ger., tsvī'shtim'mīyh). For 2 voices; in or for 2 parts.

Zwischensatz (Ger., tsvish'en-zähts'). Episode.

Zwischenspiel (Ger., tsvish'en-shpēl'). Interlude, intermezzo.

Noteworthy Musicians

Revised by Ed Berlin

Abravanel, Maurice (1903–), Greek-born conductor of the Utah State Symphony Orchestra.

Acuff, Roy (1903–), American country-music singer, fiddler, and publisher.

Adam, Adolphe (1803–1856), French composer of operas and ballets.

Adam de la Halle (c.1237–c.1287), foremost French trouvère.

Adderley, Julian "Cannonball" (1928–1975), American bebop alto saxophonist.

Addinsell, Richard (1904–1977), English composer of film music.

Adler, Larry (1914–), American virtuoso harmonica player.

Albéniz, Isaac (1860–1909), Spanish pianist and composer.

Albert, Eugène d'. See d'Albert, Eugène.

Alberti, Domenico (1710–c.1740), Italian harpsichordist and composer; reputed inventor of the "Alberti bass."

Albinoni, Tomaso (1671–1750), Italian violinist and composer.

Albright, William (1944–), American composer.

Alkan, Charles-Henri (1813–1888), French pianist and composer.

Allegri, Gregorio (1582–1652), Italian choral composer.

Allen, Steve (1921–), versatile American pianist, songwriter, and TV personality.

Alpert, Herb (1935–), popular American trumpeter, composer, and bandleader.

Althouse, Paul (1889–1954), American operatic tenor.

Amati, Nicola (or **Niccolò**) (1596–1684), violin builder and teacher of Andrea Guarneri and Antonio Stradivarius.

Amram, David (1930–   ), American composer.

Anderson, Leroy (1908–1975), American composer of popular orchestral pieces.

Anderson, Marian (1902–   ), American contralto; the first black American member of the Metropolitan Opera.

Anderson, T. J. (1928–   ), American composer.

Andrews Sisters; La Verne (1915–1967), **Maxene** (1918–   ), and **Patti** (1920–   ), popular American singing group.

Angeles, Victoria de los (1923–   ), Spanish operatic soprano.

Ansermet, Ernest (1883–1969), Swiss conductor.

Antes, John (1740–1811), Moravian-American composer; first American-born composer to write chamber music.

Antheil, George (1900–1959), American composer of the avant-garde.

Arcadelt, Jacob (c.1500–1568), Flemish composer.

Arel, Bülent (1919–   ), Turkish composer of orchestral and electronic music.

Arensky, Anton (1861–1906), Russian composer.

Argento, Dominick (1927–   ), American opera composer.

Arlen, Harold (real name **Hyman Arluck;** 1905–   ), American composer of Broadway musicals and Hollywood film scores.

Armstrong, Louis (1900–1971), American cornetist and trumpeter; the leading New Orleans jazz figure, whose style of improvisation revolutionized jazz performance on all instruments.

Arne, Thomas (1710–1778), English dramatic composer.

Arnold, Eddy (1918–   ), American country-music singer and guitarist.

Arnold, Malcolm (1921–   ), English composer.

Arnold, Samuel (1740–1802), English dramatic composer.

Arrau, Claudio (1903–   ), Chilean pianist.

Arriaga, Juan (1806–1826), Spanish composer.

Arroyo, Martina (1940–   ), American operatic soprano.

Asafiev, Boris (1884–1949), Russian composer and writer on music.

Ashkenazy, Vladimir (1937–   ), Russian emigré pianist.

Ashley, Robert (1930–   ), American avant-garde composer.

Atkins, Chet (1924–   ), American country & western guitarist.

Atterberg, Kurt (1887–1974), Swedish composer.

Auber, Daniel-François-Esprit (1782–1871), French opera composer.

Aubert, Louis (1877–1968), French opera composer.

Audran, Edmond (1840–1901), French operetta composer.

Auer, Leopold (1845–1930), Hungarian violinist; teacher of Heifetz, Zimbalist, and Elman.

Auric, Georges (1899–   ), French composer of ballets and film music.

Austin, Larry (1930–   ), American avant-garde composer.

Autry, Gene (1907–   ), American singing cowboy/actor.

Avison, Charles (1709–1770), English composer.

Ax, Emanuel (1949–   ), Polish-born American pianist.

Babbitt, Milton (1916–   ), American serial composer and theoretician.

Bach, Carl Philipp Emanuel (1714–1788), German composer of the *empfindsamer* style; third son of J. S. Bach.

Bach, Johann Christian (1735–1782), German composer of the *galant* style; eighteenth child of J. S. Bach; known as "London Bach," because of his long-term residence in London.

Bach, Johann Sebastian (1685–1750), German composer, organist, and giant of Baroque polyphony.

Bach, P. D. Q. (1807–1742), invented alter ego of composer-humorist Peter Schickele.

Bach, Wilhelm Friedemann (1710–1784), German composer, eldest son of J. S. Bach.

Bacharach, Burt (1928–   ), popular American composer of film music and Broadway shows.

Bachauer, Gina (1913–1976), Greek pianist.

Backhaus, Wilhelm (1884–1969), German pianist.

Bacon, Ernst (1898–   ), American composer.

Badings, Henk (1907–   ), Dutch composer.

Badura-Skoda, Paul (1927–   ), Austrian pianist.

Baez, Joan (1941–   ), American folk singer.

Baird, Tadeusz (1928–   ), Polish composer.

Baker, David (1931–   ), American jazz composer and educator.

Baker, Janet (1933–   ), English operatic mezzo-soprano.

Baker, Theodore (1851–1934), American musicologist; original editor of this dictionary.

Balakirev (pronounced Ba-la′-ki-rev, *not* Ba-la-ki′-rev), **Mily** (1837–1910), Russian composer.

Balfe, Michael William (1808–1870), Irish opera composer.

Bantock, Sir **Granville** (1868–1946), English composer.

Barber, Samuel (1910–   ), American composer.

Barbirolli, Sir **John** (1899–1970), English conductor.

Barenboim, Daniel (1942–   ), Israeli pianist and conductor.

Barraud, Henry (1900–   ), French composer.

Bartók, Béla (1881–1945), great Hungarian composer, whose style was intimately welded to his pioneering folk music research.

Basie, William "Count" (1906–   ), American jazz pianist and bandleader.

Bassett, Leslie (1923–   ), American composer.

Bassey, Shirley (1937–   ), Welsh singer of popular music.

Battistini, Mattia (1856–1928), Italian opera baritone.

Bauer, Harold (1873–1951), English pianist.

Bauer, Marion (1887–1955), American composer and teacher.

Bax, Sir **Arnold** (1883–1953), English composer.

Beach, Mrs. **H. H. A. (Amy Marcy Cheney;** 1867–1944), American composer.

Beardslee, Bethany (1927–   ), American concert soprano; specialist in modern music.

Bechet, Sidney (1897–1959), American New Orleans jazz clarinetist and soprano saxophonist.

Becker, John (1886–1961), American composer.

Beckwith, John (1927–   ), Canadian composer.

Beecham, Sir **Thomas** (1879–1961), English conductor.

Beeson, Jack (1921–   ), American opera composer.

Beethoven, Ludwig van (1770–1827), great German composer who bridged the Classic and Romantic periods; master of the symphony, string quartet, and piano sonata.

Beiderbecke, Bix (1903–1931), American jazz cornetist.

Beinum, Eduard van (1901–1959), Dutch conductor.

Beissel, Johann Conrad (1690–1768), German-American composer of sacred music and founder of the Solitary Brethren at Ephrata, Pennsylvania.

Belafonte, Harry (1927–   ), American folk singer and actor.

Belcher, Supply (1751–1836), American hymn writer.

Bellini, Vincenzo (1801–1835), Italian composer of *bel canto* opera.

Benedict, Sir **Julius** (1804–1885), German-English composer.

Ben-Haim, Paul (1897–   ), German-born Israeli composer.

Benjamin, Arthur (1893–1960), Australian composer.

Bennett, Richard Rodney (1936–   ), English composer.

Bennett, Robert Russell (1894–   ), American composer and arranger.

Bennett, Sir **William Sterndale** (1816–1875), English composer.

Benoit, Peter (1834–1901), Flemish composer.

Berg, Alban (1885–1935), leading Austrian twelve-tone composer and pupil of Schoenberg.

Berger, Arthur (1912–   ), American composer.

Bergsma, William (1921–   ), American composer.

Berio, Luciano (1925–   ), leading Italian composer.

Bériot, Charles de (1802–1870), Belgian violinist and composer.

Berkeley, Lennox (1903–   ), English composer.

Berlin, Irving (1888–   ), American composer of enormously popular songs and Broadway shows.

Berlioz, Hector (1803–1869), great French Romantic orchestral composer.

Berman, Lazar (1930–   ), Russian pianist.

Bernstein, Elmer (1922–   ), American film composer.

Bernstein, Leonard (1918–   ), widely celebrated American conductor, composer of popular and art music, and commentator on music.

Berry, Chuck (1926–   ), American rock'n'roll singer, guitarist, and songwriter.

Berwald, Franz Adolf (1796–1868), Swedish composer.

Bigard, Barney (1906–   ), American jazz clarinetist.

Biggs, E. Power (1906–1977), English-American organist.

Billings, William (1746–1800), American composer of ingenious "fuging tunes."

Binchois, Gilles (c.1400–1460), Flemish composer.

Bing, Sir Rudolf (1902–   ), Austrian-born opera impresario; general manager of the Metropolitan Opera, New York, from 1950 to 1972.

Birtwistle, Harrison (1934–   ), English composer.

Bishop, Sir Henry Rowley (1786–1855), English composer of *Home Sweet Home*.

Bizet, Georges (1838–1875), French composer of *Carmen* and other operas.

Blacher, Boris (1903–1975), German composer.

Blackwood, Easley (1933–   ), American composer.

Blake, James Hubert "Eubie" (1883–   ), American ragtime pianist and composer of major black musicals.

Bland, James A. (1854–1911), American minstrel and composer; wrote *Carry Me Back to Old Virginny*.

Bley, Paul (1932–   ), American jazz keyboard performer.

Bliss, Sir Arthur (1891–1975), English composer.

Blitzstein, Marc (1905–1964), American composer of socially conscious theater music.

Bloch, Ernest (1880–1959), Swiss-born, Jewish-American composer.

Blom, Eric (1888–1959), eminent English music lexicographer.

Blomdahl, Karl-Birger (1916–1968), Swedish composer of modernistic operas.

Blow, John (1649–1708), English organist and composer of church music.

Boatwright, McHenry (1928–   ), American operatic baritone.

Boccherini, Luigi (1743–1805), Italian composer of chamber music.

Boieldieu, François-Adrien (1775–1834), French opera composer.

Boito, Arrigo (1842–1918), Italian opera composer and librettist.

Bolet, Jorge (1914–   ), Cuban-American pianist.

Bolcom, William (1938–   ), American composer and ragtime pianist.

Bond, Carrie Jacobs (1862–1946), American composer of sentimental popular songs.

Bonnet, Joseph (1884–1944), French organist.

Bononcini, Giovanni (1670–1747), Italian opera composer.

Boone, Pat (1934–   ), American pop singer.

Borge, Victor (real name **Borge Rosenbaum**; 1909–   ), Danish pianist and musical humorist.

Borodin, Alexander (1833–1887), Russian opera composer.

Boulanger, Lili (1893–1918), French composer, sister of Nadia Boulanger.

Boulanger, Nadia (1887–1979), renowned French teacher of composition.

Boulez, Pierre (1925–   ), French composer and conductor.

Boult, Sir **Adrian** (1889–   ), English conductor.

Boyce, William (1711–1779), English composer.

Braham, David (1838–1905), American composer for the popular theater.

Brahms, Johannes (1833–1897), great German late Romantic composer.

Brailowsky, Alexander (1896–1976), Russian pianist.

Brian, Dennis (1921–1957), English horn virtuoso.

Brant, Henry (1913–   ), Canadian-American composer of the avant-garde.

Brian, Havergal (1876–1972), prolific English symphonic composer.

Bridge, Frank (1879–1941), English composer and teacher of Benjamin Britten.

Bristow, George Frederick (1825–1898), American composer.

Britten, Benjamin (1913–1976), one of the major opera composers of the mid-20th Century, and foremost composer of his time in England.

Brooks, Shelton (1886–1975), Canadian-American pianist, vaudeville singer, and songwriter; wrote *Some of These Days* and *The Darktown Strutters Ball*.

Broonzy, Big Bill (1898–1958), American country-blues singer and guitarist.

Brown, Earle (1926–   ), American avant-garde composer.

Brown, James (1928–   ), American soul singer.

Browning, John (1933–   ), American pianist.

Brownlee, John (1900–1969), American operatic baritone.

Brubeck, Dave (1920–   ), American composer and jazz pianist.

Bruch, Max (1838–1920), German composer.

Bruckner, Anton (1824–1896), Austrian symphonic composer.

Brumel, Antoine (1460–c.1520), Flemish composer.

Buck, Dudley (1839–1909), American organist, composer, and pedagogue.

Bull, John (c.1562–1628), English composer and organist.

Bull, Ole (1810–1880), Norwegian violinist and composer.

Bülow, Hans von (1830–1894), German pianist, conductor, and music editor.

Bumbry, Grace (1937–   ), American operatic soprano.

Burkhard, Willy (1900–1955), Swiss composer.

Burney, Charles (1726–1814), British music historian.

Burrell, Kenny (1931–   ), American jazz guitarist.

Busoni, Ferruccio (1866–1924), Italian-German composer, pianist, and writer on modern aesthetics.

Bussotti, Sylvano (1931–   ), Italian avant-garde composer.

Buxtehude, Dietrich (c.1637–1707), German organist and composer.

Byrd, Donald (1932–   ), American jazz trumpet player and educator.

Byrd, William (1543–1623), English vocal composer and organist.

Cabezón, Antonio de (1510–1566), Spanish organist and composer.

Caccini, Giulio (c.1550–1618), Italian composer; one of the originators of opera.

Cadman, Charles Wakefield (1881–1946), American opera composer and researcher on the music of American Indians.

Cage, John (1912–   ), American composer and leader of the avant-garde.

Caldwell, Sarah (1924–   ), American conductor and opera director.

Callas, Maria (1923–1977), American operatic soprano of Greek origin.

Calvé, Emma (1858–1942), French operatic soprano.

Cardew, Cornelius (1936–   ), English composer of the avant-garde.

Carissimi, Giacomo (1605–1674), Italian composer of oratorios and Masses.

Carmichael, Hoagy (1899–   ), American songwriter.

Carpenter, John Alden (1876–1951), American composer.

Carr, Benjamin (1768–1831), British-born American composer and publisher.

Carrillo, Julián (1875–1965), Mexican composer and theorist.

Carter, Benny (1907–   ), American jazz saxophonist and arranger.

Carter, Elliott (1908–   ), American composer.

Carter family; A. P. (?–1960), **Sara** (1899–   ), **Maybelle** (1909–1978), **June** (1929–   ), American family of country musicians.

Caruso, Enrico (1873–1921), legendary Italian operatic tenor.

Casadesus, Gaby (1901–   ), French pianist; wife of Robert Casadesus.

Casadesus, Jean (1927–1972), French pianist; son of Gaby and Robert Casadesus.

Casadesus, Robert (1899–1972), French pianist and composer.

Casals, Pablo (1876–1973), Spanish cellist.

Casella, Alfredo (1883–1947), Italian composer and pianist.

Cash, Johnny (1932–   ), American country singer, guitarist, and songwriter.

Castelnuovo-Tedesco, Mario (1895–1968), Italian composer.

Castro, Juan José (1895–1968), Argentinian opera composer and conductor.

Cavalli, Francesco (1602–1676), Italian composer of early operas.

Cazden, Norman (1914–   ), American composer.

Cesti, Marc Antonio (1623–1669), Italian opera composer.

Chabrier, Emmanuel (1841–1894), French composer of operas and orchestral works.

Chadwick, George Whitefield (1854–1931), American composer of symphonic music.

Chaliapin, Feodor (1873–1938), legendary Russian operatic bass.

Chaminade, Cécile (1857–1944), French composer of salon music for piano.

Charles, Ray (1930–   ), American rhythm and blues singer, pianist, and songwriter.

Charpentier, Gustave (1860–1956), French opera composer.

Charpentier, Marc-Antoine (1636–1704), French composer of stage and vocal music.

Chasins, Abram (1903–   ), American pianist and composer.

Chausson, Ernest (1855–1899), French composer.

Chávez, Carlos (1899–1978), leading Mexican composer.

Checker, Chubby (real name **Ernest Evans**; 1941–   ), American rock'n'roll singer.

Cherubini, Luigi (1760–1842), Italian composer of operas.

Chopin, Frédéric (1810–1849), incomparable Polish composer of piano music.

Chou Wen-chung (1923–   ), Chinese-American composer.

Christian, Charlie (1919–1942), American jazz guitarist.

Cimarosa, Domenico (1749–1801), Italian opera composer.

Clark, Roy (1933–   ), American folk guitarist and singer.

Clementi, Muzio (1752–1832), Italian pianist, pedagogue, and composer of piano studies.

Cliburn, Van (1934–   ), American pianist.

Cohan, George M. (1878–1942), American composer of popular shows.

Cole, Nat "King" (1917–1965), American jazz pianist and popular singer.

Coleman, Ornette (1930–   ), American saxophonist and composer; a leading exponent of "free jazz."

Coleridge-Taylor, Samuel (1875–1912), African-English composer.

Colgrass, Michael (1932–   ), American composer.

Collins, Judy (1939–   ), American folk singer.

Coltrane, John (1926–1967), American jazz saxophonist and composer.

Condon, Eddie (1904–   ), Chicago jazz guitarist.

Confrey, Zez (1895–1972), American novelty pianist and composer.

Converse, Frederick Shepherd (1871–1940), American composer.

Cook, Will Marion (1869–1944), American composer of black musical comedies.

Copland, Aaron (1900–   ), one of the outstanding American composers of the century.

Corea, Chick (1941–   ), American jazz keyboard musician.

Corelli, Arcangelo (1653–1713), Italian violinist and composer.

Corigliano, John (1938–   ), American composer.

Cornelius, Peter (1824–1874), German opera composer.

Cortot, Alfred (1877–1962), French pianist.

Couperin, François (1668–1733), French keyboard composer and organist; called "Couperin le grand."

Cowell, Henry (1897–1965), American composer, the first to use tone clusters.

Craft, Robert (1923–   ), American conductor and writer; amanuensis and literary collaborator of Igor Stravinsky.

Crawford, Ruth (1901–1953), American composer.

Creston, Paul (1906–   ), American composer.

Crosby, Bing (real name **Harry Lillis Crosby;** 1901–1977), American pop singer and actor.

Crumb, George (1929–   ), American composer.

Cugat, Xavier (1900–   ), Spanish-born popular Latin-American bandleader.

Cui, César (1835–1918), Russian composer.

Czerny, Carl (1791–1857), Austrian composer of celebrated piano exercises; pupil of Beethoven.

Dahl, Ingolf (1912–1970), American composer and teacher.

d'Albert, Eugène (or **Eugen**) (1864–1932), Scottish-German composer.

Dalcroze. See **Jaques-Dalcroze.**

Dallapiccola, Luigi (1904–1975), Italian serial composer.

Damrosch, Frank (1859–1937), German-American choral conductor.

Damrosch, Leopold (1832–1885), German-American conductor.

Damrosch, Walter (1862–1950), German-American conductor and opera composer.

Da Ponte, Lorenzo (1749–1838), Italian librettist for Mozart and other composers.

Daquin, Louis-Claude (1694–1772), French composer of keyboard music.

Dargomyzhsky, Alexander (1813–1869), Russian opera composer.

David, Ferdinand (1810–1873), German violinist.

Davidovsky, Mario (1934–   ), Argentinian-American composer of electronic music.

Davies, Peter Maxwell (1934–   ), English composer.

Davis, Colin (1927–   ), English conductor.

Davis, Miles (1926–   ), American jazz trumpet player.

Davis, Sammy, Jr. (1925–   ), American pop singer, dancer, and actor.

Debussy, Claude (1862–1918), great modern French composer; originator of Impressionism.

DeGaetani, Jan (1933–   ), American mezzo-soprano who specializes in modern music.

De Koven, Reginald (1859–1920), American composer of light operas.

Delibes, Léo (1836–1891), French composer of operas and ballets.

Delius, Frederick (1862–1934), English composer of poetic symphonic pieces.

Dello Joio, Norman (1913–   ), American composer.

Del Tredici, David (1937–   ), American composer.

de Pachmann, Vladimir (1848–1933), eccentric Russian pianist.

De Reszke, Jean (1850–1925), Polish operatic tenor.

Des Prez, Josquin (c.1440–1521), Flemish polyphonic composer, the greatest master of his generation; known also simply as "Josquin."

Diabelli, Anton (1781–1858), Austrian composer and music publisher, known chiefly through a set of variations Beethoven wrote on one of his themes.

Diamond, David (1915–   ), American orchestral composer.

Diamond, Neil (1941–   ), American folk singer and composer.

di Bonaventura, Mario (1924–   ), American conductor, educator, and music publisher.

Dichter, Misha (1945–   ), Chinese-born Russian-American pianist.

Dickinson, Peter (1934–   ), English composer.

Diddley, Bo (1928–   ), American rock'n'roll singer and guitarist.

d'Indy, Vincent (1851–1931), French composer.

Dittersdorf, Karl Ditters von (1739–1799), Austrian violinist and composer.

Dodge, Charles (1942–   ), American composer of avant-garde tendencies.

Dohnányi, Ernst von (1877–1960), significant Hungarian composer, pianist, and pedagogue.

Dolmetsch, Arnold (1858–1940), English manufacturer of lutes, recorders, and harpsichords.

Domino, Antoine "Fats" (1928–   ), American rock'n'roll singer, pianist, and songwriter.

Donizetti, Gaetano (1797–1848), prolific Italian composer of operas in the *bel canto* tradition.

Dorati, Antal (1906–   ), Hungarian conductor.

Dorsey, Jimmy (1904–1957), American jazz clarinetist and bandleader.

Dorsey, Tommy (1905–1956), American jazz trombonist and bandleader, brother of Jimmy Dorsey.

Dowland, John (1562–1626), English lutenist and song composer.

Dragonetti, Domenico (1763–1846), Italian double-bass virtuoso.

Dresden, Sem (1881–1957), Dutch composer and educator.

Druckman, Jacob (1928–   ), American composer.

Dubois, Théodore (1837–1924), French organist and pedagogue.

Duchin, Eddy (1910–1951), popular American pianist and bandleader.

Dufallo, Richard (1933–   ), American clarinetist, conductor, and composer of the avant-garde.

Dufay, Guillaume (c.1400–1474), Flemish composer.

Dukas, Paul (1865–1935), French composer.

Duke, Vernon. See **Dukelsky, Vladimir**.

Dukelsky, Vladimir (1903–1969), Russian-American composer of serious and popular music, the latter under the pseudonym "Vernon Duke."

Dunstable, John (c.1380–1453), English composer.

Duparc, Henri (1848–1933), French song composer.

DuPré, Jacqueline (1945–   ), English cellist; married to Daniel Barenboim.

Dupré, Marcel (1886–1971), French organist.

Durey, Louis (1888–   ), French composer.

Dushkin, Samuel (1891-1976), Russian violinist.

Dussek, Jan Ladislav (1760-1812), Czech pianist and composer.

Dvořák, Antonín (1841-1904), Czech composer.

Dyer-Bennet, Richard (1913–   ), English-American folk and lieder singer.

Dylan, Bob (real name **Robert Zimmerman**; 1941–   ), songwriter and one of the beacons of 1960s folk/rock.

Eckstine, Billy (1914–   ), American jazz and pop singer.

Eddy, Nelson (1901-1967), American baritone.

Egge, Klaus (1906–   ), Norwegian composer.

Egk, Werner (1901–   ), German composer.

Ehrling, Sixten (1918–   ), Swedish conductor.

Einem, Gottfried von (1918–   ), Austrian composer.

Einstein, Alfred (1880-1952), German musicologist.

Eisler, Hanns (1898-1962), German composer of politically oriented works.

Eldridge, Roy (1911–   ), American jazz trumpeter.

Elgar, Sir **Edward** (1857-1934), English composer.

Ellington, Edward Kennedy "Duke" (1899-1974), American jazz pianist, composer, and bandleader.

Elliott, Cass (1941-1974), corpulent American rock vocalist; member of the Mamas and Papas.

Elman, Mischa (1891-1967), Russian violinist.

Emerson, Keith (1948–   ), English rock keyboard musician and composer; member of Emerson, Lake and Palmer.

Emmett, Daniel Decatur (1815-1904), American composer of *Dixie* and other minstrel songs.

Enesco, Georges (1881-1955), Rumanian violinist and foremost national composer; teacher of Menuhin.

Evans, Bill (1929–   ), American jazz pianist and composer.

Evans, Gil (1912–   ), Canadian jazz arranger.

Ewen, David (1907–   ), prolific American writer on music; published some eighty books of reference and biography.

Falla, Manuel de (1876–1946), Spanish composer.

Farinelli (1705–1782), Italian castrato of legendary virtuosity.

Farrar, Geraldine (1882–1967), American operatic soprano.

Farrell, Eileen (1920–   ), American operatic and concert soprano.

Farwell, Arthur (1872–1952), American composer.

Fauré, Gabriel (1845–1924), French composer and music educator.

Faure, Jean-Baptiste (1830–1914), French baritone.

Fayrfax, Robert (1464–1521), English organist and church composer.

Feldman, Morton (1926–   ), American avant-garde composer.

Feliciano, José (c.1945–   ), Puerto Rican *salsa* vocalist and instrumentalist.

Ferguson, Maynard (1928–   ), American jazz trumpeter and bandleader.

Ferrero, Willy (1906–1954), American-born Italian conductor who began his career as a child prodigy.

Ferrier, Kathleen (1912–1953), English contralto.

Fiedler, Arthur (1894-1979), American conductor of the Boston Pops Orchestra.

Field, John (1782–1837), Irish pianist and composer.

Fine, Irving (1914–1962), American composer.

Fine, Vivian (1913–   ), American composer.

Finney, Ross Lee (1906–   ), American composer.

Firkušný, Rudolf (1912–   ), Czech pianist.

Fischer-Dieskau, Dietrich (1925–   ), German baritone and conductor.

Fitzgerald, Ella (1918–   ), American jazz vocalist.

Flack, Roberta (1939–   ), American soul singer and pianist.

Flagstad, Kirsten (1895–1962), Norwegian operatic soprano.

Flanagan, William (1923–1969), American composer.

Flatt, Lester (1914–   ), bluegrass country singer and guitarist; teamed with Earl Scruggs.

Flotow, Friedrich von (1812–1883), German opera composer.

Floyd, Carlisle (1926–   ), American opera composer.

Foote, Arthur (1853–1937), American composer.

Ford, Tennessee Ernie (1919–   ), American country & western singer.

Fortner, Wolfgang (1907–   ), German composer.

Foss, Lukas (1922–   ), German-American pianist, composer, and conductor.

Foster, Stephen (1826–1864), American composer of popular songs.

Fox, Virgil (1912–   ), flamboyant American organist.

Francescatti, Zino (1905–   ), French-American violinist.

Franck, César (1822–1890), French organist and composer.

Franklin, Aretha (1942–   ), American soul singer.

Franz, Robert (1815–1892), German lieder composer.

Freeman, Harry (1869–1954), American composer of operas on black themes.

Frescobaldi, Girolamo (1583–1643), Italian organist and composer.

Friml, Rudolf (1881–1972), Czech-born American operetta composer.

Froberger, Johann Jakob (1616–1667), German composer and organist; originator of the Baroque suite.

Fry, William Henry (1813–1864), American opera composer.

Furtwängler, Wilhelm (1886–1954), German conductor.

Fux, Johann Joseph (1660–1741), German music theorist.

Gabrieli, Andrea (c.1520–1586), Italian organist and composer.

Gabrieli, Giovanni (c.1557–1612), Italian organist and composer; nephew of Andrea Gabrieli.

Gabrilowitsch, Ossip (1878–1936), Russian pianist.

Gade, Niels (1817–1890), Danish composer.

Galilei, Vincenzo (c.1520–1591), Italian composer of songs that led to early opera; father of astronomer Galileo Galilei.

Galli-Curci, Amelita (1882–1963), Italian coloratura soprano.

Galuppi, Baldassare (1706–1785), Italian composer of *opera buffa*.

Galway, James (1939–   ), Irish flute virtuoso.

Garden, Mary (1874–1967), Scottish-born American soprano.

Garfunkel, Art (1941–   ), American folk singer; former performing partner of Paul Simon.

Garland, Judy (1922–1969), American singer and actress.

Garner, Erroll (1923–1976), American jazz pianist and composer.

Gatti-Casazza, Giulio (1868–1940), Italian impresario; director of the Metropolitan Opera, New York, from 1908 to 1935.

Gedda, Nicolai (1925–   ), Swedish tenor.

Geminiani, Francesco (1680–1762), Italian violinist and composer.

Gerhard, Roberto (1896–1970), Spanish-born British composer.

German, Sir Edward (1862–1936), British composer.

Gershwin, George (1898–1937), great American songwriter and composer of popular musicals and jazz-flavored "serious" works.

Gershwin, Ira (1896–   ), American lyricist-librettist; collaborated with his brother George Gershwin and other major composers of the American musical theater.

Gesualdo, Don Carlo (c.1560–1613), Prince of Venosa, Italian composer whose chromatic music anticipated later styles.

Getz, Stan (1927–   ), American West Coast "cool" jazz tenor saxophonist.

Giannini, Vittorio (1903–1966), American composer.

Gibbons, Orlando (1583–1625), English composer.

Gideon, Miriam (1906–   ), American composer.

Gieseking, Walter (1895–1956), German pianist.

Gilbert, Henry Franklin (1868–1928), American composer.

Gilbert, Sir William (1836–1911), English lyricist and librettist of Gilbert and Sullivan operettas.

Gilels, Emil (1916–   ), Russian pianist.

Gillespie, John Birks "Dizzy" (1917–   ), American jazz trumpet player; co-founder of bebop, with Charlie Parker.

Gilmore, Patrick (1829–1892), American bandmaster.

Ginastera, Alberto (1916–   ), world-renowned Argentinian-born composer.

Giulini, Carlo Maria (1914–   ), Italian conductor.

Glanville-Hicks, Peggy (1912–   ), Australian composer.

Glass, Philip (1937–   ), American avant-garde composer.

Glazer, Tom (1914–   ), American folk singer and instrumentalist.

Glazunov, Alexander (1865–1936), Russian composer and music educator.

Glière, Reinhold (1875–1956), Russian composer and pedagogue.

Glinka, Mikhail (1804–1857), Russian composer; "Father of Russian music."

Gluck, Christoph Willibald von (1714–1787), German composer of operas to French and Italian texts.

Godowsky, Leopold (1870–1938), Russian-American pianist and composer of virtuoso etudes.

Goldman, Edwin Franko (1878–1956), American bandmaster.

Goldman, Richard Franko (1910–   ), American bandmaster.

Goldmark, Carl (1830–1915), German composer.

Goldmark, Rubin (1872–1936), American composer and teacher.

Golschmann, Vladimir (1893–1972), French born American conductor.

Goodman, Benny (1909–   ), leading American jazz clarinetist and swing bandleader.

Goossens, Sir Eugene (1893–1962), English conductor and composer.

Gossec, François Joseph (1734–1829), Belgian composer.

Gottschalk, Louis Moreau (1829–1869), American pianist and composer.

Goudimel, Claude (c.1514–1572), French composer.

Gould, Glenn (1932–   ), Canadian pianist noted for unorthodox interpretations.

Gould, Morton (1913–   ), American composer and conductor.

Gounod, Charles (1818–1893), French opera composer.

Grainger, Percy (1882–1961), Australian pianist and composer.

Gramm, Donald (1927–   ), American bass-baritone.

Granados, Enrique (1867–1916), Spanish composer.

Grandjany, Marcel (1891–1975), French harpist and composer for harp.

Grappelli, Stephane (1908–   ), French jazz violinist.

Greenberg, Noah (1919–1966), American conductor and musicologist; specialist in Medieval and Renaissance music.

Gretchaninoff (pronounced Gre-tcha-né-nof, *not* Gretchá-ne-nof), **Alexander** (1864–1956), Russian composer.

Grétry, André (1741–1813), French opera composer.

Grieg, Edvard (1843–1907), Norwegian composer.

Griffes, Charles Tomlinson (1884–1920), American Impressionist composer.

Grofé, Ferde (1892–1972), American composer of popular orchestral pieces.

Grove, Sir **George** (1820–1900), English music lexicographer.

Gruenberg, Louis (1884–1964), American composer.

Guarneri, Giuseppe Antonio (1698–1744), Italian violin-maker; grandson of Andrea Guarneri.

Guido d'Arezzo (c.995–c.1050), Italian founder of fundamental music theory.

Guilmant, Alexandre (1837–1911), French organist.

Gulda, Friedrich (1930–   ), Austrian jazz pianist and composer.

Guthrie, Arlo (1947–   ), American folk singer, guitarist, and songwriter.

Guthrie, Woody (1912–1967), American folk singer, guitarist, and songwriter; father of Arlo Guthrie.

Hába, Alois (1893–1973), Czech composer of quarter-tone music.

Hadley, Henry (1871–1937), American composer and conductor.

Hageman, Richard (1882–1966), American song composer.

Haggard, Merle (1937–   ), American country & western singer, guitarist, and songwriter.

Haieff, Alexei (1914–   ), Russian-American composer.

Hale, Philip (1854–1934), American music critic.

Halévy, Jacques (1799–1862), French opera composer.

Haley, Bill (1927–   ), American pioneer rock'n'roll singer.

Hall, Jim (1930–   ), American jazz guitarist and composer.

Hamilton, Iain (1922–   ), Scottish composer.

Hammerstein, Oscar, II (1895–1960), American lyricist-librettist for the Broadway stage; collaborated with Richard Rodgers and others.

Hampton, Lionel (1909–   ), American jazz vibraphonist.

Hancock, Herbie (1940–   ), American jazz keyboard performer and film composer.

Handel, George Frideric (1685–1759), German organist and composer, one of the giants of the late Baroque; excelled in Italian opera and established English oratorio.

Handy, W. C. (1873–1958), American song composer; wrote *Saint Louis Blues*.

Hanon, Charles-Louis (1819–1900), French pianist, pedagogue, and composer of keyboard exercises.

Hanslick, Eduard (1825–1904), Austrian music critic and polemicist.

Hanson, Howard (1896–   ), American composer and educator.

Harris, Roy (1898–   ), American composer.

Harrison, George (1943–   ), English rock singer and guitarist; member of the Beatles.

Harrison, Lou (1917–   ), American composer.

Hart, Lorenz (1895–1943), American lyricist and collaborator of Broadway musical composer Richard Rodgers.

Harty, Sir Hamilton (1879–1941), British conductor.

Hasse, Johann Adolph (1699–1783), German opera composer.

Hassler, Hans Leo (1564–1612), German composer.

Hauer, Josef Matthias (1883–1959), Austrian 12-tone theorist and composer.

Hauptmann, Moritz (1792–1868), German violinist and theorist.

Hawkins, Coleman (1904–1969), American jazz tenor saxophonist.

Hawkins, Sir John (1719–1789), British music historian.

Haydn, Franz Joseph (1732–1809), great Austrian composer; the first master of Viennese Classicism and the "Father of the Symphony."

Haydn, Michael (1737–1806), Austrian composer; brother of Franz Joseph Haydn.

Hayes, Roland (1887–1977), American concert tenor.

Heifetz, Jascha (1901–   ), Russian-American violin virtuoso.

Heinrich, Anthony Philip (1781–1861), Bohemian-American composer of most extravagant music.

Heller, Stephen (1813–1888), Hungarian pianist and composer.

Henderson, Fletcher (1898–1952), American jazz pianist, bandleader, and arranger; developer of "big band" jazz.

Henderson, Skitch (1918–   ), popular American bandleader.

Hendrix, Jimi (1942–1970), American rock singer and guitarist.

Henry, Pierre (1927–   ), French composer; developer of *musique concrete.*

Henschel, Sir George (1850–1934), German-English bass, composer, and conductor.

Hensel, Fanny Cäcilia (1805–1847), pianist and composer; sister of Felix Mendelssohn.

Henselt, Adolf von (1814–1889), German pianist and pedagogue.

Henze, Hans Werner (1926–   ), German composer.

Herbert, Victor (1859–1924), American operetta composer.

Herbst, Johannes (1735–1812), Swabian-born American-Moravian composer and compiler of a major collection of 18th-century music.

Herman, Woody (1913–   ), American jazz clarinetist and bandleader.

Hérold, Louis (1791–1833), French opera composer.

Herrmann, Bernard (1911–1975), American composer of movie music.

Herz, Henri (1803–1888), Austrian pianist and composer of piano music.

Heseltine, Philip (1894–1930), British composer; used the pen name "Peter Warlock."

Hess, Dame Myra (1890–1965), English pianist.

Hewitt, James (1770–1827), English-born American composer.

Hill, Edward Burlingame (1872–1960), American composer.

Hiller, Ferdinand von (1811–1885), German composer.

Hiller, Lejaren (1924–   ), American composer of computer music.

Hindemith, Paul (1895–1963), German composer.

Hines, Earl "Fatha" (1905–   ), American jazz pianist.

Hirt, Al (1922–   ), American Dixieland trumpeter.

Hodges, Johnny (1906–   ), American jazz saxophonist.

Hofmann, Josef (1876–1957), Polish-born American pianist.

Holiday, Billie (1915–1959), American jazz vocalist.

Hollander, Lorin (1944–   ), American pianist.

Holmès, Augusta Mary Anne (1847–1903), French composer.

Holst, Gustav (1874–1934), English composer.

Honegger, Arthur (1892–1955), French composer.

Hooker, John Lee (1917–   ), American electric-blues singer and guitarist.

Hopkinson, Francis (1737–1791), American composer and statesman.

Horne, Marilyn (1934–   ), American operatic soprano.

Horowitz, Vladimir (1904–   ), celebrated Russian-American pianist.

Hovhaness, Alan (1911–   ), American composer.

Howard, John Tasker, (1890–1964), American musicologist.

Hubay, Jenö (1858–1937), Hungarian violinist.

Hubbard, Freddie (1938–   ), American jazz trumpeter.

Huberman, Bronislaw (1882–1947), Polish violinist; founder of Israel Philharmonic.

Hummel, Johann Nepomuk (1778–1837), Czech-born pianist and composer.

Humperdinck, Engelbert (1854–1921), German composer of the children's opera *Hänsel und Gretel*.

Husa, Karel (1921–   ), Czech-born American composer.

Huss, Henry Holden (1862–1953), American pianist and composer.

Hutcheson, Ernest (1871–1951), American pianist and teacher.

Ibert, Jacques (1890–1962), French composer.

Imbrie, Andrew (1921–   ), American composer.

Indy, Vincent d'. See d'Indy, Vincent.

Ippolitov-Ivanov, Mikhail (1859–1935), Russian composer.

Ireland, John (1879–1962), English composer.

Isaac, Heinrich (c.1450–1517), Renaissance composer of vocal works, active in Germany and Italy.

Istomin, Eugene (1925–   ), American pianist.

Iturbi, José (1895–   ), Spanish pianist and conductor.

Ives, Burl (1909–   ), American folk singer and actor.

Ives, Charles Edward (1874–1954), American composer whose individual genius was universally recognized late in his life.

Jackson, Mahalia (1911–1972), American gospel singer.

Jackson, Milt (1923–   ), American jazz vibraphonist.

Jadassohn, Salomon (1831–1902), German music theorist and pedagogue.

Jagger, Mick (1943–   ), lead singer of the English rock group, the Rolling Stones.

James, Harry (1916–   ), popular American trumpeter and bandleader.

James, Philip (1890–1975), American composer.

Janáček, Leoš (1854–1928), Czech composer.

Janequin, Clément (c.1475–c.1560), French composer.

Jacques-Dalcroze, Émile (1865–1950), Austrian-Swiss composer; inventor of eurhythmics.

Joachim, Joseph (1831–1907), German violinist and pedagogue.

Johannesen, Grant (1921–   ), American pianist.

Johansen, Gunnar (1906–   ), American pianist.

John, Elton (1947–   ), English rock singer.

Johnson, J. Rosamond (1873–1954), American singer and composer for the black musical stage.

Johnson, James P. (1891–1955), American stride pianist and composer; teacher of "Fats" Waller.

Johnson, Thor (1913–1975), American conductor.

Jolivet, André (1905–1974), French composer.

Jolson, Al (1886–1950), American popular singer.

Jommelli, Niccolò (1714–1774), Italian opera composer.

Jones, Hank (1918–   ), versatile American jazz and studio pianist.

Jones, Lindley Armstrong "Spike" (1911–1965), American musical satirist whose big-band spoofs created a unique cacophonous genre.

Jones, Philly Joe (1923–   ), American modern-jazz drummer.

Jones, Quincy (1933–   ), American jazz trumpeter, pianist, and film composer.

Jones, Thad (1923–   ), American jazz trumpet and band-leader.

Jones, Tom (1940–   ), Welsh pop singer.

Joplin, Janis (1943–1970), American rock singer.

Joplin, Scott (1868–1917), American ragtime pianist and composer.

Joseffy, Rafael (1852–1915), Hungarian pianist and peda-gogue.

Josquin. See **Des Prez, Josquin.**

Josten, Werner (1885–1963), German-American composer.

Joubert, John (1927–   ), South African composer.

Judson, Arthur (1881–1975), American impresario.

Juilliard, Augustus D. (1836–1919), French-American music patron; founder of the Juilliard School of Music in New York.

Kabalevsky, Dmitri (1904–   ), Russian composer.

Kalkbrenner, Friedrich (1785–1849), German pianist and composer.

Karajan, Herbert von (1908–   ), Austrian conductor.

Karg-Elert, Sigfrid (1877–1933), German organist and com-poser.

Kay, Ulysses (1917–   ), American composer.

Keiser, Reinhard (1674–1739), German opera composer.

Kelley, Edgar Stillman (1857–1944), American composer.

Kenton, Stan (1912-1979), American bandleader.

Kern, Jerome (1885–1945), American composer of musical comedies.

Khachaturian, Aram (1903–1978), Russian-Armenian composer.

Kindler, Hans (1892–1949), Dutch-American cellist and conductor.

King, B. B. (real first name **Riley**; 1925–   ), American urban blues singer, songwriter, and guitarist.

Kinkeldey, Otto (1878–1966), American musicologist.

Kipnis, Alexander (1891–1978), Russian-American operatic bass; father of Igor.

Kipnis, Igor (1930–   ), American harpsichordist.

Kirchner, Leon (1919–   ), American composer.

Kirk, Rahsaan Roland (1936–1977), American jazz musician.

Kirkpatrick, John (1905–   ), American pianist and Charles Ives scholar.

Kirkpatrick, Ralph (1911–   ), American harpsichordist and Scarlatti scholar.

Kirnberger, Johann Philipp (1721–1783), German theorist.

Kleiber, Erich (1890–1956), Austrian conductor.

Klemperer, Otto (1885–1973), German conductor.

Klindworth, Karl (1830–1916), German pianist and teacher.

Klosé, Hyacinthe-Éléonore (1808–1880), French clarinetist and pedagogue.

Kneisel, Franz (1865–1926), German-American violinist.

Köchel, Ludwig von (1800–1877), Austrian mineralogist; compiler of the standard Mozart catalogue.

Kodály, Zoltán (1882–1967), Hungarian composer and music educator.

Koechlin, Charles (1867–1950), French composer.

Kogan, Leonid (1924–   ), Russian violinist.

Köhler, Louis (1820–1886), German pianist and pedagogue.

Korngold, Erich Wolfgang (1897–1957), Austrian-American composer of operas and film music.

Kostelanetz, André (1901–   ), Russian-born American conductor.

Koussevitzky, Serge (1874–1951), Russian conductor and virtuoso on the double bass.

Kraft, William (1923–   ), American composer and percussion virtuoso.

Krauss, Clemens (1893–1954), Austrian conductor.

Krehbiel, Henry Edward (1854–1923), American music critic.

Kreisler, Fritz (1875–1962), Austrian violinist and composer of solo pieces for the violin.

Krenek, Ernst (1900–   ), Austrian-American composer.

Kreutzer, Rodolphe (1766–1831), French-born violinist to whom Beethoven dedicated his *Kreutzer Sonata.*

Krips, Josef (1902–1974), Austrian conductor.

Kristofferson, Kris (1937–   ), American country singer, songwriter, and actor.

Krupa, Gene (1909–1973), American jazz drummer.

Kubelík, Jan (1880–1940), Czech violinist and composer of violin pieces.

Kubelík, Rafael (1914–   ), Czech conductor.

Kubik, Gail (1914–   ), American composer.

Kuhnau, Johann (1660–1722), German composer.

Kullak, Theodor (1818–1882), German pianist and teacher.

Kupferman, Meyer (1926–   ), American composer.

Laderman, Ezra (1924–   ), American composer.

Lalo, Édouard (1823–1892), French composer.

Lamb, Joseph F. (1887–1960), American composer of "classic" ragtime.

Lambert, Constant (1905–1951), English composer.

La Montaine, John (1920–   ), American composer.

Lamoureux, Charles (1834–1899), French conductor.

Landau, Siegfried (1921–   ), German-American conductor and composer.

Landowska, Wanda (1877–1959), Polish harpsichordist largely responsible for that instrument's revival.

Landré, Guillaume (1905–1968), Dutch composer.

Lane, Burton (1912–   ), American composer of Broadway musicals.

Lang, Eddie (1904–33), American jazz guitarist.

Lanner, Joseph (1801–1843), Austrian composer of dance music.

Lanza, Mario (1921–1959), American tenor who sang popular songs and operatic arias on records and in movies.

Larrocha, Alicia de (1923–   ), Spanish pianist.

Lassen, Eduard (1830–1904), Danish-German conductor.

Lassus, Roland de (c.1532–1594), great Flemish composer.

Lateef, Yusef (1921–   ), American jazz musician.

Lavry, Marc (1903–1967), Israeli composer.

Law, Andrew (1749–1821), American composer, singing master, and developer of "shape notes."

Leadbelly (real name **Huddie Ledbetter;** 1885–1949), American folk singer, guitarist, and songwriter.

Lear, Evelyn (1927–   ), American soprano.

Leclair, Jean Marie (1697–1764), French violinist and composer.

Lecuona, Ernesto (1896–1963), Cuban composer of popular music.

Lee, Peggy (1920–   ), American pop and jazz singer.

Lees, Benjamin (1924–   ), American composer.

Leginska, Ethel (1886–1970), English-born American pianist and composer.

Legrand, Michel (1932–   ), French composer of popular music.

Lehár, Franz (1870–1948), Austrian composer of famous operettas.

Lehmann, Lilli (1848–1929), German soprano.

Lehmann, Liza (1862–1918), English soprano and song composer.

Lehmann, Lotte (1888–1976), German soprano.

Leibowitz, René (1913–1972), Polish-born French composer and conductor.

Leinsdorf, Erich (1912–   ), Austrian conductor.

Le Jeune, Claude (1528–1600), French composer.

Lennon, John (1940–   ), English rock singer, guitarist, and songwriter; member of the Beatles.

Lenya, Lotte (1900–   ), German actress who cultivated a coarse, pungent singing style; married Kurt Weill.

Leoncavallo, Ruggiero (1857–1919), Italian composer of the opera *Pagliacci.*

Leoninus (active, mid-12th century), master of the Notre Dame School of Paris.

Lerner, Alan Jay (1918–   ), lyricist-librettist for Broadway musicals; collaborated with Frederick Loewe.

Leschetizky, Theodor (1830–1915), Austrian pianist and pedagogue.

Lev, Ray (1912–   ), Russian-American pianist.

Levant, Oscar (1906–1927), American pianist, composer, actor, and wit.

Levine, James (1943–   ), American conductor.

Lewenthal, Raymond (1926–   ), American pianist; specialist in the works of neglected Romantic composers.

Lewis, Henry (1932–   ), American conductor.

Lewis, Jerry Lee (1935–   ), American rock 'n' roll singer.

Lewis, John (1920–   ), American jazz pianist and composer, member of the Modern Jazz Quartet.

Lewis, Mel (1929–   ), American jazz drummer and bandleader; co-leader of the Thad Jones-Mel Lewis Orchestra.

Lhévinne, Joseph (1874–1944), Russian pianist and teacher.

Lhévinne, Rosina (1880–1976), Russian pianist and teacher; married Joseph Lhévinne.

Liadov, Anatol (1855–1914), Russian composer.

Liberace (real name **Wladziu Valentino;** 1919–   ), American popular pianist.

Liebermann, Rolf (1910–   ), Swiss composer and opera impresario.

Lieberson, Goddard (1911–1977), American composer and recording industry executive.

Ligeti, György (1923–   ), Hungarian composer of avantgarde music.

Lind, Jenny (1820–1887), celebrated Swedish soprano, nicknamed "Swedish nightingale."

Lipatti, Dinu (1917–1950), Rumanian pianist and composer.

Liszt, Franz (1811–1886), Hungarian pianist and composer; the greatest piano virtuoso of the Romantic period.

Little Richard (real name **Richard Penniman;** 1935–   ), American rock 'n' roll singer and songwriter.

Locatelli, Pietro (1695–1764), Italian violinist and composer.

Loeffler, Charles Martin (1861–1935), Alsatian-born American composer.

Loesser, Arthur (1894–1969), American pianist and author.

Loesser, Frank (1910–1969), American composer of Broadway musicals.

Loewe, Carl (1796–1869), German song composer.

Loewe, Frederick (1904–), Austrian-American composer of Broadway musicals, including *My Fair lady*.

Lombardo, Guy (1902–1977), Canadian-born American bandleader.

London, George, (1919–), American operatic baritone.

Long, Marguerite (1874–1966), French pianist.

Loomis, Harvey Worthington (1865–1930), American composer.

Lopatnikoff, Nikolai (1903–1976), Russian-American composer.

Lortzing, Albert (1801–1851), German composer.

Löschhorn, Albert (1819–1905), German pianist and teacher.

Luening, Otto (1900–), American composer, pioneer in electronic music.

Lully, Jean-Baptiste (1632–1687), Italian-born composer of the French royal court.

Lutoslawski, Witold (1913–), Polish composer.

Lutyens, Elisabeth (1906–), English composer.

Lynn, Loretta (1927–), American country & western singer and songwriter.

Maazel, Lorin (1930–), American conductor.

MacDowell, Edward Alexander (1860–1908), European-trained American composer.

Machaut, Guillaume de (c.1300–1377), major polyphonic composer of the late Middle Ages; composed the first complete polyphonic Mass.

Maderna, Bruno (1920–1973), Italian composer and conductor.

Mahler, Gustav (1860–1911), Austrian symphonic composer and conductor.

Makeba, Miriam (1932–), South African singer.

Malipiero, Gian Francesco (1882–1973), Italian composer.

Mancini, Henry (1924–   ), American film and TV composer.

Mantovani, Annunzio Paolo (1905-   ), Italian-English conductor of bland popular music.

Marenzio, Luca (1553–1599), Italian madrigal composer.

Markevitch, Igor (1912–   ), Russian-French composer and conductor.

Marschner, Heinrich (1795–1861), German opera composer.

Martenot, Maurice (1898-   ), French inventor of electronic instruments.

Martin, Frank (1890–1974), Swiss composer.

Martin, Mary (1913–   ), American soprano famed for roles in Broadway musicals.

Martinelli, Giovanni (1885–1969), Italian opera tenor.

Martini, Giovanni Battista (1706–1784), Italian composer, theorist, and teacher; known as "Padre Martini."

Martinon, Jean (1910–1976), French composer and conductor.

Martinu, Bohuslav (1890–1959), Czech composer.

Martirano, Salvatore (1927–   ), American avant-garde composer.

Mascagni, Pietro (1863–1945), Italian composer of the opera *Cavalleria Rusticana.*

Mason, Daniel Gregory (1873–1953), American composer and pedagogue.

Mason, Lowell (1792–1872), American organist and music educator.

Mason, William (1829–1908), American pianist and teacher.

Massenet, Jules (1842–1912), French opera composer.

Matthay, Tobias (1858–1945), English pianist and famous pedagogue.

Mattheson, Johann (1681–1764), German composer and music theorist.

Maxfield, Richard (1927–1969), American avant-garde composer.

McCartney, Paul (1942–   ), English rock singer, songwriter, and guitarist; member of the Beatles.

McCormack, John (1884–1945), legendary Irish tenor.

McPartland, Jimmie (1907–   ), American Chicago-style jazz cornetist.

McPartland, Marian (1920–   ), English-American jazz pianist.

McPhatter, Clyde (1933–1972), American popular singer.

Mehegan, John (1920–   ), American jazz pianist and educator.

Mehta, Zubin (1936–   ), Indian-born American conductor.

Méhul, Étienne-Nicolas (1763–1817), French opera composer.

Melba, Nellie (1859–1931), Australian operatic soprano.

Melchior, Lauritz (1890–1973), Danish-American operatic tenor.

Mendelssohn, Felix (1809–1847), German early Romantic composer.

Mendes, Sergio (1941–   ), Brazilian pop pianist, composer, and bandleader.

Mengelberg, Willem (1871–1951), Dutch conductor.

Mennin, Peter (1923–   ), American composer and music educator.

Menotti, Gian Carlo (1911–   ), Italian-born composer of highly successful operas to his own librettos (in English).

Menuhin, Yehudi (1916–   ), American violinist.

Merman, Ethel (1909–   ), American Broadway musical performer.

Merrill, Robert (1917–   ), American baritone, active in opera and popular music.

Messiaen, Olivier (1908–   ), French composer.

Mester, Jorge (1935–   ), Mexican-American conductor.

Metastasio, Pietro (1698–1782), Baroque opera librettist.

Meyerbeer, Giacomo (1791–1864), German-born French opera composer.

Miaskovsky, Nikolai (1881–1950), Russian symphonic composer.

Michael, David Moritz (1751–1825), German Moravian composer who worked in the U.S.

Milhaud, Darius (1892–1974), French neo-Classic composer.

Miller, Glenn (1904–1944), popular American trombonist and bandleader.

Milstein, Nathan (1904–   ), Russian-American violinist.

Mingus, Charles (1922–1979), American jazz bassist and composer.

Mitropoulos, Dimitri (1896–1960), outstanding Greek-born conductor.

Monk, Thelonious (1918–   ), American bebop pianist and composer.

Monteux, Pierre (1875–1964), French conductor.

Monteverdi, Claudio (1567–1643), first great Italian opera composer; bridged Renaissance and Baroque eras.

Moog, Robert A. (1934–   ), American inventor of the Moog synthesizer.

Moore, Douglas (1893–1969), American composer.

Morath, Max (1926–   ), American ragtime pianist.

Morley, Thomas (1557–1602), English madrigal composer.

Morton, Jelly Roll (real name **Ferdinand Joseph La Menthe**;

1885–1941), pioneer American jazz pianist, composer, and arranger.

Moscheles, Ignaz (1794–1870), German composer and pianist.

Mossolov, Alexander (1900–1973), Russian composer.

Moszkowski, Moritz (1854–1925), Polish-German pianist and composer of piano music.

Mozart, Leopold (1719–1787), Austrian violinist and composer; father of Wolfgang.

Mozart, Wolfgang Amadeus (1756–1791), Austrian pianist and composer; universal genius of 18th-century classical music; master of the opera, symphony, and concerto.

Mulligan, Gerry (1927–), American baritone saxophonist, arranger, and composer of "cool" West Coast jazz.

Munch, Charles (1891–1968), Alsatian conductor.

Münz, Mieczyslaw (1900–1976), Polish-American pianist.

Musgrave, Thea (1928–), Scottish composer.

Mussorgsky, Modest (1839–1881), Russian opera composer.

Nabokov (pronounced Nah-bo′-kov, *not* Nah′-bo-kov), **Nicolas** (1903–1978), Russian-American composer.

Nardini, Pietro (1722–1793), Italian violinist and composer.

Nelsova, Zara (1924–), Canadian cellist.

Nevin, Ethelbert (1862–1901), American composer.

Newman, Alfred (1901–), American film composer.

Newman, Ernest (1868–1959), English music critic.

Nielsen, Carl (1865–1931), Danish composer.

Nikisch, Arthur (1855–1922), German conductor.

Niles, John Jacob (1892–), American folk singer, instrumentalist (dulcimer, lute, piano), and composer.

Nilsson, Birgit (1918–), Swedish Wagnerian soprano.

Nilsson, Bo (1937–), Swedish avant-garde composer.

Nin, Joaquín (1879–1949), Spanish composer.

Noble, Ray (1903–1978), English bandleader and songwriter.

Nono, Luigi (1924–   ), Italian composer of the avant-garde.

Nordica, Lillian (1857–1914), American operatic soprano.

Nyiregyházi, Erwin (1903–   ), Hungarian pianist who abandoned his concert career in the early 1930s only to reappear in 1974 as a recording artist.

Obrecht, Jacob (c.1450–1505), Flemish church composer of the Renaissance.

Ochs, Phil (1940–1976), American folk singer and songwriter.

Ockeghem, Johannes (c.1420–1495), Flemish church composer of the Renaissance.

Odetta (original name **Odetta Holmes**; 1930–   ), American folk singer and guitarist.

Offenbach, Jacques (1819–1880), French operetta composer.

Ogdon, John (1937–   ), English pianist.

Oistrakh, David (1908–1974), Russian violinist.

Oistrakh, Igor (1931–   ), Russian violinist.

Oliver, Henry Kimble (1800–1885), American hymn composer.

Oliver, Joe "King" (1885–1938), American New Orleans jazz cornetist.

Oliver, Sy (1910–   ), American jazz trumpeter and arranger.

Oliveros, Pauline (1932–   ), American avant-garde composer.

Orff, Carl (1895–   ), German composer and music educator.

Ormandy, Eugene (1899–   ), Hungarian-American conductor; has led the Philadelphia Orchestra since 1938.

Ornstein, Leo (1892–), Russian-American "futurist" composer and pianist.

Overton, Hall (1920–1972), american composer and occasional jazz pianist.

Ozawa, Seiji (1935–), Japanese conductor; permanent conductor and music director of the Boston Symphony Orchestra.

Pachelbel, Carl Theodorus (1690–1750), German-American organist and composer; son of Johann.

Pachelbel, Johann (1653–1706), German organist and composer.

Pachmann, Vladimir de. See de Pachmann, Vladimir.

Paderewski (pronounced Pah-deh-rev′-skee), **Ignace** (1860–1941), Polish piano virtuoso, composer, and statesman.

Paganini, Niccolò (1782–1840), fabled Italian violin virtuoso and composer.

Paik, Nam June (1932–), Korean-American avant-garde, mixed-media composer.

Paine, John Knowles (1839–1906), American composer and educator.

Paisiello, Giovanni (1740–1816), Italian opera composer.

Palestrina, Giovanni Pierluigi da (c.1525–1594), Italian Renaissance choral composer whose sacred works are the apotheosis of Catholic Church music.

Palmgren, Selim (1878–1951), Finnish composer.

Panufnik, Andrzej (1914–), Polish composer and conductor.

Parker, Charlie (1920–1955), American alto saxophonist; creator of bebop.

Parker, Horatio (1863–1919), European-trained American composer and pedagogue; taught Charles Ives at Yale.

Parry, Sir Charles Hubert (1848–1918), English composer and pedagogue.

Partch, Harry (1901–1974), American composer of experimental music and inventor of instruments.

Parton, Dolly (1946–   ), American country-music singer and songwriter.

Pasatieri, Thomas (1945–   ), American opera composer.

Patti, Adelina (1843–1919), Italian coloratura soprano.

Paxton, Tom (1937–   ), American folk singer and guitarist.

Peerce, Jan (1904–   ), American operatic tenor.

Penderecki, Krzysztof (pronounced Krshishtof Pen-dehrets′-kee; 1933–   ), Polish composer of the avant-garde.

Pennario, Leonard (1924–   ), American pianist.

Pergolesi, Giovanni Battista (1710–1736), Italian composer of early *buffa* operas.

Peri, Jacopo (1561–1633), Italian composer and one of the originators of opera.

Perlman, Itzhak (1945–   ), Israeli-born violinist.

Perotin (c.1155–c.1200), Medieval French composer.

Persichetti, Vincent (1915–   ), American symphonic composer.

Peter, Johann Friedrich (1746–1813), Dutch-born American-Moravian composer.

Peter, Simon (1743–1819), Dutch-born American-Moravian composer; brother of Johann Friedrich Peter.

Peters, Roberta (1930–   ), American operatic soprano.

Peterson, Oscar (1925–   ), Canadian jazz pianist.

Petrassi, Goffredo (1904–   ), Italian composer.

Petrucci, Ottaviano dei (1466–1539), early Italian music printer.

Peyser, Joan, (1931–   ), American musicologist, journalist, author, and editor of *The Musical Quarterly*.

Pfitzner, Hans Erich (1869–1949), German composer.

Philidor, François André (1726–1795), French opera composer and chess master.

Philipp, Isidor (1863–1958), Hungarian-born French pianist and celebrated teacher.

Piaf, Edith (1915–1963), French popular singer.

Piatigorsky, Gregor (1903–1976), Russian master cellist.

Piccinni, Niccolò (1728–1800), Italian opera composer.

Pijper, Willem (1894–1947), Dutch composer.

Pinza, Ezio (1892–1957), Italian bass, active in both opera and the Broadway musical theater.

Piston, Walter (1894–1976), American composer and teacher.

Pleyel, Ignaz Joseph (1757–1831), Austrian composer and founder of the piano manufacturing firm bearing his name.

Ponce, Manuel (1882–1948), Mexican composer.

Ponchielli, Amilcare (1834–1886), Italian opera composer.

Pons, Lily (1898–1976), French-American coloratura soprano active in opera, radio, and the movies.

Popper, David (1843–1913), Czech violoncellist and composer.

Porter, Cole (1891–1964), leading American composer and lyricist of the musical theater.

Porter, Quincy (1897–1966), American composer.

Poulenc, Francis (1899–1963), French composer.

Pousseur, Henri (1929–   ), Belgian composer of avant-garde music.

Powell, Earl "Bud" (1924–1966), American bebop pianist.

Powell, John (1882–1963), American pianist and composer.

Powell, Mel (1923–   ), American composer and one-time jazz pianist.

Praetorius, Michael (1571–1621), German organist and theorist.

Presley, Elvis (1935–1977), immensely popular pioneer American rock'n'roll singer.

Previn, André (1929–   ), German-born American conductor and one-time jazz pianist.

Prey, Hermann (1929–   ), German baritone.

Price, Florence B. (1888–1953), American composer; the first black woman to write symphonies.

Price, Leontyne (1927–   ), American operatic soprano.

Prokofiev, Sergei (1891–1953), great Russian composer.

Prout, Ebenezer (1835–1909), English music theorist.

Pryor, Arthur (1870–1942), American virtuoso trombonist, bandleader, and composer.

Puccini, Giacomo (1858–1924), Italian opera composer.

Purcell, Henry (c.1659–1695), great English composer.

Quantz, Johann Joachim (1697–1773), German composer, theorist, and virtuoso flute player.

Rabaud, Henri (1873–1949), French composer and conductor.

Rachmaninoff, Sergei (1873–1943), Russian virtuoso pianist and composer of enduring piano favorites.

Raff, Joachim (1822–1882), German composer and teacher.

Rainey, Gertrude "Ma" (1886–1939), American blues singer; teacher of Bessie Smith.

Rameau, Jean-Philippe (1683–1764), French composer and theorist.

Ravel, Maurice (1875–1937), French Impressionist composer.

Read, Daniel (1757–1836), American composer and singing master.

Read, Gardner (1913–   ), American composer.

Rebikov, Vladimir (1866–1920), Russian composer of Romantic piano music.

Reese, Gustave (1899–1977), American musicologist.

Reger, Max (1873–1916), German contrapuntal composer, organist, and teacher.

Reicha, Anton (1770–1836), Bohemian-born composer and important theorist.

Reinagle, Alexander (1756–1809), Anglo-American keyboard performer, composer, and impresario.

Reinecke, Carl (1824–1910), German pianist, composer, and conductor.

Reiner, Fritz (1888–1963), Hungarian conductor.

Reinhardt, Django (1910–1953), Belgian jazz guitarist.

Reményi, Eduard (1830–1898), Hungarian violinist.

Resnik, Regina (1922–), American operatic soprano.

Respighi, Ottorino (1879–1963), Italian composer of colorful symphonic scores.

Reszke, Jean De. See De Reszke, Jean.

Revueltas, Silvestre (1899–1940), Mexican composer.

Reynolds, Roger (1934–), American avant-garde composer.

Rheinberger, Josef (1839–1901), German composer and teacher.

Ricci, Ruggiero (1918–), American violinist.

Rich, Buddy (1917–), American jazz drummer.

Richter, Hans (1843–1916), Hungarian-born German conductor.

Richter, Sviatoslav (1914–), Russian pianist.

Riddle, Nelson (1921–), American arranger and conductor of popular music.

Riegger, Wallingford (1885–1961), American composer.

Riemann, Hugo (1849–1919), German music scholar and lexicographer.

Ries, Ferdinand (1784–1838), German pianist and composer.

Rieti, Vittorio (1898–), Italian composer.

Riley, Terry (1937–   ), American avant-garde composer.

Rimsky-Korsakov, Nikolai (1844–1908), Russian composer and master of orchestration.

Ritchie, Jean (1922–   ), American folk singer and instrumentalist.

Ritter, Tex (1905–1974), American country & western singer, guitarist, and actor.

Roach, Max (1925–   ), American modern-jazz drummer.

Robeson, Paul (1898–1976), American bass singer and actor.

Rochberg, George (1918–   ), American composer.

Rodgers, Jimmie (1897–1933), American country-music singer, guitarist, and songwriter. Father of country music and originator of the blue yodel.

Rodgers, Richard (1902–1979), American musical theater composer and writer of hit songs.

Rodzinski, Artur (1892–1958), Polish-born American conductor.

Roger-Ducasse, Jean Jules (1873–1954), French composer.

Rogers, Bernard (1893–1968), American composer.

Rogers, Roy (1912–   ), American singing cowboy/actor.

Romberg, Sigmund (1887–1951), Hungarian-born American composer of popular operettas.

Ronstadt, Linda (1943–   ), American country-rock singer.

Root, George Frederick (1820–1895), American composer and publisher.

Rorem, Ned (1923–   ), American composer of songs.

Rosbaud, Hans (1895–1962), Austrian conductor.

Rose, Leonard (1918–   ), American cellist.

Rosen, Charles (1927–   ), American pianist and musicologist.

Rosenberg, Hilding (1892–   ), Swedish composer.

Rosenthal, Moriz (1862–1946), Polish-born pianist.

Ross, Diana (1944–   ), American pop/soul singer.

Rossini, Gioacchino (1792–1868), Italian opera composer.

Rostropovich, Mstislav (1927–   ), Russian cellist and conductor; active in U.S.

Rousseau, Jean-Jacques (1712–1778), French philosopher and opera composer.

Roussel, Albert (1869–1937), French neo-Classic composer.

Rózsa, Miklós (1907–   ), Hungarian-born American composer of symphonic pieces and film music.

Rubbra, Edmund (1901–   ), English symphonic composer.

Rubinstein, Anton (1829–1894), Russian virtuoso pianist and prolific composer.

Rubinstein, Artur (1887–   ), enormously successful and beloved Polish-born American pianist.

Rudel, Julius (1921–   ), Viennese-American opera conductor.

Rudolf, Max (1902–   ), German-American conductor.

Ruggles, Carl (1876–1971), American composer of few but highly significant works.

Rushing, Jimmie (1903–1972), American blues singer, known as "Mister Five-by-Five."

Russolo, Luigi (1885–1947), Italian futurist composer of "noise music."

Sachs, Hans (1494–1576), foremost Meistersinger.

Saint-Georges, Joseph Boulogne, Chevalier de (1739–1799), West Indian violinist and composer active in France.

Saint-Saëns, Camille (1835–1921), French composer.

Salieri, Antonio (1750–1825), Italian composer of operas and church music.

Salzman, Eric (1933–   ), American composer active in mixed-media "happenings."

Salzedo, Carlos (1885–1961), French-American harp virtuoso and composer.

Sammartini, Giovanni Battista (1701–1775), Italian composer and organist.

Sanders, Pharoah (real first name **Farrell**; 1940–   ), American jazz saxophonist.

Sankey, Ira David (1840–1908), American composer of gospel hymns.

Sarasate, Pablo de (1844–1908), Spanish virtuoso violinist.

Satie, Erik (1866–1925), French composer of eccentric piano pieces and ballet numbers.

Sax, Adolphe (1814–1894), Belgian inventor of the saxophone.

Scarlatti, Alessandro (1660–1725), Italian opera composer.

Scarlatti, Domenico (1685–1757), Italian composer for the harpsichord; son of Alessandro Scarlatti.

Schaeffer, Pierre (1910–   ), French acoustician, composer, and originator of *musique concrète.*

Schaefer, R. Murray (1933–   ), Canadian composer and educator.

Schat, Peter (1935–   ), Dutch composer of electronic and mixed-media theatrical events.

Scheidt, Samuel (1587–1654), German organist and composer.

Schein, Johann Hermann (1586–1630), German composer of church music.

Schelling, Ernest (1876–1939), American pianist and composer.

Schenker, Heinrich (1868–1935), Austrian theorist.

Scherchen, Hermann (1891–1966), German conductor.

Scherman, Thomas (1917–   ), American conductor; founder of the Little Orchestra Society.

Schickele, Peter (1935–   ), American composer and musical humorist; creator of P. D. Q. Bach.

Schifrin, Lalo (1932–   ), Argentinian-American jazz musician and composer for film and TV.

Schillinger, Joseph (1895–1943), Russian-American composer and author of the influential "Schillinger system of musical composition."

Schipa, Tito (1890–1965), Italian opera tenor.

Schippers, Thomas (1930–1977), American conductor.

Schirmer, Gustav (1829–1893), German musician, founder of the music publishing house bearing his name.

Schmitt, Florent (1870–1958), French composer and music critic.

Schnabel, Artur (1882–1951), Austrian pianist and teacher.

Schoeck, Othmar (1886–1957), Swiss composer.

Schoenberg, Arnold (1874–1951), Austrian-born composer who revolutionized music with extreme expressionistic dissonance; originator of 12-tone music.

Scholes, Percy (1877–1958), English music scholar, author, and lexicographer.

Schreker, Franz (1878–1934), Austrian composer of expressionistic neo-Romantic operas.

Schubert, Franz (1797–1828), Austrian early Romantic composer and master of the art song.

Schuller, Gunther (1925–   ), American horn player, composer, and conductor.

Schuman, William (1910–   ), American composer and music educator.

Schumann, Clara (1819–1896), German pianist and composer; wife of Robert Schumann.

Schumann, Elisabeth (1885–1952), German operatic soprano.

Schumann, Robert (1810–1856), a leading figure in German Romanticism, both as a composer and as a writer on music; master of the art song and short piano piece.

Schumann-Heink, Ernestine (1861–1936), Bohemian-born contralto.

Schütz, Heinrich (1585–1672), German Baroque composer who transferred the Italian choral style to German semi-dramatic church music.

Schwarzkopf, Elisabeth (1915–   ), German operatic soprano.

Schweitzer, Albert (1875–1965), Alsatian-born organist, philosopher, writer on music, and medical missionary in Africa.

Scott, Cyril (1879–1970), English composer of Impressionistic piano pieces.

Scott, James Sylvester (1886–1938), American ragtime pianist and composer.

Scriabin, Alexander (1872–1915), Russian composer of harmonically and technically innovative piano and orchestral pieces with mystical connotations.

Scruggs, Earl (1924–   ), American bluegrass banjoist, teamed with Lester Flatt.

Searle, Humphrey (1915–   ), English composer and writer on music.

Seeger, Charles (1886–1979), Mexican-born American musicologist and folklorist; married Ruth Crawford; the father of Pete Seeger.

Seeger, Pete (1919–   ), American folk singer, instrumentalist, and composer.

Seeger, Ruth Crawford. See Crawford, Ruth.

Segovia, Andrés (1893–   ), Spanish virtuoso guitarist.

Seiber, Mátyás (1905–1960), Hungarian composer and teacher.

Seidl, Anton (1850–1898), Hungarian conductor.

Sembrich, Marcella (1858–1935), Austrian coloratura soprano.

Serkin, Peter (1947–   ), American pianist.

Serkin, Rudolf (1903–   ), Austrian pianist; father of Peter Serkin.

Serly, Tibor (1900–1978), Hungarian-American composer.

Serov, Alexander (1820–1871), Russian opera composer.

Sessions, Roger (1896–   ), American composer and teacher.

Severinsen, Carl "Doc" (1927–   ), American popular trumpeter and bandleader.

Shakespeare, William (1849–1931), English tenor and singing teacher.

Shaliapin, Feodor. See Chaliapin, Feodor.

Shank, Bud (1926–   ), American saxophonist associated with West Coast jazz.

Shankar, Ravi (1920–   ), Indian sitarist and composer; known for collaboration with Western musicians.

Shapero, Harold (1920–   ), American neo-Classic composer.

Shapey, Ralph (1921–   ), American conductor and neo-Classic composer.

Sharp, Cecil (1859–1924), English organist and folk song collector.

Shaw, Artie (1910–   ), American jazz clarinetist and popular bandleader.

Shaw, Oliver (1779–1848), American organist, composer, and singing teacher.

Shaw, Robert (1916–   ), American choral conductor

Shchedrin, Rodion (1932–   ), Russian composer.

Shearing, George (1919–   ), English-American bebop pianist.

Shepherd, Arthur (1880–1958), American composer and teacher.

Shepp, Archie (1937–   ), American bebop saxophonist.

Shostakovich, Dmitri (1906–1975), Russian Soviet composer.

Sibelius, Jean (1865–1957), Finnish composer of nationalistic symphonic works.

Siegmeister, Elie (1909–   ), American composer.

Siepi, Cesare (1923–   ), Italian operatic bass.

Sills, Beverly (1929–   ), American operatic soprano.

Siloti, Alexander (1863–1945), Russian pianist and conductor.

Silver, Horace (1926–   ), American jazz pianist.

Simon, Paul (1941–   ), American folk/rock singer and songwriter; teamed with Art Garfunkel.

Sims, Zoot (1925–   ), American jazz saxophonist.

Sinatra, Frank (1915–   ), American pop singer and actor.

Sinding, Christian (1856–1941), Norwegian composer.

Skalkottas, Nikos (1904–1949), Greek composer.

Skilton, Charles Sanford (1868–1941), American composer.

Slezak, Leo (1873–1946), Austrian operatic tenor.

Slonimsky, Nicolas (1894–   ), Russian-American pianist, conductor, composer, and lexicographer; early champion of Varèse, Ives, and Ruggles.

Smetana, Bedrich (1824–1884), Bohemian national composer of operas and symphonic works.

Smith, Bessie (c.1895–1937), great American blues singer, "Empress of the Blues."

Smith, Clarence "Pinetop" (1904–1929), American blues singer and boogie-woogie pianist.

Smith, John Stafford (1750–1836), English organist and composer who wrote the song *Anacreon in Heaven,* the tune of which was used for *The Star-Spangled Banner.*

Smith, Kate (1909–   ), popular American singer.

Smith, Willie "The Lion" (1897–1973), American stride pianist.

Smyth, Ethel (1858–1944), British composer and militant suffragist.

Solomon (real name **Solomon Cutner**; 1902–   ), English pianist known by his first name alone.

Solti, Sir George (1912–   ), Hungarian-born British-American conductor.

Sondheim, Stephen (1930–   ), American lyricist and composer of Broadway musicals.

Sonneck, Oscar (1873–1928), pioneering American musicologist.

Sousa, John Philip (1854–1932), celebrated American bandmaster and composer of exciting marches.

Sowerby, Leo (1895–1968), American composer.

Speaks, Oley (1874–1948), American songwriter.

Spitalny, Phil (1890–1970), Russian-American bandleader; led an "all-girl" orchestra.

Spohr, Ludwig (1784–1859), German violinist, conductor, and prolific composer.

Spontini, Gasparo (1774–1851), Italian opera composer.

Stamitz, Carl (1745–1801), Bohemian violinist and composer, son of Johann Stamitz.

Stamitz, Johann (1717–1757), Bohemian composer of symphonies and chamber music; founder of the Mannheim School.

Starer, Robert (1924–   ), American composer.

Starker, Janos (1924–   ), Hungarian-American cellist.

Starr, Ringo (real name **Richard Starkey**; 1940–   ), English rock drummer; member of the Beatles.

Steber, Eleanor (1916–   ), American operatic soprano.

Steffani, Agostino (1654–1728), Italian composer of choral music.

Steinberg, William (1899–1978), German-born American conductor.

Steinway, Heinrich Engelhard (1797–1871), German piano manufacturer; founder of the Steinway firm.

Stern, Isaac (1920–   ), American violinist.

Steuermann, Eduard (1892–1964), Polish-American pianist.

Stevens, Halsey (1908–   ), American composer and teacher.

Stevens, Risë (1913–   ), American operatic and popular mezzo-soprano.

Stewart, Slam (1914–   ), American jazz bassist.

Still, William Grant (1895–1978), foremost black American composer.

Stitt, Sonny (1924–   ), American bebop saxophonist.

Stockhausen, Karlheinz (1928–   ), contemporary German composer; leading proponent of electronic and aleatory types of composition.

Stokowski, Leopold (1882–1977), illustrious English conductor; led the Philadelphia Orchestra from 1912 to 1938, and continued an active musical life until age 95.

Stradella, Alessandro (1642–1682), Italian composer of choral music.

Stradivarius, Antonio (1644–1737), Italian, the greatest violin maker.

Straus, Oskar (1870–1954), Austrian operetta composer.

Strauss, Eduard (1835–1916), Austrian composer; brother of Johann Strauss, Jr.

Strauss, Johann, Jr. (1825–1899), Austrian composer of infectious waltz tunes.

Strauss, Johann, Sr. (1804–1849), Austrian composer, father of Johann Strauss, Jr.

Strauss, Josef (1827–1870), Austrian waltz composer; brother of Johann Strauss, Jr.

Strauss, Richard (1864–1949), German composer; creator of the modern tone poem.

Stravinsky, Igor (1882–1971), celebrated Russian-born master of modern music.

Strayhorn, Billy (1915–1967), American jazz composer and arranger, active with Duke Ellington.

Streisand, Barbra (1942–   ), American pop singer and film actress.

Styne, Jule (1905–   ), American composer for the Broadway stage.

Subotnick, Morton (1933–   ), American composer of electronic and mixed-media works.

Sullivan, Sir **Arthur** (1842–1900), English composer; the creator, with W. S. Gilbert, of the perennially attractive series of comic operas; also wrote religious hymns and serious operas.

Sullivan, Joe (1906–   ), American Chicago jazz pianist.

Sun Ra (original name **Herman "Sonny" Blount**; c.1915–   ), American keyboard performer and bandleader.

Suppé, Franz von (1819–1895), Austrian composer of vivacious orchestral overtures and successful operettas.

Süssmayr, Franz Xaver (1766–1803), Austrian composer and student of Mozart; completed Mozart's *Requiem*.

Sutherland, Joan (1926–   ), Australian operatic soprano.

Sweelinck, Jan Pieterszoon (1562–1621), Dutch organist and composer; a major figure in the development of fugal writing.

Swingle, Ward (1927–   ), American singer and arranger; leader of the Swingle Singers.

Szell, George (1897–1970), Hungarian-American conductor.

Szigeti, Joseph (1892–1973), Hungarian violinist.

Szymanowski, Karol (1882–1937), foremost Polish composer of his time.

Tallis, Thomas (c.1505–1585), English composer of religious choral music.

Talma, Louise (1906–   ), American neo-Classic composer.

Taneyev, Sergei (1856–1915), Russian composer and teacher.

Tansman, Alexandre (1897–   ), Polish-French composer.

Tartini, Giuseppe (1692–1770), Italian violin virtuoso, composer, and notable theorist.

Tatum, Art (1910–1956), blind American jazz pianist.

Tausig, Carl (1841–1871), Polish virtuoso pianist.

Taylor, Cecil (1933–   ), American avant-garde jazz pianist.

Taylor, Deems (1885–1966), American composer and distinguished writer on music.

Taylor, Raynor (c.1747–1825), English-American composer and impresario.

Tchaikovsky, Peter Ilyich (1840–1893), great Russian composer.

Tcherepnin, Alexander (1899–1977), Russian pianist and composer.

Tcherepnin, Nicolas (1873–1945), Russian composer, teacher, and conductor; father of Alexander Tcherepnin.

Teagarden, Jack (1905–1964), American jazz trombonist and singer.

Tebaldi, Renata (1922–   ), Italian operatic soprano.

Telemann, Georg Philipp (1681–1767), prolific German composer of secular and sacred music.

Terry, Charles Sanford (1864–1936), Scottish composer, teacher, and musicologist.

Terry, Sonny (1911–   ), American folk harmonica player.

Tertis, Lionel (1876–1975), English violinist.

Tetrazzini, Luisa (1871–1940), Italian coloratura soprano.

Thalberg, Sigismond (1812–1871), Swiss-born virtuoso pianist.

Theodorakis, Mikis (1925–   ), Greek film composer and statesman.

Theremin, Leon (1896–   ), Russian inventor of the Thereminovox, the first electronic musical instrument.

Thibaud, Jacques (1880–1953), French violinist; part of a trio including Cortot and Casals.

Thomas, Ambroise (1811–1896), French opera composer.

Thomas, Michael Tilson (1944–   ), American conductor.

Thomas, Theodore (1835–1905), German-American conductor.

Thompson, Oscar (1887–1945), American music critic and lexicographer.

Thompson, Randall (1899–   ), American composer of symphonic and choral music.

Thomson, Virgil (1896–   ), American composer of beguiling modern operas; a brilliant music critic.

Thorne, Francis (1922–   ), American composer and patron of avant-garde composers.

Tibbett, Lawrence (1896–1960), American baritone.

Tiomkin, Dmitri (1894–   ), Russian-American film composer.

Tippett, Sir Michael (1905–   ), English composer.

Toch, Ernst (1887–1964), Austrian composer of romantically inspired symphonies and finely crafted chamber music.

Torelli, Giuseppe (1658–1709), highly esteemed Italian violinist and Baroque composer; originator of the solo violin concerto.

Torkanowsky, Werner (1926–   ), German-American conductor; director of the New Orleans Philharmonic Symphony Orchestra.

Torme, Mel (1925–   ), American pop singer and author.

Toscanini, Arturo (1867–1957), supreme Italian master of operatic and symphonic conducting.

Tourel, Jennie (1900–1973), Russian-American operatic mezzo-soprano.

Tovey, Sir Donald Francis (1875–1940), English pianist, conductor, composer, and music critic.

Trampler, Walter (1915–   ), German-American violinist.

Traubel, Helen (1899–1972), American operatic soprano and novelist; attracted to pop-singing for night-club and movie performances.

Travis, Merle (1917–   ), American country-music singer and guitarist.

Trumbauer, Frankie (c.1900–1956), American jazz saxophonist.

Tubb, Ernest (1914–   ), American folk singer, guitarist, and composer.

Tucker, Richard (1913–1975), American tenor.

Tucker, Sophie (1884–1966), Russian-American pop singer, "The Last of the Red Hot Mamas."

Tuckwell, Barry (1931–   ), Australian French horn virtuoso.

Tudor, David (1926–   ), American avant-garde pianist and composer.

Tureck, Rosalyn (1914–   ), American pianist and harpsichordist; a specialist in Bach.

Turina, Joaquín (1882–1949), Spanish composer.

Turner, Joe (1911–   ), American blues singer.

Ugarte, Floro (1884–1975), Argentinian composer.

Uribe-Holguín, Guillermo (1880–1971), foremost Colombian composer.

Ussachevsky, Vladimir (1911–   ), Russian-American composer and pioneer in electronic music.

Vaet, Jacobus (1529–1567), Flemish church composer.

Vallee, Rudy (1901–   ), popular American saxophonist, singer, bandleader, and film actor.

Vanhal, Johann Baptist (1739–1813), Bohemian violinist and composer.

Van Vactor, David (1906–   ), American composer and conductor.

Varèse, Edgard (1883–1965), French-American composer of innovative music using both pitched and non-pitched sound.

Vaughan, Sarah (1924–   ), American jazz vocalist.

Vaughan Williams, Ralph (1872–1958), English composer.

Vecchi, Orazio (1550–1605), Italian madrigal composer.

Venuti, Joe (1904–1978), American jazz violinist.

Verdi, Giuseppe (1813–1901), Italy's most celebrated opera composer; wrote works that combine *bel canto* lyricism with great dramatic power.

Viardot-García, Pauline (1821–1910), French mezzo-soprano.

Victoria, Tomás Luis de (c.1549–1611), Spanish composer of the Palestrina school.

Vieuxtemps, Henri (1820–1881), Belgian violinist and composer.

Villa-Lobos, Heitor (1887–1959), Brazilian composer.

Vincent, John (1902–1977), American composer.

Viotti, Giovanni Battista (1775–1824), Italian violinist and composer.

Vitali, Giovanni Battista (c.1632–1692), Italian composer.

Vitry, Philippe de (1291–1361), French composer and theorist.

Vivaldi, Antonio (1678–1741), prolific Italian Baroque composer; a major figure in the development of the concerto.

Vladigerov, Pantcho (1899–   ), foremost Bulgarian composer.

Vogel, Wladimir (1896–   ), Russian-born Swiss composer.

Vogelweide, Walther von der (c.1170–c.1230), German Minnesinger.

Vogler, Georg Joseph (1749–1814), important German music theorist and composer of numerous vocal and instrumental works.

Wagenaar, Bernard (1894–1971), Dutch-American composer and teacher.

Wagenseil, Georg Christoph (1715–1777), Austrian pianist and composer.

Wagner, Joseph Frederick (1900–1974), American composer.

Wagner, Richard (1813–1883), German composer and harmonic innovator; creator of operas which attempted a synthesis of song, drama, and orchestral music.

Waldstein, Ferdinand Ernst Gabriel, Graf von (1762–1823), amateur musician, friend and patron of Beethoven, and dedicatee of Beethoven's *Waldstein Sonata,* Op. 53.

Waldteufel, Emil (1837–1915), French waltz composer.

Wallenstein, Alfred (1898–   ), American cellist and conductor.

Waller, Thomas "Fats" (1904–1943), American jazz pianist, songwriter, and ebullient popular vocalist.

Walter, Bruno (1876–1962), German conductor.

Walton, Sir William (1902–   ), English composer.

Ward, Robert (1917–   ), American composer excelling in stage works.

Warfield, William (1920–   ), American baritone and educator.

Waring, Fred (1900–), American choral conductor.

Warlock, Peter. Pseudonym of Philip Heseltine, which see.

Warwick, Dionne (1941–), American pop singer and pianist.

Washington, Dinah (1942–1963), American blues singer.

Waters, Ethel (1896–1977), American singer and actress.

Waters, "Muddy" (real name **McKinley Morganfield**; 1915–), American blues singer.

Watts, André (1946–), American pianist.

Weber, Ben (1916–), American composer.

Weber, Carl Maria von (1786–1826), creator of German Romantic opera.

Webern, Anton von (1883–1945), Austrian serial composer; pupil of Schoenberg.

Weelkes, Thomas (c.1575–1623), English composer of madrigals and airs.

Weill, Kurt (1900–1950), German-American composer of operas and musicals of social significance.

Weinberger, Jaromir (1896–1967), Czech opera composer.

Weingartner, Felix (1863–1942), Austrian conductor.

Weisgall, Hugo (1912–), American composer.

Welk, Lawrence (1903–), American accordionist and bandleader.

Wellesz, Egon (1885–1974), Austrian musicologist and composer.

White, Clarence Cameron (1880–1960), American violinist and composer.

White, Josh (1908–1969), American folk singer.

Whiteman, Paul (1890–1967), American conductor of "symphonic jazz."

Whiting, Arthur (1861–1936), American organist and composer.

Widor, Charles-Marie (1844–1937), French organist, teacher, and composer.

Wieck, Friedrich (1785–1873), German pianist and pedagogue; father of Clara Schumann and teacher of Robert Schumann.

Wieniawski, Henryk (1835–1880), Polish violinist and composer for the violin.

Wilbye, John (1574–1638), English madrigal composer.

Wilder, Alec (1907–   ), American composer, songwriter, and author.

Wilhelmj, August (1845–1908), German violin virtuoso and teacher.

Willaert, Adrian (c.1480–1562), Flemish contrapuntist.

Williams, Alberto (1862–1952), Argentinian composer.

Williams, Bert (1874–1922), popular comic singer of musical theater.

Williams, Cootie (1908–   ), American jazz trumpeter.

Williams, Hank (1923–1953), American country-music singer, guitarist, and songwriter.

Williams, Joe (1918–   ), American blues singer; associated with Count Basie.

Williams, John M. (1884–1974), American pianist.

Williams, Mary Lou (1910–   ), American jazz pianist and composer.

Wilson, Teddy (1912–   ), American jazz pianist.

Wilson, Olly (1937–   ), American composer.

Winding, Kai (1922–   ), Danish-born bebop trombonist, often teamed with trombonist J. J. Johnson.

Winner, Septimus (1827–1902), American composer of popular songs; wrote under the pseudonym Alice Hawthorne.

Wittgenstein, Paul (1887–1961), Austrian one-armed pianist; commissioned concertos for left-hand alone from Ravel, Strauss, Prokofiev, and others.

Wolf, Hugo (1860–1903), Austrian lieder composer.

Wolf-Ferrari, Ermanno (1876–1948), Italian-German opera composer.

Wolff, Christian (1934–   ), French-American composer of the avant-garde.

Wolpe, Stefan (1902–1972), German-American composer and teacher.

Wonder, Stevie (1951–   ), blind American soul singer, composer, and keyboard artist.

Wood, Sir **Henry** (1869–1944), English conductor.

Work, Henry Clay (1832–1884), American popular composer; wrote *Marching Through Georgia* and other popular songs.

Wuorinen, Charles (1938–   ), American composer of advanced, complex music.

Xenakis, Iannis (1922–   ), Rumanian-born Greek composer, trained in engineering and architecture, who derived a "stochastic" method of composition from scientific principles and formulae.

Yannay, Yehuda (1937–   ), avant-garde Israeli-American composer.

Youmans, Vincent (1898–1946), American composer of popular musicals.

Young, La Monte (1935–   ), American avant-garde composer.

Young, Lester (1909–1959), American jazz tenor saxophonist.

Ysaÿe, Eugène (1858–1931), Belgian violinist.

Yun, Isang (1917–   ), expatriate Korean composer of operas.

Zádor, Eugen (1894–1977), Hungarian-American composer.

Zappa, Frank (1940–   ), American rock singer, guitarist, and composer; leader of the Mothers of Invention.

Zarlino, Gioseffo (1517–1590), Italian music theorist.

Zelter, Carl Friedrich (1758–1832), German composer of art songs.

Zemlinsky, Alexander von (1871–1942), Austrian composer and conductor.

Zimbalist, Efrem (1889–   ), Russian-American violinist and teacher.

Zimmermann, Bernd-Alois (1918–1970), German composer.

Zukerman, Pinchas (1948–   ), Israeli violinist.

Zukofsky, Paul (1943–   ), American violinist who specializes in avant-garde music; son of poet Louis Zukovsky.